Hopeful Influence

A Theology of Christian Leadership

Jude Padfield

scm press

© Jude Padfield 2019

Published in 2019 by SCM Press
Editorial office
3rd Floor, Invicta House,
108–114 Golden Lane,
London EC1Y 0TG, UK
www.scmpress.co.uk

SCM Press is an imprint of Hymns Ancient & Modern Ltd
(a registered charity)

Hymns Ancient & Modern® is a registered trademark of
Hymns Ancient & Modern Ltd
13A Hellesdon Park Road, Norwich,
Norfolk NR6 5DR, UK

British Library Cataloguing in Publication data

A catalogue record for this book is available
from the British Library

978-0-334-05749-9

Typeset by Regent Typesetting
Printed and bound by
CPI Group (UK) Ltd

Contents

*For St Mellitus College and the
Diocese of Liverpool.
With gratitude.*

Foreword

God is sovereign over all time. But we live in a world where – for us – the arrow of time points in one direction only. So as a Christian leader, my own work has been orientated to the future – to God's future – and I seek through story and language to magnetize people to that future. For this reason I resonate strongly with the idea of 'Hopeful Influence' in this book.

Of course, magnetizing people to the future is not always easy:

A bishop talks to a churchwarden:
'How long have you been churchwarden here?'
'Oh, forty years, bishop.'
'Forty years? You must have seen a lot of changes in that time.'
'Yes, bishop. And I've opposed every one of them!'

God is sovereign over all time, and so as people of faith we naturally look to the past for wisdom and enrichment, as well as for the wellsprings of God's revelation in Scripture and tradition. But as a leader in this generation, that churchwarden was magnetized to the past. It is not a way of being that gives hope and strength. It is not a model I seek to follow.

In the Diocese of Liverpool, we're asking God for a bigger Church to make a bigger difference, and we say: 'More people knowing Jesus, more justice in the world.' To bring this vision to earth in the journey of each disciple we have a simple Rule of Life: we're *called* to pray, read and learn; and we're *sent* to tell, serve and give. In so doing, we respond to the promptings of the Spirit, often made manifest through others, and we offer ourselves as conduits to others of those same Holy Spirit-led initiatives. Or in shorthand, we try to lead one another together in community.

In laying out such a vision in a world of time, I am speaking of the future and asking my friends and fellow-disciples to work with me in calling that future into being. I affirm and encourage people to step out in this generation, and I remind them that their forebears did exactly that in their own time – but my affirmation is worthless without the extra step that says: 'Look ahead, then. Live hopefully. Take a risk, and I'll support you. Make something new for Jesus, even if it's only a big mistake.'

Language of risk is inevitable as we live towards the future, because the future is uncertain. How can we see what is to come when, in the words of the poet Ted Hughes, 'The World is dark one inch ahead.'[1] So a hopeful eschatology demands courage and confidence in the God who is sovereign over all time.

My leadership depends on my faith in the God whom I know from the past, but who comes to me now from the future, as each future moment becomes 'now' for me and my Diocese. To live in this faith is to live in daily need of courage. So as a future-facing person and as one who tries to shape a vision for the future, I must ask God daily for strength and for creativity. That strength and creativity is what I see in all the leaders I respect – including the author of this book. And I pray it for you, too, who are reading it. 'And I am sure of this, that he who began a good work in you will bring it to completion at the day of Jesus Christ.'[2]

Rt Revd Paul Bayes of Liverpool

Notes

1 Ted Hughes, 'Song for a Phallus', from *Crow* (London: Faber, 2001), p. 71.
2 Philippians 1.6, ESV.

Acknowledgements

As a church leader attempting to get a better handle on my role, I am hugely grateful for the chance to learn and grow within the pioneering St Mellitus community, and for their teaching and influence on me in the early formation of this book. I am grateful, too, for the support of the Diocese of Liverpool in providing a study break during which to write it, and to Gladstone's Library in Wales for providing a warm welcome and helpful space for the book to take shape.

Significant thanks are due to each of the eleven commentators who have helped anchor the ideas of the book in experience and practice beyond my own, and to Bishop Paul in Liverpool for the book's Foreword and his general affirmation of the direction of travel. Revd Michael Leyden, Director of St Mellitus, North West, deserves a special mention for his theological clarity and unwavering support as the book was in its developmental phase.

I am extremely grateful for my church family at St James': much of the book's material has developed in conversation with them. There are of course many others – too numerous to mention – who have contributed to my leadership understanding over the years.

I would also like to thank the team at SCM Press, particularly David Shervington for his wisdom and encouragement, and Miranda Lever, for her helpful independent editing.

And finally. Thank you to my wife, Hannah, and our children Jake and Sophia. The book's development has run slowly across the last 18 months or so, so the impact on them hasn't been too significant, but I thank God for their continual love, encouragement and patience.

Hope leads everything,
for faith only sees what is,
but hope sees what will be.
Charity only loves what is,
But hope loves what will be –
In time and for all eternity.

Charles Péguy (1873–1914), 'Hope'

Introduction

It is interesting the way parenting affects you. Suddenly you have this remarkable opportunity to love someone else into life from a place of rather intense proximity. A bit like marriage, you could say, although the direction of travel with marriage is towards greater intimacy. With parenting, the direction of travel is towards greater autonomy and independence. Thank goodness, you might say.

I'm certainly still a learner when it comes to parenting, but I know that I have already learned much and been remoulded greatly by the experience. In some ways it's a microcosm of leadership: we love, we help – and we ourselves grow through the experience. My most significant formations, certainly as an adult, have happened through leadership experiences. And some of the greatest joys too, on the occasions when I know I've helped someone else develop or achieve something they wouldn't otherwise have been able to do. Perhaps the extremes of formation and joy are most evident in parenting, but they are there in myriad other roles and relationships too. Leadership is real and leadership matters.

So I'm a follower of Jesus who is trying to reflect on my own leadership experience and make better sense of this thing that seems to affect so much of our lives. From an early point in my own Christian journey, I've had a clear sense that Jesus is inviting people into a richer, fuller and better kind of life. With almost equal clarity has been the conviction that we need each other to enter into that life, and that God is calling me, in some sense, to serve this wider vision of the Church. Today I'm helping to lead a church in Liverpool as an Anglican vicar, working mostly with a demographic of younger people, and consistently inspired by God's work among them and their hopes for a better future.

As I've journeyed in both my faith and sense of vocation before God, I am very aware of the way others have helped me and the increasing ways in which I have been able to help others. In the communal life we lead, God seems to bring people together to learn from each other and to do things and achieve things together. In a sense I have a formalized role in that process as a vicar but, much wider than that, there seems to be this powerful social dynamic at work within the Church, to an extent within any community, where we help each other on our collective journeys into the future. You might call it expressions of leadership.

Yet I've found myself writing this book from a place of frustration. Frustration that these processes of leadership go so badly wrong. That, as human creatures, we seem to follow people and things that often lead to mess and destruction rather than life. But frustration as well that the Church's understanding of leadership isn't more coherent. Yes, there are many great books on the methods of leadership and the kinds of shapes that distinctive Christian leadership can take. However, among this material there is insufficient theological exploration of what God is actually doing in our leadership. We don't want to define what leadership actually is or what it's for under God's advancing rule, so we don't anchor our arguments well enough, and we allow space for disagreement and disunity on the subject, of which there is a great deal. The reality is this: we follow Jesus, we also follow others who point us to Jesus and others follow us when we point them to Jesus. Through this mutual series of activities we get to partner with God in the wider renewal of the whole earth. Yet we seem unable to talk about this across the Church with more agreed clarity, and particularly *theological* clarity.

As such, this isn't a book primarily about how to lead. First and foremost it is a book about the nature and purpose of leadership and whether we can identify a theologically adequate and pastorally unifying motif that helps anchor the wider leadership conversation. Yes, I do attempt to sketch out some of the practical implications of such a motif, and start to connect the theological thinking with some of the wealth of good leadership material that is out there. But, at its core, this book is trying to answer the double-edged question: What is God doing in and through our leadership – and how do we need to talk about it to enact that leadership more faithfully? To approach the subject of leadership, and certainly to speak authoritatively on it, without a handle on this question seems to me to be potentially dangerous and damaging.

This is a book, then, about leadership, but it is also a book about the Kingdom of God and about hope. The Kingdom of God is an often under-developed and under-utilized theological reality that is vital for helping us understand the right shapes of the Christian life. Jesus has ascended to the right hand of the Father and is, right now, on the throne. His rule and reign is advancing in the hearts of his followers, but it's spilling over through them into the wider life of humanity and all of creation. There is a movement back to God, but also forwards into a new future; and we're invited into that if we are willing to surrender the deep, inherited self-centredness of our hearts. Jesus demands nothing from us, yet paradoxically asks us to give everything as we take our place in this emerging future. When we look closer at this Kingdom theology, we begin to understand better how central hope is to the Christian experience. The Kingdom of God is here now. And yet, the Kingdom of God is not yet here in all its fullness. We look forward to the Kingdom advancing more fully. Tomorrow. The day after. And one day perfectly. Hope is what moves us into that new future and what informs the shape of our Christian activity.

When I use the language of Kingdom and of hope, I have these precise meanings in mind, which I will attempt to develop more fully within this exploration of Christian leadership. It is certainly true that much of the world seems to be acting independently from the rule of Jesus. And yet, I want to suggest that a great deal of our inherited life has been shaped by people who were active agents of the Kingdom, and as such there is far more conformity to Jesus' rule around us than we might necessarily think. Humanity is being rescued from idolatry, chaos and destruction. Yes, these things consistently emerge and re-emerge through the human story, but there is a great deal of structural and societal goodness that has been drawn into a degree of alignment with that Kingdom.

In exploring leadership, the Kingdom of God and hope, I want to acknowledge that aspects of leadership take different shapes and have different emphases within the different spheres of life that we occupy. There are lots of ways in which we can categorize our spheres of life, and for this book I have chosen five: the Church, politics, business, third sector and leadership towards the next generation. There's plenty of overlap between these spheres and in some ways the categorization is artificial. However, in trying to explore the shape of Christian leadership, acknowledging and engaging with the variety of contexts feels important and this is why I've employed this method.

The book, put simply, is a first stab at trying to sharpen our theological language within the discourse on Christian leadership. The outline is fairly simple. Part One is a navigation of some of the painful expressions of leadership, the theological and practical confusion on the subject and a possible starting place for a hope-filled theology of leadership. Part Two unpacks this theology of leadership and tries to connect the motif of Hopeful Influence with a wider understanding of what Christian leadership looks like. Part Three explores the shape of Hopeful Influence in the different spheres of life, connecting recognizable good practice with the proposed theology, and attempting to inspire further thought.

It's a book, then, for every Christian – for all Christians have the potential to lead. In fact, in the way that I've defined leadership, everyone is exercising forms of leadership at different times. The better resourced we are to do that, the more effective our leadership should become. However, it is also a book specifically for every Christian person engaged in a more formalized position of leadership. Part of what we do as human creatures, recognizing this inherent potential for collective movement within our humanity, is to formalize positions of leadership within our social groupings. We appoint people. We promote people. We recruit people. We ordain people. We elect people. We train people. We ask people to hold positions of leadership in our churches, governments, businesses and third sector organizations. And, of course, we recognize people as leaders in our community and family structures: caring for each other and nurturing others into the world.

Christian leadership then, for every person, begins with the purposes of God for our lives. It finds us within a hugely complex web of relationships we call family, friends and society, through which we exert and respond to myriad influences. It sees a pilgrim people, undergoing an inward and outward transformation, journeying towards a very particular destination. A city on a hill, a sunrise of golden light, a place of clean air and clear thoughts, of knowing and being known, of vitality, a place where we become our truest selves. Most centrally of all, within these social networks and affecting the shape of our journey, the call to lead is also a call to follow. A call to follow Jesus. A call that manifests in and through one another, a sharing of leadership if you will, even coming from the most unexpected places. It is this manifestation of call and response that I want to explore in the pages of this book. A call and response grounded in the Christian hope.

PART ONE

Is There Hope for Leadership?

I

Pain

So there you sit. And how much blood was shed
That you might sit there.
Bertolt Brecht (1898–1956)[1]

For many at the time, Bill Clinton's rise within the Democratic Party
and election as President of the USA in 1993 was a political triumph:
the centrist, Third Way political ideology seemingly sweeping aside some
of the petty and ineffectual political caricatures of the past. Finally the
political pursuit of prosperity and social justice were articulated together,
a new world lay waiting to be discovered and here was someone we could
trust to lead us into it. It wasn't until Clinton was in his second term that
it came to light that he had been having an affair with Monica Lewinsky,
a White House intern 27 years his junior. Just as painful as the infidelity
to his wife and the seeming abuse of sexual power, Clinton then began
a long period of denial and imaginative reworking of his memory and
description of events as he and the team around him clung to office. Most
of those in the States and overseas who had cheered him into the presi-
dency felt hugely disappointed and even a sense of betrayal. But in a sense
there was nothing new here, and nothing to be surprised about.

Delving into what Bishop Steven Croft pictures as 'an old, deserted
mine shaft, in the shadow of the bright lights of the business school' we
find resonance and even answers as to why these things happen with such
regularity. Bishop Croft is talking about the Judeo-Christian reflection
on leadership, which, at over 3,000 years, he notes to be the 'longest
continuous tradition of reflection on leadership in the entire history of
human culture'.[2] There we find the stories of Saul, David and Solomon:
men holding the highest political offices of leadership, who were simply
unable to inhabit the leadership clothes with sustained personal integrity.
The pressures on the self, and the contradictions, inadequacies and compromises found therein ultimately led to failure and eventual destruction.
The particular temptation to use power for sexual fulfilment is illustrated
best by King David's pursuit of Bathsheba and his role in the murder
of her husband to make way for her betrothal[3] – and it has happened
many, many times before and since. While those in positions of lesser
power looked on in disappointment, perhaps the potential for this kind

of failure, and pain of failed self-leadership, is much closer to each of us than we imagine.

How can we lead better?

As well as the trials of self-leadership, the internal conflicts within teams and the leader's role as overseer and peacemaker within a leadership team are sources of equal challenges. Within the business world, competing factions lead to the splintering of interests and sometimes to the break-up of businesses themselves. Organizations, public services, sports teams – even churches – can become nests of division, competing priorities and personalities pulling collaborations apart. Often the most intriguing conflicts are the political ones, played out on the public stage. Fortunately, modern democracies seem to have outgrown the violent enactments of Caesar and Brutus, although you don't have to look far around the current world to find similarly murderous fallouts.

Again, the contours of team disharmony are well sketched in the biblical narratives and, among myriad other examples, Paul's perpetual call to unity, mutual submission and love stands as a counterweight to what can happen in destructive team situations. Leading teams well requires these deep resources of selflessness, and they aren't easily tapped into. Sadly, perhaps the most painful conflicts within teams, if I can apply that term in this way, are within families. The generational gap has always put pressure on the parent–child relationship, but the increasing levels of divorce and family breakdowns, to say nothing of the difficult external pressures families now have to navigate, make good leadership in the family extremely difficult. The safe place, the loving harbour of mutual encouragement and reflective growth, has been badly eroded, at untold cost, and much support is needed to resource those striving to protect family life. In every environment, there is great pain when teams fail, and it is often a tremendous challenge for those in leadership to keep their teams united and effective.

How can we lead better?

I remember sitting in a packed auditorium in the late 1990s, with hundreds of other graduates on the GEC-Marconi development programme, listening to Lord Simpson and John Mayo outlining their vision for the company with triumphalist zeal. Carol Vorderman was parachuted in to act as compère, and there was a tinge of arrogance around the stage that the company and those present were destined for greatness. And they said such wonderful things about each other. The following couple of years or so are now recognized as being one of the biggest boom-to-bust periods of any company anywhere, let alone a British manufacturing one. In mid-2000, the share price was at £12.50 with the company valued at £35 billion. A year later that share price would fall to 29 pence. Very quickly the company's credit rating would be 'junk status' and, within a few years, despite valiant attempts to restructure, the company would no longer exist in any recognizable form. The leadership of GEC-Marconi showed what appeared to be a total inability to lead the organization into a place of productivity and growth. In fact, the opposite was true: a small group of leaders led thousands of employees and shareholders into turmoil and loss.

But the pain of failed organizational leadership is nothing new. Six hundred years or so before the birth of Jesus, the small kingdom of Judah was the last remaining stronghold of what had been the extensive province of Israel. The northern kingdom was overcome, and within a few years, all of Judah was routed and most of the surviving people taken into exile in Babylon. The Bible offers a blow-by-blow account of how, within a few generations, a small number of rulers had led a flourishing people group into destruction and captivity. An isolated leadership, without relationship and proper accountability beyond itself, detached from the organization's true purpose, compromised in its dealing, exuding excessive self-confidence and an unwillingness to seek help beyond the confines of the corridors of power are characteristics that are all too common in large organizations.

How can we lead better?

If the pain of failed self-leadership, team leadership and organizational leadership abounds, what price the failure of leadership beyond an organization – that which Steven Croft calls 'outward facing leadership'?[4] At the beginning of the twentieth century, certainly in Europe and North America, human confidence could hardly have been higher. Industry and trade had revolutionized societies. Advances in science, medicine, engineering and travel were utterly transforming people's life experiences. There was a sense that life could only get better: human progress was unstoppable. And then there were the two World Wars. Tens of millions of people killed and injured in the first. A population the size of Britain today killed in the second, alongside a cultish embodiment of hatred, prejudice and genocide to add to the horrors of the war zone. This happened across societies that had been at least nominally Christianized and where the Church was significantly active and engaged.

When the politicians of the Western world tried to pick up the pieces in the middle of the twentieth century, there was an urgency to build political structures that would stand against the tribalism and propensity for violence that clearly hadn't been overcome through the advances of human progress. With this backdrop, it isn't entirely surprising to see the historic fading of the Church and the marginalization of Christian influence on wider society which took place from the end of the Second World War onwards. Where had the Church been when society needed it most? What leadership had it exercised in pulling the politicians and wider society back towards peace? The institutional Church's role, to take a moral lead in society, had been painfully absent, and the results were as horrific as human beings can imagine. Yet again, even in the age of the Church, God's people had failed to be the blessing they were called to be to wider society. Yet again, like so many times through the Judeo-Christian story, the tide of blood and violence had swept across nations as a result. Yet again, the pain of failed leadership, or failing to exercise proper responsibility beyond an organization, was felt in the most extreme way.

How can we lead better?

I share these negative pictures at the outset of this book because, in different ways, they illustrate the pain of failed leadership. Of course, at their most basic they illustrate failed humanity – broken images of personhood twisted and warped out of its intended shape. However, for our purposes, which are about drawing the bigger pictures of human flourishing and the mechanisms to achieve it, it is the failed leadership that I want to concentrate on. The four pictures represent failure on four different levels – what Croft goes on to define as leadership of the self, leadership of the team, leadership of the organization and outward-facing leadership from an organization into the wider world.[5] We'll explore what leadership is, in a theological sense at least, as the book develops. At this stage I simply want to recognize that leadership has something to do with the exercise of power, something to do with how we move as communities and something to do with how we grow into personal responsibility and inhabit it, hopefully with integrity. Clearly this thing called 'leadership', whatever it is exactly, is exercised in a positional sense within an organization, but can also exist in a much more relational and organic sense without formal structures of command and control. There are untold numbers of books on leadership, all with varying ways into the notion of leadership, and this isn't the moment in my exploration to unpick what different commentators mean by the term. But if it is true that so much of human flourishing and failure rests on leadership activity, then despite the plethora of leadership material available, recent history says we still have a lot of work to do.

The challenge couldn't be greater. Over the past few years, certainly in my own cultural context in Britain, it feels as though there's been a shaking of the recognized power structures as more and more instances of destructive leadership have come to light. The 2008 banking crisis exposed a hugely broken financial system – even today the pursuit of wealth has become so institutionally dominant that moral and sensible practices are extremely difficult to identify and apply. The British government required a significant shake-up after the MPs' expenses scandal in 2009 and is still playing catch-up on claims of bullying and abuse. The

News International phone-hacking scandal of 2011 was the tip of an iceberg of journalistic malpractice. Car-makers tampering with emissions tests, clothing and food brands employing slave labour, huge corporations tax dodging are stories that have become normalized. The new industries, supposedly without some of the old baggage, are suddenly just as open to corruption, only in more creative ways – social media platforms and their network of application and data providers are a case in point – to say nothing of the sexual abuse that has tarnished every major institution in the land. People within the institutional Church have harboured and protected sexual predators for generations. Characters like Jimmy Savile used their celebrity status to sexually dominate and abuse many. The Weinstein saga revealed the film industry to be rife with sexual exploitation, full of people deliberately using their power and influence to coerce others into sex, and full of people willing to look the other way to preserve the beneficial status quo. Even our charities aren't exempt from this kind of behaviour, an example being the small number of senior staff from Oxfam who were revealed to have used their relational power for abusive sexual gratification in troubled parts of the world. Fault lines run through our finances, our political structures, our industries, social institutions and our relationships.

And throughout this picture of broken power structures, Christians live and work. Not just Christians, but a huge swathe of people who have been broadly Christianized in terms of social values and behaviour and who are deeply sympathetic to the person of Jesus. And not just the de-churched community, but myriad folks of other faiths and none who understand enough about the intended shape of things to feel deeply pained by the current leadership crisis and are convinced there is a better way. Certainly many of them will have big questions about the relevancy of the Church and its historic messages, but good people are out there and in abundance. However, for many of them the general hubris of the culture around is too confusing or intimidating to swim against: the status quo is too comfortable and sometimes the minor temptations and indulgences too attractive.

For all these reasons and more, a coherent shape and manifesto for truly good leadership is lacking and, for reasons that will hopefully become explicit through this book, I believe the best place to start is with a theology of Christian leadership. How misshapen humanity takes form, how it gets passed around and gets a hold needs to be understood so we can catch it and reverse it. More positively, how do we begin the cycle with an understanding of leadership that leads to fullness of life for all? As such, this isn't so much a *how to* book, of which there are plenty, but more of a *why* leadership, and *where* is God in all this?

These are the big interests of this book, and to help us I'd like to sketch out the aforementioned five spheres of life within which our expressions of leadership operate: Church, politics, business, third sector and finally family, which, for the purposes of this book, I'll refer to as next generation. While I don't think life is meant to be neatly compartmentalized, nor that these five spheres sufficiently cover all of life by any means, I do think these spheres operate sufficiently differently, in general terms at least, to be used helpfully as different lenses into human relations.

The pain of failed leadership in the Church

So let us begin with the Church. Getting at accurate numbers is tricky but, for most of the period since the Second World War in Britain, church attendance was probably declining at around one per cent a year. Bob Jackson is helpful on the statistics behind church decline and growth, and his account suggests that actual turnaround, certainly in the Church of England, has only begun to happen since the turn of the new millennium after a top-down transition in outlook that probably reflected what some grassroots folks had been hankering after for years.[6]

The Church is a missionary organization, it's meant to be reaching out to those around it and growing in numbers, depth of faith and influence. At the heart of its shared life is a message of hope and love that connects with the deepest needs of every human person. Propagation of the Christian gospel and the subsequent growth of the Church is meant to be normal. Yes, there have been massive cultural shifts in Britain during this period, and part of the challenge for the Church has been how to navigate these. But clearly, in a sustained way over a long period of time, much of the institutional Church became disconnected from its core message and the kind of life Christians are invited and empowered to live. It's an oftentimes sad story of tears, disappointments and a whole generation of people left spiritually empty and looking elsewhere for the fulfilment our souls seek.

Of course, the picture is varied in different contexts. During that same post-war period, the Church in Africa, South America and parts of Asia has grown at an extraordinary rate. While the Anglican and Roman Catholic Churches have struggled in Britain and Europe, the independent Churches in these contexts have been growing, often picking up the folks opting out of the mainline denominations. However, having served as a missionary in an African country where the Church is fast growing, and having been quite well connected with a variety of independent Churches that are flourishing in the UK, I have observed that intrinsic to the challenge of church growth is an even bigger challenge: are churches sufficiently equipping Christians to lead lives that are genuinely Christian? We might be good at some aspects of evangelism and Christian community, but are our discipleship foundations strong enough? That, for me, sharpens the leadership question.

Part of my own story will hopefully serve as an illustration. I grew up with some church experience. My parents were active in church life without ever being particularly evangelical about it. When I hit the teenage years, I opted out of church as did my younger brother (and seemingly most of my generation). I then spent ten years without any church attendance, and basically forgot about God as a person to talk to and do life with. Wonderfully, I encountered God through the influence of a friend and a book, and my life took a new direction.

Looking back, I would say that the first ten years of my Christian life were characterized by two things. First, a deeply personal, emotionally fulfilling, real and vivid experience of the presence of God which was both satisfying and sustaining as I tried to work out my general life direction as a young adult. Second, a conviction that the good news about Jesus was something to be shared. Despite my evangelistic timidity, being attentive and brave enough to seek out opportunities to share my faith seemed a natural part of the Christian life. However, as I continued my Christian journey, this combination of personal spirituality and evangelistic energy led me to a significant question: beyond the personal experience of God, what kind of life was I inviting people into?

During this period, I had the privilege of being part of some fantastic church communities, each one of them alive and growing. But I must say that in those first ten years as a Christian, I don't think I ever got a sufficient answer to this question. There are some obvious quick answers, the biggest one being the eternal significance of the decision to follow Jesus, and the hope of a life beyond this one. However, I quickly became sure that that wasn't entirely sufficient on its own, particularly with Jesus' emphasis on fullness of life[7] and the often overlooked translation issue that 'eternal life' in the New Testament has as much of a qualitative emphasis as a quantitative one.

It was probably Tom Wright's influence, first with the more academic *The Resurrection of the Son of God* and then in the easier to read *Surprised by Hope*, that really got me and some of my friends at the time thinking about what Jesus meant by fullness of life and why the resurrection and ascension are so important for informing life today as well as life tomorrow. Encouragingly, as we'll see, today it feels like there's an emerging cluster of church leaders who have got their heads round this: the initiatives of Mark Greene, James Lawrence and LICC, and books like *Imagine Church* by Neil Hudson, being illustrative of the UK context.

However, the sorry fact is that the vast majority of Christians across the world are still hugely under-resourced in their understanding of what it means to be Christian in the contexts we find ourselves in today. By and large, church leaders have failed to build a strong enough bridge between our hope for eternity and the implications for the kind of lives Christians are meant to live. That seems to be the crux of the leadership challenge within the Church. Yes, like every other institution, the pitfalls of leadership abound, the situation with Bill Hybels at the time of writing being the latest sorry story of a seemingly successful but abusive church leader. But at its core, perhaps linked to the moral failures in part, lies this burning question about the appropriate shape of the Christian life in the contemporary world. Even for those of us who have begun to get our heads round the implications of Jesus' lordship, actually teaching and equipping people to live in ways aligned with the coming Kingdom can feel like a vain struggle against the tide. I have a haunting thought that now, as a full-time church leader, I have come to this role in part through a 'survival of the fittest' natural order of selection. Despite the absence of a worked-through theology for Christian life today, I have managed to hang in there when others drifted away, and here I am, ready to continue a form of leadership that has consistently sold Christians short and failed to energize and equip the saints for their true and proper role in the world. My prayer is that I will do a bit better than that.

The pain of failed leadership in politics

If church leadership hasn't quite been the shining example of informed, practical yet visionary leadership, then where do you start with politics? In truth, most of the politicians I've got to know personally have been extraordinarily gifted and compassionate people. But like the struggles of the Church, our inherited political system and the language and form of our politics often seems to come from a distant age, unable to really cut it where the contemporary needs lie. And, unfortunately, there is still far too much room for abuses of power. I can't even begin to start on the political stories of the likes of Donald Trump, as appealing as some of their policies clearly are to a section of the electorate.

So let's start with some political theory. For Aristotle, politics is about marshalling social partnerships that lead to the greatest common good.[8] In slightly more specific terms you could say that the purpose of our political system is to create space for reasoned discourse about our shared life together, to make mutual decisions around the best shape of that shared life and, in agreed forms, to marshal the exercise of power to achieve those ends. Taking the post-war European-American context, this has essentially played out through the emerging consensus around a liberal democracy, with a relatively free and open capitalist market-driven economy, and a plethora of social services designed to educate and care for a growing population. Given the advances we've made in life expectancy, social infrastructure and household income, you'd have to say we've achieved incredible things. However, in recent years the cracks in the system have opened into great abysses of discontent.

The gap between rich and poor has been steadily increasing and the IMF argues that this presents the greatest social challenge of our era.[9] We are seemingly heading for climate disaster because of our inability to rein in fossil fuel consumption. There are more slaves in the world than there ever have been, and child labour rates are still incredibly high. Our farming methods, particularly of livestock and fish, have been thoroughly barbaric and inhumane. The actions of a small minority of religious extremists and the West's crude responses have caused turmoil in the Middle Eastern region, with millions of deaths and displaced peoples. As participants in this consumerist society, we can't even get dressed, have breakfast or drive to work without participating in a deep violation of someone's human dignity, or the wider dignity of creation for that matter. Confidence and trust in our elected representatives is consequently very low, with little more than half of the eligible voters in the USA even bothering to vote, and the percentage not much better in most European nations.

Chris Hedges is well worth a read from an American perspective, *The World As It Is* offering a provocative critique of the status quo. At its heart, I'd side with the likes of Will Hutton, who offers probably the best recent analysis of the British political malaise in *How Good We Can Be*. While he offers a very particular critique of the British system, many of his ideas are translatable to different contexts, and the heart of that critique is the suggestion that the government has failed to understand its leadership role and to broker the right kinds of relationships with other power brokers in both wider society and the wider world. Hutton imagines a creative, well-informed government, which is able to hold organizations to account and to know when the market best serves wider society's long-term aspirations. As he puts it:

A democracy has both the right and the duty to ask tough questions of the effectiveness of all its institutions, public and private: moreover there is a public realm and public interest that can only be represented by public institutions with public values.[10]

Now clearly there is still significant debate about where those public and private boundaries lie, and whether some elements of what is traditionally understood as public might be best served by that which is private. However, that is simply nuance next to the major failure of such unfettered power being given to the market, largely because of misunderstood first principles about the role of the market in wider society. A significant imbalance has formed and Figure 1 might prove helpful.

Figure 1: Interplay of politics, business and third sector

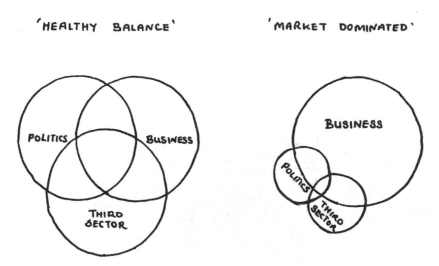

Now, to avoid misunderstanding, I should say that I don't see the market as an inherently broken place, and I'm certainly not wanting to put excessive burdens on it. The market has consistently proved itself to be the place where we humans can express our greatest creative vitality in ways that lead to human flourishing: employment, products and services are things that have massive potential to generate wealth and improve well-being. Part of this book's agenda is about underpinning a theology for a thriving market. We need it. However, part of the political function is to legislate how the market operates and, as per our earlier definition, to create space for discourse about what is good and healthy, to make decisions towards the common good and to forcefully ensure businesses operate within well-determined boundaries. There has been considerable failure at all these levels, at great cost to both humanity and the wider planet.

Into this messy imbalance I would also have to throw the difficulty that Christians have with engaging in the current political arena. I will argue later in this book that the real, true and lasting answers to our political malaise are to be found in practical Christian theology, translated and proclaimed through a Christian community winning the right to be at the secular decision-making table and showing the world that we can help it become a better place for all. That's the argument that the Church has historically been able to win, in the British landscape at least. How sad it was then that under a recent Labour government we were told, despite the fact that many front-bench politicians were professing Christians, not least the Prime Minister himself, that the government 'didn't do God'. This stands as a poor reflection on the government of the day, but even more saddening is that the fractured and muddled caricature of the Church had become so open to disdain in the media-dominated political arena, despite the Church's extraordinary history of shaping the political life of the nation. Granted, the secular press was a tad militant, but we simply failed to explain why the voice of Christian faith, diverse in itself, was important to the wider political conversation. The recent pressure Tim Farron felt as leader of the Liberal Democrat party reflects another angle on this. While being a champion of liberal policy, with liberal views about human freedom deeply informed by his Christian faith, Tim was under attack for his personal conviction about sexual ethics. Despite his being a living example of someone mature enough to lead a broad-based secular party and still fighting hard to protect his personal integrity, he was effectively pressured out of frontline politics. Christians are marginalized, our political foundations are imbalanced and, for a multitude of people, the political journey our leaders are taking us on globally feels disastrous.

The pain of failed leadership in business

As we've touched on already, for a business to be successful it must deliver products or services that customers want. To achieve this, it needs to build the right kind of relationships within and without the business, and to find the right internal gearing of production and delivery for the operating conditions of any given market the business engages in. Relationships and gearing are market-driven but can be helpfully brokered by government. In a free-market economy, businesses will always be competitive environments, pushing for growth in the products and services they deliver and the retail opportunities around them. Inherent in this process are demands for future innovation, increased efficiency, wider networks of sales distribution as well as improved quality of life for a company's employees. Businesses in a free-market economy are vehicles that either self-improve or die, and that's why we have such confidence in them as a catalyst for wider social benefit. But businesses make mistakes and go wrong, and when they do there are painful consequences. So let's examine that and, specifically, where the pain of poor leadership is most manifest.

For me, the greatest sell-out of a business's purpose is encapsulated by Thomas Murphy, the former chairman of GM, when he infamously said 'General Motors is not in the business of making cars. It is in the business of making money.' It is a desperately sad truth that many of our business leaders not only think the same but are taught to think the same. When the leaders of a company focus exclusively on profitability and not adequately enough on the wider purposes of that business in the world, then the business isn't being built on firm enough ground. I'll explore why this is so fundamental later, but again Will Hutton's analysis is helpful. Essentially he argues that exclusive focus on profitability, particularly short-term profitability, leads to a mercenary culture that fundamentally restricts the intrinsic self-improvement at the heart of the free-market business model, and therefore compromises the wider social benefits inherent therein.

When I worked for a large data services company, the regional director, on one occasion, addressed staff to outline our strategy for tackling competition. Our business unit was the dominant player in the market, and we enjoyed a rather fat profit margin of something approaching 50 per cent of our turnover. A new player had come to the market, and our strategy for competition was initially an attempt at an aggressive take-over. This director played to our tribalism, was a scaremonger about potential job losses due to competition, and essentially depicted our competition as something to be snuffed out at all costs. In contrast to the director's presentation, the truth was that our sector badly needed healthy competition. As a business we hadn't sufficiently innovated, had historically overcharged for under-developed technology, and we'd used our wider influence in the market to segment a suite of data services that other businesses weren't then able to develop. The real purpose of the business was preventing fraud and effectively managing consumer and commercial identity. In reality we were acting as a parking brake on the true development of fraud and identity management tools in our sector and getting in the way of where the market needed to go. Instead of rallying the troops and managing the business through the creative opportunity presented by the competition, the director chose to do as much as possible to shore up the status quo. Was the director a bad egg who just needed replacing? Actually, no. He was a good strategist who was operating simply within short-term parameters that the government, the market and the shareholders had allowed to be set. Our structures can create monsters.

If we've misunderstood the purpose of our businesses – their 'teleology' if you like – and failed to gear our markets to ensure those purposes flourish, then we also haven't worked hard enough on the detail of how our businesses operate, on our particular strategies for growth within moral and environmental parameters. Not finding a solution to adequately connect share prices, remuneration, promotion and so on to both long-term as well as short-term financial goals is one well-documented problem. Another has been how we've failed to respond to the challenge and opportunity of globalization. Europe and America have had a good stab at getting decent employment rights, ethical forms of production and appropriate community engagement within our businesses, but then we allow products and services to be accessed from all parts of the globe where none of these things exist. Down the supply chains of almost everything we own and use lies untold exploitation and environmental degradation. The power holders, the de-facto leaders if you like, have given little thought to making these global supply chains morally and ethically accountable.

As a final stain on the leadership of our businesses, alongside the failures of purpose and the gaping holes in our strategy for business operations, there is something very specific about the failure of most businesses to properly care for and protect their employees. Our business leaders, and the shapers of our employer–employee relationship, have insufficiently reflected on the complexities of our human connection and attachment to our place of work. Yes, trade unions have done a great deal to help correct this. But through my 15 or so years working in commercial life, I frequently saw the value and dignity of my colleagues trampled over because of the demands of the business. Excessive hours worked. Unimaginative methods of working. Remuneration not properly reflecting contribution. Hire and fire, with inadequate severance or employment protection, to say nothing of unfair and abusive power holders forming minor fiefdoms within the empire. I was always fortunate in these regards. I loved my jobs and wanted to work hard at them. I enjoyed flexibility in how I worked. I was always at the higher end of peer remuneration. I never got fired, consistently got promoted and got on well with those in managerial roles above me. But, frankly, when I look back I can see how far I'd bought into the status quo and how uncritical I was of what was happening around me. My personally positive experience was unusual, and many and deep are employees' scars from business leadership that is rooted in destructive paradigms.

The pain of failed leadership in the third sector

Like the business sector, the third sector's greatest leadership challenge has been how it has brokered its life and energy within wider society. For the third sector, there has been a high degree of suffocation in an environment dominated by a particular view of the market. Having to harness expertise and resources in a world that devalues the social capital provided by the third sector has made it very difficult for some, often brilliant, organizations to flourish. Where possible, it seems absolutely right that voluntary organizations, charities and social enterprises are able to enjoy peppercorn rents and gain access to products and services at less than commercial rates. However, this is often the exception rather than the norm. In Liverpool in the UK where I live, there has been a good history of the third sector operating alongside and supported by local government, faith groups and businesses. However, it seems to me that this has typically happened through local champions, fired up by issues of justice, leveraging relational networks, and who work extremely hard against, and despite, the structures of society. We need more of these heroes elsewhere, but our social leadership needs to rethink the role of the third sector and incentivize the existing power brokers to give this sector the leg-up it needs.

The situation around support for asylum seekers seems like a good case in point. Millions of refugees from the Middle East and northern Africa have migrated into Europe since the two Gulf wars, the growth of IS and the conflict in Syria. As a Christian minister I've listened to people's stories, helped run English language and cultural integration groups, welcomed strangers into my home and attended court to support people's applications for asylum. What I've noticed is that there are some brilliant third sector organizations helping these people find their feet in a strange country, but that the wider landscape of support, legal assessment and subsequent social integration is disconnected and often inadequate, which is to everybody's detriment. The long-term benefits of successful migrant assessment and effective integration are enormous. The reality is that the significant majority of asylum seekers will end up making this country their permanent home, and failing to give them dignity and integrate them into British life is simply storing up prejudice and division for future generations. Third sector groups that have a heart for this task should be drawn into the fabric of city life, not only accessing funding from local government and businesses, but helping to sketch out a wider framework of support that draws in the faith groups, educational institutions, health care and businesses that can all support the aim of assessment and social inclusion. Frankly, leading these organizations in the present climate is excessively difficult and frustratingly limited in terms of effect.

We will look at ways in which third sector leadership can respond to these challenges, but I'd also like to offer two further observations that are perhaps more critical of leadership within third sector operations themselves. First, given the dominance of the market and the effects of its particular values at the present time, many third sector leaders are deeply suspicious of commercial business models and the appropriateness or otherwise of revenue-generating activities. While some suspicion is understandable, it is often the case that third sector organizations could simply do with some smart business know-how, increased technical efficiency, appropriate branding, and making use of a whole load of commercial practices that aren't ideologically flawed within themselves, but that tend to help organizations work better.

Another aspect that warrants some reflection is the level of paternalism inherent in some third sector organizations. Helping others is a beautiful thing. 'The poor you will always have with you' says Jesus in Matthew's Gospel,[11] which is another way of saying that we'll always be called to help those around us less fortunate than ourselves. But helping others is sometimes more complicated than we want to admit. The increase in the prevalence of food banks in the UK over recent years is testimony to the generosity and neighbourly love most of us feel towards one another. However, if we limit our action to just food banks, then we are essentially propping up a system that is allowing people to fall into abject poverty. This can't be right. Not all of us will be able to fight for economic justice at the different levels in society, but leaders in the third sector must be clear that the actions of their organizations are often testimony to a greater injustice that, in some form or another, needs addressing. Opportunities to campaign for change, to essentially pursue a world where your organization is no longer necessary, or looks different, should be a high priority.

There's something here about how expressions of altruism become woven into an organization's purpose that we'll need to look at in more detail later. In brief, altruism is wonderful, but those who are used to intentionally helping others will know that there is an emotional, identity-strengthening payback: we feel good about helping others and it bolsters our sense of significance in the world. Because of this there is a danger that our shadow sides, those self-seeking parts of us that are hidden but still active, pursue this payback more for our own benefit, sometimes without our really thinking through what is properly helpful for other people. Robert Lupton, a social activist and entrepreneur in the USA, dissects the actual impact of some of our well-intentioned activity in the book *Toxic Charity*.[12] He argues that, while we may not want to hear it, we often aren't willing to take the hard road to really empower and support people out of the cycles of poverty they are trapped in. A much more complex relational solution is often required that is more costly to us, so we give people things, which in turn makes us feel better, but that potentially disempowers them and isn't what they really want. We need to open up the space for third sector organizations to thrive, but we also need to ask the harder questions to prevent well-intentioned leadership from becoming destructive.

The pain of failed leadership to the next generation

Alongside, but in some sense running across, the particular spheres of Church, politics, business and the third sector is a further sphere that I will call *next generation*. We could call it *family*, but I think it is wider than that. I am talking about the networks of relationships that are very specifically about passing the baton of leadership on to the generation that follows us, of which the family is certainly one expression.

In the church of which I am part, we have a particular emphasis on developing young leaders. One of the implications of this is that every year we have people who want to explore the possibility of ordained leadership within the Church of England. I'm a vicar, so in a sense I have a very particular opportunity to hand the baton of ordained leadership on, by envisioning, giving experience to and helping others taste a little of what ordained ministry might be like. This is different, I think, from just leadership in the Church. This is a very specific activity in which I offer leadership to the next generation coming after me, to those who will inhabit a role like my own. In so doing, I need to be careful about projecting my own sense of calling and purpose onto someone else. I need to help people identify the things inside them that are aligned with this particular ministry. I need to make space for others to grow into their vocation without imposing the particular shape, confines or limitations that I might have experienced or embraced for myself. It is a difficult job, and one that can go badly wrong without careful attention.

As another example, consider parenting. My wife and I adopted our two children, and it was very interesting how much dissection of motivations, reflection on our own experiences of parenting and intense preparation on our parenting strategies was required to fulfil the basic requirements to adopt. For us, preparing to be a parent was 18 months of personal and collective formation. We were a couple in our late thirties with plenty of life experience, who had gone through years of formational work already in preparing for full-time Christian ministry. Passing the baton of our humanity on to our children has been difficult enough, even with all this preparation. I don't want to throw out statistics on divorce rates, parental absence, or simply the enormous pressures that many families are under, but good leadership in the family context is hard. Like the structural brokenness that poisons business and political life, so, in most contexts within the so-called developed world, we have a societal brokenness that puts significant strain on family life and makes it intrinsically harder than it should be. Family life can't be commoditized, it doesn't have a monetary value and it often comes last in the series of priorities we find ourselves juggling. As a Christian minister who gets to hear the inside track from quite a number of families within and without the Church, I'd say that most parents feel under-resourced and out of their depth in their ability to maintain a healthy family life. Many of the others are probably too scared to admit it.

I accept that leadership may seem a funny term to use in the family context, and I don't want to simply equate it to parenting. My big observation looking at the pain of failed leadership within the family is that we often don't realize the main event. We are there to facilitate change, and to embrace change for ourselves. In a sense, family life is the primary place where adults and children are together shaped and reshaped as human becomings. Passing on the baton requires our own transformation as we come into relationship with those that follow us, and as such family life inherently brings some of our greatest challenges. Nowhere else do we have the opportunity to help others grow or find the same potential for our own growth. When we fail to see that, when we miss what God is up to in our midst, we are the most vulnerable to failure and pain.

In a sense, the same is true for leadership to the next generation in the widest sense. I get to play a specific *next generation* leadership role on a host of different fronts, but particularly where I have the opportunity to pass on the baton to people who are travelling a similar road to the one that I have travelled. Younger families in my social network. Students and young adults that I know. People who, like me, spent a number of years working nine to five and developing a career in the corporate world. As I've referred to already, people exploring ministry in the Church. In a very specific sense, because of my journey, I have something to offer each of these groups and, if I allow myself to travel closely with these people, they also have something very specific to offer me. The interaction between generations comes loaded with challenge and opportunity and hence, as well as looking at leadership in the different spheres of life that we occupy, I want to explore leadership that happens between generations and want to try to establish the underlying shape that helps us best move towards collective health and well-being. How might we better resource ourselves to pass the baton on well and to be open to the potential for significant soul formation – in our lives and the lives of others?

The call to understand leadership better

We have seen that there is a huge amount of pain caused by inadequate and destructive forms of leadership, to say nothing of the loss of unrealized human potential. However, it seems to me that this is strongly connected to a misunderstanding of what leadership is all about; that is, what we are meant to be and do as leaders, and how that fits into what God is being and doing in the world. As we look to the future, I believe that the technological and social changes around us are forcing a dramatic confrontation over how leadership is realized in the world, and pretty much all of our inherited way of life is up for grabs. The plethora of leadership material suggests that many people understand this, at least in part, which is a good start. But it's not enough. We can't just dialogue around the edges of leadership. The self-help guides and leadership gurus are often positive, but my sense is that we need to go much deeper. In short, a significant first step that we have struggled to take is to show how the bigger theological picture of God's re-creation of the world informs our understanding of human leadership.

Even then, the fact remains that understanding true forms of leadership is no guarantee that we will be able to live in a way that is consistent with them. Anyone who has held a position of significant leadership will tell you that the myriad ways our human soul is fractured constantly manifest as counterweights to the way of the angels. We are shot through with holes, and our need for significance, security and identity comes through even more forcefully, and with selfish twists and connotations, when we have increasingly powerful ways of meeting those needs. However, through shared understanding we can build checks and balances into our systems of leadership. We can hold people accountable. We can opt into supportive communities that help us pursue shared values together. We can commit ourselves, with others, to different ways of leading, and that surely is part of the way forward.

Despite the sad fact that much of life is a mess; despite the disappointment that, given our social and technological advancements, we are far behind where we should be in terms of a just and fair world village; despite the myriad pains of failed leadership around us, there is still hope. I believe we can turn the ship around with greater societal momentum. So much of history makes me believe that good will triumph, when the pathways to that good are properly articulated and promoted. The quest started many moons ago, and in historical terms we are perhaps a few steps from an important next summit. This is something for every person to engage with – but particularly, I believe, for the Christian, as we take the next step in locating our human activity in God's re-creation of the world. As a first step, let's consider how the Church talks about and enacts leadership, before deepening our theological journey.

Comment
Tim Farron, Liberal Democrat MP,
Westmorland and Lonsdale

One of the few things that everyone seems able to agree upon is that politics is broken. It seems as if the idea of government working for the common good of the people has been lost. Instead we watch politicians vying for power, and the damaging results of selfish political ideologies that are deepening poverty, harming our planet and escalating the divisions in our society. These are the pains resulting from failed leadership. The ancient story that power can corrupt even the best of intentions is played out at every level today.

And this is where the Church is called to step in: to equip Christians to exercise leadership, act as salt and light, and create a better society that points people to an eternal Kingdom. The Church's mission is to preach the gospel and to bring people to salvation, but the Bible also tells us to obey God in the here and now: to look after the most vulnerable in society, to be responsible stewards of creation and to love others as ourselves.

Jesus got his hands dirty. He cared for people's bodies as well as their souls. He fed the hungry, healed the sick and restored those who were physically and emotionally wounded. As Tom Wright puts it, Jesus' birth was the moment that God broke into this world, to put it to rights from within.

A well-meaning friend of mine once suggested that Christians should steer clear of politics because it is a mucky business. Yes it is. But so is life. And I strongly believe that Christians must continue to roll up our sleeves and get stuck in.

And we should expect to face opposition: from those with conflicting world views; from people who think that faith no longer has the right to a place at the table of public debate; from those who find Christian beliefs unpalatable and offensive. And we need to support one another through the church family; to equip our members to serve faithfully in Babylon as Daniel did.

This is not to say that we should be seeking to make people who are not Christians live as if they were. We are not seeking to install a theocracy or change people's hearts and minds through passing 'Christian laws'. In a culture where everyone is expected to create their own truth, this is both counterproductive and ineffective. But we become like that which we worship, and if we worship God, we should start to reflect his love to those around us.

So what should it look like to live out our faith in society? Government cannot do everything, and many churches are involved in helping the homeless, running food banks, toddler groups, street pastors; they are reaching out to their communities in many ways. Their motivation is their Christian faith: the two go hand in hand. And people see the love of Jesus through our actions.

We should be concerned for our neighbours – for their material needs *and* for their spiritual needs. This is the outworking of our faith. This is the work of the Church, at a grassroots level across society and through equipping Christians to serve in politics at every level. And this way we seek to fulfil the two greatest commandments until Christ returns: to love God and to love one another.

Notes

1 Bertolt Brecht, 'To the Students of the Workers' And Peasants' Faculty', in *Poems: 1913–1956*, ed. John Willett and Ralph Manheim (London: Methuen, 2000).

2 Steven Croft, https://blogs.oxford.anglican.org/adventurous-and-courageous-leadership/ (accessed 19 August 2019).

3 2 Samuel 11.

4 Steven Croft, https://blogs.oxford.anglican.org/adventurous-and-courageous-leadership/ (accessed 19 August 2019).

5 Steven Croft, https://blogs.oxford.anglican.org/adventurous-and-courageous-leadership/ (accessed 19 August 2019).

6 Bob Jackson makes a helpful observation about the decade of evangelism that the Church of England implemented in the 1990s. On the one hand it was a complete failure: 'Church attendance went down 17 per cent ... double the decline rate in the 1980s.' On the other hand, a long overdue transition in outlook was required. The Anglican Church had seen itself as an ever-present pastoral function for the entire land and by the turn of the century: 'evangelism was increasingly being accepted as an integral part of the Church's core business.' (*What Makes Churches Grow?: Vision and Practice in Effective Mission*, London: Church House Publishing, 2015, p. 29.)

7 John 10.10.

8 Aristotle, *Politics*, 1252a1, www.perseus.tufts.edu/hopper/text?doc=Perseus:-text:1999.01.0058 (accessed 12 July 2019).

9 Era Dabla-Norris et al., *Causes and Consequences of Income Inequality: A Global Perspective* (International Monetary Fund, 2015), www.imf.org/external/pubs/ft/sdn/2015/sdn1513.pdf (accessed 12 July 2019).

10 Will Hutton, *How Good We Can Be* (London: Little, Brown, 2015), p. 130.

11 Matthew 26.11.

12 Robert B. Lupton, *Toxic Charity: How Churches and Charities Hurt Those They Help (And How to Reverse It)* (New York: HarperOne, 2012).

Reflection

Presence Amid Brokenness

Job 24.1–9

Why does the Almighty not set times for judgement?
  Why must those who know him look in vain for such days?
There are those who move boundary stones;
  they pasture flocks they have stolen.
They drive away the orphan's donkey
  and take the widow's ox in pledge.
They thrust the needy from the path
  and force all the poor of the land into hiding.
Like wild donkeys in the desert,
  the poor go about their labour of foraging food;
  the wasteland provides food for their children.
They gather fodder in the fields
  and glean in the vineyards of the wicked.
Lacking clothes, they spend the night naked;
  they have nothing to cover themselves in the cold.
They are drenched by mountain rains
  and hug the rocks for lack of shelter.
The fatherless child is snatched from the breast;
  the infant of the poor is seized for a debt.

Questions

1 In what ways does this chapter resonate with your own experience and observations of the pain of failed leadership?
2 Do you find Stephen Croft's four levels of leadership helpful? Which areas are most significant for you in your leadership today? Why?
3 How has the leadership of others caused you pain? How might healing come?
4 How has your leadership caused pain for others? How might you seek forgiveness and restoration?
5 Why does God seem to allow so much painful leadership?

6 In which sphere of life do you need most help with your leadership? Why?

7 What kind of leadership do you aspire to? How might you inhabit this better?

Prayer

Father God, you know the times the leadership of others has hurt us. Mend the pains of the past and give us courage to resist destructive influence. We confess also the times when our leadership has been painful to others. Help us to say sorry when we get it wrong and to seek better forms of influence on others. In the different spheres of life where we can exercise leadership, help us to bring life and love and goodness to others. Help us to lead ourselves well. To lead our teams well. To lead our organizations well. To lead those outside and beyond us well, as much as we have the opportunity. Grant us your Spirit, so we may truly serve you and others. In Jesus' name, amen.

2

Confusion

Every one has heard people quarrelling ... however it sounds,
I believe we can learn something very important from listening
to the kind of things they say.
C. S. Lewis (1898–1963), Mere Christianity[1]

I was looking forward to the conversation. For a few months now, some of the church leadership had been praying for the younger adults in our congregation, and asking God how we might help this group grow in numbers and depth of spirituality. Encouragingly, two of the women in that group had begun talking about their desire to deepen relationships, to organically create social space where people could just hang out and get to know one another better. Less about programmes they had indicated, as important as they are, but more about community and varying up the times when people could easily draw alongside each other.

So, my turn to join in the conversation, I was the vicar and all that. With a listening ear I asked them to talk me through their ideas, and tried to work out with them how what they were planning might fit alongside the other rhythms and shapes of our shared church life. As we listened and talked there was agreement and mutual excitement. This was important and good, and God's timing seemed to be all over it. As we seemingly came in to land with the planning, I made what I thought was an encouraging summary of what we'd talked about and where we might go. As I finished up, almost as an afterthought, I affirmed them both as leaders within our community and said I was thrilled to be supporting them in their leadership. Before I'd even got to the end of the sentence, though, I knew my language had provoked a different type of reaction. 'Leaders?' one of them replied, 'No, no, no. We don't want to be leaders.'

As I'd spoken about leadership, it was as if the conversation, which had been light and airy, had suddenly clouded with heavy responsibility and formalized relationship. I don't think it's an overstatement that one of them looked visibly repulsed. The other, the one who replied, was upright, alert, ready to push back on what clearly felt like a complete misinterpretation of their role in all this. Yet I thought I had been speaking of something positive and energizing. Recognizing the faux pas, I think I said, 'OK, let's ditch that word', or something equivalent, as I then attempted to pull the conversation back to where we'd just come from. Fortunately, we made it, and we finally concluded the conversation in the positive mood to which we'd originally been heading. However, I was deeply struck by our completely different perceptions of the word *leader*. And how quickly the whole conversation could have been derailed if I hadn't been able to convince them that what I meant by *leader* wasn't the same as what they thought I meant.

What does the Church say about leadership?

While the world may ache with the pain of failed leadership, struggling to understand the dynamite it plays with – particularly without moral, spiritual or philosophical consensus – the Church on the other hand should be well placed to offer a coherent and consistent theological picture of what leadership is. Unfortunately, as the account I've just offered illustrates, there remains an extraordinarily varied opinion and reaction to leadership within the Church, perhaps most significantly in postmodern contexts where the remnants of failed leadership lie all too close in physical and historical terms. Indeed, having spent a few years trying to piece together contemporary and historic Christian reflections on leadership, I'm sorry to say that there is just as much confusion around both the nature of leadership and how it should become manifest in academic circles as with your everyday Christian.

First, there is a lot of confusion about whether leadership is even a Christian term. Leonard Sweet wrote a beautiful book, *I Am a Follower*, with the provocative additional comment on the cover, 'It's never been about leading'. In it, Sweet basically argues that Christians have overplayed the leadership ticket and bought into a worldly paradigm that is more about power and status. Sweet thinks that, almost by definition, when we pursue leadership we are either subconsciously massaging our ego or simply positioning ourselves over others so we get what we want or avoid doing things we don't want to do. He summarizes his view of leadership neatly as, 'It's more that the whole category is corrupt or even a category mistake. Leadership is an alien template that we have laid on the Bible, and followership is a key not tried in any lock.'[2] When you work your way through Sweet's masterly critique, it's hard not to side with his analysis and certainly there are some shocking blunders within the Church that he is quick to reference.

Henri Nouwen takes a similar view. He'd reached a certain zenith of leadership in his role at Harvard, but when he moved to work in a L'Arche community, it was as if he saw his previous leadership position as a vain outworking of a desire for significance and status that hadn't been properly deconstructed. On reflection, if leadership was going to mean anything at all for Nouwen, it now meant being willing to follow others, as he summarizes: 'leadership, for a large part, means to be led.'[3]

This doesn't seem too far removed from the biblical emphasis either. When you get into the New Testament texts, there are a number of words used to describe functional roles within the Christian community, some of which could be argued to resonate with an assumed leadership concept. However, alongside these you would expect to find the most commonly used Greek word for leader, *archon*. This was the word used for leaders in all aspects of society and, guess what? The New Testament doesn't use it at all. The early Christian writers had plenty of opportunity to use this term and give it a Christian slant, but instead they chose to ignore it.[4] It seems, at first glance, as if the New Testament writers wanted to dissociate themselves from the specific word 'leader' altogether. Anyone wanting to write about leadership had better have a convincing way around that one.

As the earlier account illustrated, there are plenty of Christian folks who just don't see leadership as something Christians should be engaged with. There was more than a sniff of this when I began to explore ordination in the Church of England. Now, I actually think the Anglican discernment process and methods of training are generally very good, but it was very striking to me that the term 'leadership' didn't fit comfortably into the frames of reference set out for the discernment process, at least not when I was going through in 2007 and 2008. In discussions with the diocesan advisers, I was repeatedly steered away from using my variety of leadership experiences as an evidence base for Christian vocation. There were reasons for this, which I'll revisit, but given Jerome's early pronouncement that 'there can be no Church community without a leader or team of leaders'[5] this did feel somewhat strange. I must say as well, that as I've gone on in Anglican ministry, the training offered is remarkably thin on both a theology of leadership and the different methods and embodiments of leadership that can be employed to fulfil this ministry. Some would say this is absolutely right; some find it very odd indeed.

Second, even among Christian writers who embrace the term, there is plenty of confusion over what leadership is and how it is expressed. A good example of this disagreement can be seen in the 2014 release of the Green report in the Church of England and some of the response it generated.[6] The Green report presented a comprehensive programme for how senior church leaders are to be trained and receive ongoing review and development. Produced by a steering group chaired by Lord Stephen Green, ex-Group Chairman of HSBC, and with management consultancy input from Christopher McLaverty, the former Global Head of Talent and Learning for BP, the report attempts to pull significant wisdom from the corporate leadership world.[7] It specifically recommends that the leadership development programme is run by a major university or business school, and not internally or by a theological college, due to a perceived 'lack of challenge' within the Church's internal training environment. The report identifies some core competencies around growth, common good, reinventing ministry and building healthy organizations. It also requires the completion of a mini MBA-style module of organizational leadership. As well as training current senior leaders, the report recommends the identification of a talent pool of high-performance future leaders who can receive specific training before taking up a senior leadership role, such as Bishop, Dean or Archdeacon. The report goes as far as stating an aspiration that all future senior leadership posts will be filled by people who have come through this talent pool of training.

As one might imagine, there has been some critique of this approach. Martyn Percy, theologian and Dean of Christ Church, Oxford, suggests that the report offers no theological framework for defining leadership but prefers 'basic contemporary approaches to executive management'.[8] Percy bemoans the absence of biblical language in defining the shape of senior leadership roles. Worryingly, he sees the potential for an inadequately informed leadership development pipeline, not developing leaders in a proper Christian sense, but simply affirming a particular leadership style that, guess what, reflects the small group of leaders who shaped it. Percy argues that the report is seemingly unaware of the widespread critique of some of its proposals, and concludes:

> The Green report represents a straightforward bid for power from a small group of elite executive managers ... this needs challenging and resisting, and the proponents need reminding that their ministry is serving and supporting the Church, not leading and controlling it.[9]

This kind of public disagreement around leadership is typical of the way different Christian camps can set themselves up. Another example can be seen in the contention around Bill Hybels' ministry. Prior to the scandal around Bill's leadership he was widely acclaimed for helping grow one of the biggest churches in America and providing resources for church leaders across the globe. Leadership is the key to church health and growth, argued Hybels in his prime, and he voiced frustration at the Church for being slow to pick up good practices from the world, happily borrowing management speak and approach when it suited. Leonard Sweet openly critiqued Hybels, in one place quoting Isaiah 31.1–3 and asking whether Hybels was building pagan alliances outside the Christian community much like the rebellious Israelites. Leaving the moral malpractice aside, Sweet questions whether Hybels' *successful* ministry was actually fundamentally compromising the identity and future viability of the Christian community because of his particular emphasis on leadership. Was Hybels setting the Church up to fail with a variety of very worldly wisdom? Who is right?

For me, the problem all stems from a lack of consensus about what we really mean by leadership. Listening to the debates, I get the feeling that some of these urgent commentators have been very influenced by their own subjective experiences of leadership and are arguing past each other without hearing what other experienced practitioners are really saying. Right at the core of the Christian dialogue around leadership lies a dangerously ambiguous sense of what we are talking about. And no one seems to want to do the hard work.

At this stage of the argument a well-acknowledged leadership guru makes a good case in point. John C. Maxwell is a Christian writer on leadership who writes for both Christian and secular audiences. In the 1990s he wrote one of the most influential contemporary books on leadership: *The 21 Irrefutable Laws of Leadership*. It sold over a million copies and the book had a significant revision ten years later which extended its reach further still. John spoke in the UK recently at a Christian leadership conference, and I had the privilege of listening to him reflect on leadership and ministry; both his passion for Jesus and his desire to enable good leadership was inspirational. I left equipped to lead better. The strapline of his book on the irrefutable laws is 'Follow them and people will follow you', and I think he's right. But given the urgency for true Christian leadership, it is important to be clear about what John has done and precisely how his contribution fits in the wider landscape of what Christian leadership actually is. If you go through the 21 laws, John's primary concern is the methodology of leadership, and in painting a rich picture of *how to lead* he essentially applies sociology and Christian truisms, accessibly embellished through personal anecdote and examples from history. At no point in the book, though, does John press up against the purpose, or teleology, of leadership and makes no effort to inform the reader how to weigh the impact of their influence. A case in point is found in the very first words of his first chapter. John narrates the story of Dick and Maurice McDonald, who of course began the McDonald's empire. They aren't held up as the success story though. They began a successful chain, but the emphasis of the first chapter is that some leaders aren't able to *lift the lid*, which for Maxwell means they are unable to see the full scope and potential of their current activity. It took the arrival of Ray Kroc, who founded the franchise model and bought the rights, to turn McDonald's into the global brand it is today. Kroc is identified as someone whose leadership lid was far higher than Dick or Maurice's. It is Kroc's leadership to which we should aspire. On one level, of course, John is right.

But hold on a second! What has the true influence of the McDonald's franchise empire been? Back when Dick and Maurice first started, they purchased supplies from local suppliers. Their outlets were clean, tidy, relaxed places to be and their quality of food – well, it was always faster food – but their venture was a small slice of the commercial food market and as such they made an effort to compete on quality with the more established restaurants. What we have today, what the brand has become, is very different. Through the influence of McDonald's, we have popularized fast food. We have normalized the most unhealthy meals, excessively full of fats, salts, sugars and all the rest. We have developed environmentally unfriendly supply chains on enormous scales that, among other wrongs, have led to deeply inhumane farming methods – all to push down the price of as much processed beef, chicken and pork as we can get our hands on. Chasing the fast-food buck has meant paying staff the lowest wages possible, reducing staffing activity to the most basic food production as opposed to more human skills of improving customer service and experience. We've decreased the quality of the product, we've decreased the quality of employee experience and we've decreased our quality of stewardship of the world. Why have we done this? To increase the financial gain of a small number of intelligent, gifted and relatively wealthy people acting as senior managers and shareholders within the franchise. We've applied very effective forms of leadership in the wrong direction and taken steps away from the world as it should be. Perhaps the most confusing thing of all, because we haven't understood what Christian leadership actually is, is that we elevate the likes of Maxwell in thoroughly uncritical ways. To whom do we turn?

Even for commentators writing about leadership for an exclusively Christian audience, we still see this same unwillingness to get to grips with the underlying purpose of Christian leadership. James Lawrence is a commentator who has contributed much to the understanding of Christian leadership. We will return to some of his thinking later, but it is important at this stage to observe that in his seminal book on Christian leadership, *Growing Leaders*, he suggests that trying to define who or what is a leader is a potentially fruitless task that may ultimately limit what is a very wide and diverse term.[10] Could that be right? Should we just overlook definitions and keep trying to develop forms of practice? Leadership coach Simon Western seemingly agrees. In attempting to get past some of the muddled, cultural thinking on leadership, he applies critical theory to the subject in his book *Leadership*.[11] Western very helpfully provokes our assumptions, and undoubtedly achieves his aim of stimulating leaders to look outside established models to engage with leadership more authentically. Like most other commentators though, he makes no effort to anchor leadership first in the activity of God. Perhaps suffering one of the modernist problems of separating the academy from the Church, I would suggest the discussion between the theological nature and purpose, the true ontology and teleology if you like, of leadership and its practical operation in the life of the everyday Christian has been sadly lacking. We simply don't understand enough about the essence of leadership to properly anchor our dialogue about how it's expressed.

Third, even if you get past the initial problems with the term leadership, duck the disagreements about what it means and select a couple of trusted voices to steer you somewhere helpful, there is still confusion about how to theologically get at leadership. Specifically, there is confusion about how to appropriately apply the Bible to the concept of leadership. What do I mean?

Well, for those actively writing about Christian leadership, a common approach is to look at the life and example of Jesus, as well as the social ethics of the early Christian community, and to find examples and illustrations of how Christians are meant to exercise leadership today. While there's surely lots of deeply biblical truth that can be harvested using this approach, there are some significant questions of method. It's interesting to apply this back to Lawrence, who is probably the best contemporary British thinker on Christian leadership. In his analysis in *Growing Leaders*, Lawrence draws out six distinctive qualities of Christian leadership. To do this he selects some verses about God, some behavioural teachings from both Jesus in the Gospels and from Paul in the epistles.[12] Contrast that with a similar voice from a different context – Heuser and Shawchuck in *Leading the Congregation* – and you find that they choose to emphasize some of the interior attitudes of a leader and a Christian leaders' spirituality as their set of a Christian leaders' distinctive qualities.[13] There's plenty of overlap in the points being made, and it's hard to say any of them are necessarily wrong, just that they feel somewhat arbitrary because the lists of attributes and the way they are presented is different. Looked at together they can seem confusing and very open to the criticism of projection. Are they just good ideas that the commentators have then tried to build a case around with subjective selection of biblical texts to reinforce these ideas?

For more blatant examples, consider again Sweet and Hybels. For all its brilliance, at the outset of *I Am a Follower*, Sweet quotes Jesus' call for others to follow,[14] and he then references another call of Jesus to serve.[15] The second example specifically refers to when Jesus called the disciples away from worldly status to a posture of servanthood. Without any detailed exegesis of these points, but with plenty of stories and subjective reflections, he then arrives at the conclusion that 'You and I are never leaders, only followers.'[16] Whether it's true or not isn't my point; the theological method is highly questionable. To be a Christian means to be a follower of Jesus, but that doesn't, by definition, negate the possibility of our also exercising leadership towards others, and to try and make the Bible say that with a few choice verses is manipulative. Hybels, on the other hand, looks at positional and hierarchical leaders from the Old and New Testament, gets all excited about their strong-willed, directive, results-based leadership and concludes categorically that the future of the Church 'rests primarily in the hands of its leaders'.[17] As he does this, it's fairly clear that his emphasis is on a particular type of positional or hierarchical leader exercising leadership in a particular way. I'm not saying that sometimes this kind of leadership isn't important; just that Hybels has a personal conviction already in mind when he selects his texts, and he may have missed other important things the Bible wants to say about where the future of the Church rests. They've just made the Bible say what they want, and if we use these subjective projections as the basis for our biblical method, we run the risk of saying things that are untrue, inadequate or probably both. As I've shown, with this approach commentators arrive at varying and even conflicting conclusions and haven't helped the Church get to the essence of Christian leadership at all.

Even the most rigorous assessments of leadership can come slightly unstuck in this way. Simon Walker's *The Undefended Leader Trilogy* material is a remarkable exploration of how our shadow sides play out in leadership, and he offers a framework for a much more accountable, self-aware and personally transforming approach. His thesis is that our effectiveness in leadership starts with our inner character: we lead out of who we are, and he takes us on a journey to surrender our propensity to defend ourselves and embrace a trusting, *undefended* posture. I've read the books, done the course and got the t-shirt, and it's been a great blessing to me and lots of others. However, even with Walker's richly informed material, the question of theological method still lingers. Figure 2 represents his illustration in *The Undefended Leader Trilogy*.[18]

Walker spends about a page explaining why, appealing purely to common sense, this is a model that fundamentally describes what is happening in the leadership dynamic. There's lots of good stuff here, but no mention of Scripture, of theology, or even rigorous sociology. Just a quick presentation of apparent reality and then, if you happen to agree, we're off into a dialogue about how to apply the model. I'm sorry, but if I'm to invest a large amount of life energy in something, I need slightly firmer foundations. Equally, as Walker's model develops, we're presented with a world in which our preoccupation with security is *the* overriding psychological instinct that shapes our leadership. Hence the paradigm, *undefended leadership*. Again, big theological questions remain untouched. What about our need for significance? What about our need for identity? The foundations are convincing in their own right,

Figure 2: Simon Walker's illustration of the intersections between leader, goal and follower

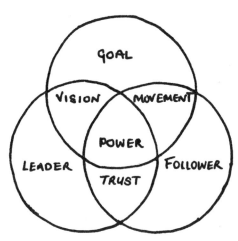

but are they exhaustive? And if so, can you show me how, please? I'm left feeling like I've got an important piece of the jigsaw, but I'm confused about how the material relates to the bigger picture of Scripture and to other aspects of our inner humanity. Ultimately, I don't have enough confidence to make it a significant controlling paradigm for helping me understand my own expressions of leadership.

So at a scholarly level, confusion arises from our theological method. I'd suggest this abounds even more so at a popular level. As a quick example, there's a fantastic leadership conference every year in the UK run by the HTB network of churches. I'm in with this group, so it's probably helpful to reveal my colours. For years this conference has rerun the mantra that we are all leaders, if only because we have a responsibility to lead ourselves. But how much of our internal workings can be genuinely described as leadership? Certainly the conference is much less concerned with internalized forms of leadership. Suggesting that we are leaders because we lead ourselves isn't wrong, it's just another example of leadership development that isn't rooted first in a convincing definition, and ultimately in a convincing theology. There must be other reasons why leadership is a fundamental activity for every person to become equipped in, and we send our folks out uncertain about the theological ground we're standing on.

While it's perhaps overly critical to say that all contemporary exegesis and instruction on Christian leadership is flawed in this regard, I do think the lack of sufficiently robust, first-principle theological foundations for Christian leadership creates a vacuous discussion into which it is all too easy to project our own leadership preferences and prejudices – both at scholarly and at popular levels. Even when there is resonance with different biblical texts, good ideas and well-chosen exemplar forms of leadership might not always be appropriate in resourcing the diverse actualization of what leadership should look like in different contexts.

What impact does this confusion have?

So there's confusion. Confusion about whether leadership is a Christian term, what leadership is and how it's expressed, and even confusion about the theological methods we use to get at the nature of leadership. Amid this confusion I think we see at least three different reactions within the life of the Church.

One reaction, the biggest one I'm sure, is that we see plenty of Christians simply opting out of intentional forms of leadership. Leadership becomes a term reserved for specific positions of authority in our workplace, which many of us will never hold. Or leadership is only for those carrying a certain responsibility, either in the Church or outside; again, which many of us will never carry. Or leadership is just for those who caricature particular personalities: mostly extrovert, domineering or expert types. For this final strand, Susan Cain offers the most brilliant analysis of the ways in which more introverted types have been relegated from leadership at all sorts of levels in society, not least the Church;[19] our shared humanity being deeply impoverished when we allow certain personality caricatures to dominate. The result is that most Christians don't end up seeing themselves as leaders and many just don't want to engage with the term. I suspect that if you go into most churches, just as in the story I shared earlier, and try and call the average Judy or Joe Christian into leadership, they will run a mile. If you put on a course for people in the congregation who exercise leadership at work or in the community, you'll only get a very select few signing up. If you use the term 'leadership', most people disqualify themselves. Therefore, if you want to call people into leadership within most churches, you'll need to start using a very different set of language to get traction: it's just a massive turn-off for most people.

A second reaction is that some Christians just crack on, but crack on inadequately. As well as those who opt out of leadership there are a group of folks who basically can tell that good leadership is an essential part of any social organization. They might be a bit unclear on the theology of it, but they know that they need to get on with it. You could call them the pragmatic activists. They read Lawrence or Hybels, perhaps more specialist material from Walker or Western, take what they can and try a bit harder. On one level this is absolutely fine. We don't necessarily need to understand something completely before we do it, and the Holy Spirit is presumably more than able to help us through our deficiencies. The main problem, as I see it, is that we aren't clear enough with this approach about what aspects of our activities and behaviour can accurately be described as 'Christian leadership', and which bits are just our personalities at play, or inaccurate assumptions about what Christian leaders should be doing. At its worst, by adopting this kind of approach, we just do things the way they seem to work, and we end up surrounding ourselves with people who like us, or who are like us, and we have our imperfect caricatures reinforced. Or, worse still, we simply keep leading in ways that aren't particularly Christian without any deeper critique.

In many ways, this is where the historical Anglican discomfort with leadership is a strength. As an aside, I tend to find that Anglican peculiarities are often based on some seasoned truth that younger denominations perhaps haven't learned yet, even if the peculiarities themselves are sometimes a blocker to the new wine of the Spirit. In this case, the diocesan advisers were right to ask me to think beyond my secular experiences of leadership in considering a call to ordination. Just because I might be able to lead in a particular context outside the Church didn't mean I was qualified to lead within the Church. The aspects of leadership I'd excelled in outside the Church may be much less appropriate in the Church. And there's more at stake leading in the Church as well. I walk in as a more extrovert type – white male, happy to take control – exuding all types of caricatures, and it's a jolly good thing the harder questions were asked. This is Susan Cain all over: the danger of the status quo perpetuating itself to the detriment of the quieter, more thoughtful majority, unless we factor in a different way of doing things. Unfortunately, very few organizations are geared up as the Anglican Church is to navigate this terrain. Despite the lengthy periods of ordination discernment, I'm thankful that the Anglican Church has a rigorous process, at least as a filter for the more aggressive activists among us.

A third reaction comes from the group of folks who fundamentally mistrust the leader and the notion of leadership, either because they've experienced the pain of failed leadership themselves, or because they simply see the shadow sides and broken aspects of various leaders' methods and personalities all too clearly. These folks essentially fight against the leadership of others, either through a posture of direct critique or passive-aggressive counter-play. They might be correct in much of their analysis, but the problem here is that, as with the splinter and the branch, the human condition is very good at finding faults in others, less good at spotting them in ourselves. Either the leadership baby gets thrown out with the bath water, or the endless wear and tear of their critical attrition simply dissipates any positive leadership energy around. The biggest problem with this third reaction of course is that, as Michel Foucault found, if you go around popping everyone else's intellectual balloon then you have to pop your own as well. My observation is that often those who are most critical of the concept of leadership seem to be the most subtly adept at drawing people towards their ways of thinking and behaviour: they are very good at leading themselves, at least within a critical sub-group which they represent. Despite my sympathy for these more nuanced criticisms of leadership, I can't side with a philosophy that doesn't find ways of positively reconstructing something that seems so fundamental to human community, and is often laced with such obvious self-contradiction. I like these folks, but I can't side with them.

Is there any hope for leadership?

At its worst, if leadership is truly something for all of us, then despite the plethora of current resources, this twin combination of pain and confusion massively stifles the proper realization of this aspect of our humanity. The world is a poorer place. Our churches lose their mojo. Many of us fail to find the significance and fulfilment for which we are made. People opt out and the leadership mantle is carried by those of us who best evidence cold caricatures. Or, just as bad, official leaders are simply thrown out and replaced by those exercising the strongest and most subtle forms of coercion. One of the principal reasons I have for writing this book is because I feel called to lead within the Church. But in truth I'm not confident in my own theological understanding of leadership, and therefore I'm afraid I might build something counter to God's purposes. A worrying dilemma.

If we pause, however, and allow ourselves to breathe for a moment, the picture is not perhaps as bleak as it first appears. Despite their apparent differences, there may be ways of reconciling some of the disparate ideas and opinions about Christian leadership. While one can always pick holes in the detail, the Christian commentators I've referenced are all saying some important and truthful things about the nature of leadership. The fact that they appear at first glance to conflict doesn't necessarily mean that they do so in their entirety. There are good reasons for the disagreements, and people with different experiences are bringing important notions and critiques to a complicated subject. The observation from C. S. Lewis about arguments at the start of the chapter is helpful, and the very presence of disagreement around leadership – loud and complex disagreement for that matter – suggests that there may be something worthy of discovery.

On reflection, perhaps there is more alignment between the different contributors on leadership than might be apparent. Sweet and Nouwen would seem to be absolutely right in saying that a leader's faithful follower-ship of Jesus is more vital for them personally than any ability they may have to lead others. And that their willingness to follow Jesus through the influence of others is a vital part of their credibility and effectiveness as leaders themselves. They would also appear to be right in saying that if we always associate leadership with extrovert, strong power types then we are right to reject the term. On the other hand, Hybels is surely correct to emphasize the significance of the role of the leader on the wider community because so much of the health of the community does depend on that role. And he's also right to have a go at robustly unpacking how leadership works because we need those insights. Additionally, Percy was right to question some of the managerialism of the Green report, even if an initiative like it was probably a generation or more overdue. Walker was right to connect the findings of secular psychology with a leader's character and build a helpful picture of some of the ways leadership goes wrong and can go right. Western, too, was right to take a different viewpoint to help shake up how we get at the practicalities of leadership. On one level all of these commentators are right. The question for us is, can we tie all these different views of leadership together with a sufficiently robust and overarching theological understanding of what leadership is? Might there be a theology that stretches across them? There are tremendous signs of life: people are on to the answers, so let's not give up hope just yet!

Comment
Rt Revd Dr Jill Duff, Bishop of Lancaster

I am passionate about encouraging people to discover their God-given gifts. This can often be a calling to leadership. I distinctly remember a presentation by one trainee vicar I was teaching, a woman in her forties. She had resisted a sense of call to ordination for many years. 'I didn't think I was a leader, because I wasn't like Donald Trump.' We all breathed a sigh of relief: 'We are glad you're not like Donald Trump!'

For me, this cameo sums up the confusion around leadership. We have a leader in mind. And we're not like them, so we're not a leader. We are confused. We slide down the slippery slope to imposter syndrome. We listen to the lies of the evil one, rather than the voice from the open heaven: 'You are my own dear son/daughter and with you I am well pleased.' The Spirit of God is endlessly, immeasurably creative. He brings myriad different colours, voices, tones, gifts. If we truly believe that Jesus was fully man and fully God, then the more filled we are with the Spirit of Jesus, then the more ourselves we become. The more uniquely ourselves; the more uniquely ourselves as leaders. As Oscar Wilde brilliantly put it: 'Be yourself, everyone else is taken.'

Yes, the typical word of the day for leader, *archon*, is not used in the New Testament, except for the forces of evil. This should give us a clue about the revolutionary work of the Spirit of God. A king born in a stable, a victory on a cross, a persecutor who became the best publicist; a scaredy-cat runaway who became the rock. But that journey of Peter to become the rock on which Jesus built his church, started on a beach by a fire when, with all the memories of betrayal still fresh, Jesus said: 'Feed my sheep.'[20] Jesus gave him authority again. He gave him a leadership role.

Shot through Scripture is the concept that human beings are created to 'have dominion'.[21] Jesus repeatedly tells his disciples: 'I have given you authority.'[22] My sense is that confusion in leadership arises when people don't take up their God-given authority. Well of course they don't take up their authority: who are they to be the leader? Everyone knows they're the imposter ... someone else would do it better than you. In many institutions, we even taunt ourselves by displaying pictures of the great leaders of the past, sneering down on our contemporary fumblings. How could we fill those big shoes of the gilt-framed oil-painted portrait?

We need to take our authority because confusion in leadership occurs when authority is dissipated, when leaders feel their face doesn't fit so shrink back from the leader's role: who am I to lead? Then authority dissipates to those who shout the loudest, bully their colleagues, or in an institution close to my heart, to those who write the longest papers. My husband often refers to his top tip of leadership advice, given to him as a new vicar by the then Archdeacon of Warrington: 'Ask yourself, where does the power lie?' Watch out when authority dissipates.

But perhaps God has chosen you. And perhaps he has chosen you to lead.

A year ago, I became bishop in the Diocese of Blackburn in Lancashire; one of only four Dioceses who voted against the ordination of women. The thirteenth female bishop in the Church of England. There weren't shoes to fill – as a wife and a mum, I simply couldn't be a carbon copy bishop of any one who had gone before. And in a wonderful gift of God's grace, my two bishop colleagues, Julian Henderson and Philip North, have persistently encouraged me to be myself. I have found this incredibly freeing. To lead in a unique way. To be a bishop in a way that's not been done before. And the incredible thing seems to be that as I am more myself in leadership, this frees others to find their own voices, styles, colours, ways of leading. Catherine of Sienna said: 'Be who God called you to be, and you will set the world on fire.'

The more we follow Jesus, who was fully man and fully God, the more we are ourselves, filled with the Spirit of hope, the more hopeful I am for leadership across the five spheres of society outlined in this book. 'May the God of hope fill you with all joy and peace as you trust in him, so that you may overflow with hope by the power of the Holy Spirit.'[23]

Notes

1 C. S. Lewis, *Mere Christianity* (London: Collins, 2012).

2 Leonard Sweet, *I am a Follower: The Way, Truth and Life of Following Jesus* (Nashville, TN: Thomas Nelson, 2012), p. 26.

3 Henri J. M. Nouwen, *In the Name of Jesus: Reflections on Christian Leadership* (London: Darton, Longman and Todd, 1989), p. 57.

4 Graham Tomlin, *The Widening Circle: Priesthood as God's way of Blessing the World* (London: SPCK, 2015), p. 141.

5 Saint Jerome, *Dialogus contra Ludiferianos*, chapter 21, as quoted in Roger Heuser and Norman Shawchuck, *Leading the Congregation: Caring for Yourself While Serving Others* (Nashville, TN: Abingdon Press, 2010), p. 182.

6 www.thinkinganglicans.org.uk/uploads/TalentManagement.pdf (accessed 20 August 2019).

7 www.thinkinganglicans.org.uk/uploads/TalentManagement.pdf, pp. 9–18 (accessed 20 August 2019).

8 Martyn Percy, 'Are these the leaders that we really want?', *Church Times*, 12 December 2014, www.churchtimes.co.uk/articles/2014/12-december/comment/opinion/are-these-the-leaders-that-we-really-want.

9 Martyn Percy, *The Future Shapes of Anglicanism: Currents, Contours, Charts* (London: Routledge, 2017), p. 36.

10 James Lawrence, *Growing Leaders: Reflections on Leadership, Life and Jesus* (Abingdon: CPAS and The Bible Reading Fellowship, 2004), pp. 22–3.

11 Simon Western, *Leadership: A Critical Text* (London: SAGE, 2008).

12 Lawrence, *Growing Leaders*, pp. 30–9.

13 Heuser and Shawchuck, *Leading the Congregation*, pp. 20–8 and 40–50.

14 Luke 9.23.

15 Luke 22.24–30.

16 Sweet, *I am a Follower*, pp. 19–27.

17 Bill Hybels, *Courageous Leadership: Field-Tested Strategy for the 360° Leader* (Grand Rapids, MI: Zondervan, 2012), pp. 26–7.

18 Simon P. Walker, *The Undefended Leader Trilogy* (Human Ecology Partners, 2011).

19 Susan Cain, *Quiet: The Power of Introverts in a World that Can't Stop Talking* (London: Penguin, 2012).

20 John 21.17.

21 Genesis 1.28, ESV.

22 Luke 10.19 and Matthew 28.18.

23 Romans 15.13.

Reflection

Searching for Truth

John 20.11–18

Now Mary stood outside the tomb crying. As she wept, she bent over to look into the tomb and saw two angels in white, seated where Jesus' body had been, one at the head and the other at the foot.

They asked her, 'Woman, why are you crying?'

'They have taken my Lord away,' she said, 'and I don't know where they have put him.' At this, she turned around and saw Jesus standing there, but she did not realise that it was Jesus.

He asked her, 'Woman, why are you crying? Who is it you are looking for?'

Thinking he was the gardener, she said, 'Sir, if you have carried him away, tell me where you have put him, and I will get him.'

Jesus said to her, 'Mary.'

She turned towards him and cried out in Aramaic, 'Rabboni!' (which means 'Teacher').

Jesus said, 'Do not hold on to me, for I have not yet ascended to the Father. Go instead to my brothers and tell them, "I am ascending to my Father and your Father, to my God and your God."'

Mary Magdalene went to the disciples with the news: 'I have seen the Lord!' And she told them that he had said these things to her.

Questions

1 In what ways does this chapter resonate with your own experience and observations of the confusion around leadership?
2 What is your first reaction to the word leadership? Is leadership generally positive or negative? Why?
3 How would you define leadership? Is leadership Christian?
4 Are there biblical accounts, pictures or imagery that you find particularly helpful in your leadership? What are they, and why are they important?

5 Do you agree that there is confusion around the term leadership? If so, how does that confusion impact you?

6 Where is there agreement around leadership? Are there particular leadership commentators that you have found helpful?

7 What might true Christian leadership look like?

Prayer

Father God, have mercy on us with our small minds and lack of understanding. Help us to listen and learn from each other and from you. Reveal your intentions for human leadership more clearly among us. Inspire us for what is possible with you. Draw us into unity that we may serve you better. May your strength overcome our weakness and your radiance transform our blindness. In Jesus' name, amen.

3

Hope

... the deepest and most important
form of hope, the only one that can keep us above water
and urge us to good works,
and the only true source of the breathtaking dimension of the human
spirit and its efforts, is something we get, as it were, from 'elsewhere'.
Václav Havel (1936–2011), Disturbing the Peace[1]

I can well remember the moment I became a Christian. I was in my early twenties, in my first job out of university, and for a variety of reasons I'd decided to read a Christian book given to me by a good friend. As I skimmed the pages over a period of days, a picture of such beauty and goodness invaded my thoughts and imagination. To this day, I cannot conceive of anything more wonderful than the notion of a personal God coming to rescue humanity from our self-centred trajectories; from mine. More than that, this God inviting us, me, into a much grander movement of redemption and renewal to become who we truly are. As I pondered these things, deep in my heart I knew that if I responded, then the ultimate future would be good. I also had enough self-awareness, just, to know that responding would, in a more immediate sense, be costly and painful, with a host of complex implications. As I sat at that existential crossroads, I experienced what I now understand to be Christian hope. A certainty within that by following the person of Jesus everything would be OK. That I would one day inhabit a world made right. As I made resolute agreement within myself to take that path, I experienced an overwhelming sense of excitement and strength; like a tidal wave of power, I knew that whatever pains this life could throw at me, this source of hope was greater.

As with many such moments of encounter and inspiration on the Christian journey – mountaintop experiences if you like – the testing would come in the normal and the mundane, through the valley to come. For me, this testing came quickly through the invitation to lead a small group within our church community and then to explore more public forms of ministry like preaching on a Sunday. What I found, as I stepped out of my comfort zone and into some of those activities, was that I felt almost overwhelmed by fear and inadequacy. While I knew God had invited me into something, to participate and use what skills and gifts I might have, so much of my adult formation had left me ill-equipped to serve in this kind of way. I felt exposed. Vulnerable. Alone. And yet – the more I ventured into these things, the more I found that there were people around me who could help. People who would encourage. Wisdom and insight from others. I began to find new ways of being and doing things, and the promise that I felt God had spoken to me, of my own renewal within this wider renewal of creation, began to take shape.

As I reflect back on some of that early Christian formation, twenty or so years ago now, I can see a consistent pattern that has emerged and re-emerged throughout my Christian journey. A pattern of being called to serve in ways that demand more of me than I feel able to give. But also a pattern where, as I step into these things, often reluctantly and hesitantly, the encouragement, support and direction of others enables me to find my place and to begin to experience a measure of fruitfulness in what I feel called to do. Undoubtedly we are meant to grow together. Growing to inhabit the kind of life that God calls us into, or perhaps I should say growing up to become who we truly are. Growing so that we can help others to go on that journey also, to pass the baton on from all we have learned and have become.

Despite having started this book exploring the pain and confusion around leadership, I do think we have plenty of grounds for hope. Hope because, as we touched on in the last chapter, despite the disagreements in what Christian commentators have been saying about leadership, there are certainly more grounds for agreement than might first be apparent. Hope because, on closer inspection, amid the available writings on leadership, there is ample material to construct a stronger theological foundation for Christian leadership; and where there is clearer theological insight, there is much greater potential for faithful embodiment and increased agreement. Hope because that specifically Christian hope I'd experienced right back at the start of my Christian journey seems to lie at the heart of our communal movement into the future. God comes to us, and promises transformation. Transformation within and transformation without. If we let it, this ironclad promise has the effect of motivating us into that new future, and enabling us to reach out and help others move there too. This is why, as we shall explore, Christian hope is so central to the nature of true human leadership.

How to define Christian leadership?

To begin then, let's see if we can identify a theology of Christian leadership – although we'll need to start with a large brush to sweep the floor rather than a fine-tooth comb to dissect the analysis, because the first problem we have is with a definition of terms. In some ways 'Christian leadership' doesn't make sense. A Christian is a person, not a particular human activity. The best thing we can probably say, and it's really important to be clear at the outset, is that when a Christian exercises whatever this thing called leadership is, there is a sense in which their faith has the potential to affect their character and behaviour so that their leadership takes a very particular *Christian* shape. God at work in us affects the way we do things and essentially can straighten them into something right and true. Therefore, if we are exploring a theological definition of Christian leadership, in a sense we are primarily asking: is there something about who God is and what God might be doing that helps us understand the essence of this thing called leadership? Once we've understood that better we can then ask, for each and every leadership opportunity a person faces: what is the distinctive Christian shape of our leadership?

It's worth saying that these possible shapes of what we might call Christian leadership are not necessarily found among Christians. It's also worth saying that, by definition, Christians should be the first people to declare this surprising truth. It would be easy to assume that because some people are Christians they therefore evidence Christian leadership, or at least predominantly exercise it. Not so. While there may be positive things to say about any given Christian's leadership, Christians should be the first to speak of the unavoidable flaws and broken aspects of even the most sanctified Christian leader. Such is the state of our fallen nature which will only ever be partially redeemed: if we know anything, we should know our limitations, and be careful about assuming the quality of any given leadership contribution.

As well as declaring that none of us will get it perfectly right, and that many of us get it consistently wrong, Christians should also want to affirm that, because we are talking about something that is embodied, leadership can take many different forms when it is actualized, and each of them could still have the potential to be *Christian*. Put another way, my style and technique of leadership may look quite different from that of another Christian leader, but I want to assume that my leadership can be just as *Christian*. Granted, there may be aspects of these styles and techniques that manifest in ways that aren't particularly Christian, and these require work, but at its heart I don't want to believe that the pursuit of Christian leadership requires conformity to one particular personality style or necessitates perfection expressed in uniformity of any leadership technique. That seems to go against the very essence of God's creative celebration of human diversity and the colourful reality that godliness encompasses much difference. Just travel around the world and observe the different expressions of good leadership in a variety of contexts for a reminder of that. Instead, what we seek is a wide and rich enough foundational shape of the distinctive part of Christian leadership, which will then manifest itself in different ways in different situations.

So Christian leadership isn't necessarily found among Christians, nor is it neatly packaged up in particular styles or techniques. But before we can get closer to what it actually is, there's another problem: we often aren't clear about how to actually define something. What do I mean? Well, I don't want to stray too far into detailed philosophy, or the etymology of how words develop and carry meaning, but it's important to state that leadership can be defined in a variety of ways: leadership *is* many things. Leadership is a noun, which is how we categorize its linguistic use. Leadership is a field of study, which is a way of saying we use the word to mean something in a particular context, in this case education. Leadership is difficult, which is how we describe one particular experience of it. All of these statements are true, but none of them take us to the heart of what leadership is *in essence*. I want to suggest, from a simple philosophical basis, that there are two key words that are fundamental to our exploration of the definition of leadership but that are too often neglected. First, the *ontology* of leadership: what is its fundamental nature? This will presumably be something within a social dimension, as leadership essentially is part of human identity and behaviour. Second, the *teleology* of leadership: what is its purpose, or perhaps God's purpose for it? This will presumably be where we have to work a bit harder theologically amid God's wider purposes for the world. To these types of definitions we will now turn.

The ontology of leadership: exploring its fundamental nature

So before we consider particularly *Christian* leadership, we need to ask: what is the ontology of leadership per se? What is this thing called leadership in its most fundamental sense? Well, as I read around that question, I came across Bernard Bass. Bass started with a PhD in psychology and engaged in a vast amount of research into the nature and methods of leadership. Most well known for his development of 'transformational leadership', Bass argued that there were multiple ways into the thinking of leadership but, in its root form, he suggests that leadership is essentially influence. Rather than tying the essence of leadership to methods or particular embodiments of leadership, Bass argued that leadership is a universal phenomenon, something that is happening all the time in social contexts as human beings exert influence on one another.[2] When a person or group influence a person or groups, there is a sense of movement – of things happening, of activities or behaviour changing – and it is at that point of influence that leadership is exercised and embodied. As such, the actualization of leadership happens when someone positively responds to, or follows, the influence of another person.

Leadership is *influence*.

'That's it!' I thought. 'Someone's managed, after years of secular research,' which on reflection is often the way of things, 'to say clearly what in hindsight feels like the most blindingly obvious statement of reality.' We do lots of things with the word 'leadership', but at its essence it is about people influencing other people. If you wanted to introduce caveats, then you might say that leadership is *influence positively responded to*, because if people react negatively and, for example, don't choose to follow, then leadership hasn't actually happened. Granted. Equally you'd probably want to say something about the free choice of the follower to *willingly* respond positively to leadership. I don't think leadership includes the manipulation of robots. The sense with leadership is that a social interaction has happened that has engaged the will of the follower, and the follower has chosen to exercise their will positively. Leadership that is entirely forced doesn't make sense. I would argue that the extent to which leadership is forced, or coercive even, is the extent to which it is no longer leadership, which is why the language of influence is much more accurate than that of control. For leadership to be leadership, then, it has to be responded to *willingly* as well as *positively*. As a final caveat, if you were being really pernickety you might say that leadership is *intentional* influence on the part of the leader. However, to this last point I'd argue that given that a good proportion of our influence is beyond our immediate self-awareness, it's probably worth including in the definition of leadership the influence we don't intend as well as the influence we do. So, fundamentally, as in Figure 3, leadership is influence; influence that is responded to positively and willingly.

Interestingly, Simon Western, who offers a tighter definition of leadership than most Christian commentators, does observe that the essence of leadership is found 'all around us, in the processes, behaviours, and … social systems'.[3] Despite his objections to ontological first principles, Lawrence also concurs that, 'leadership is exercised whenever anyone influences another person.'[4] This definition of leadership manages to transcend, but still include, institutional or hierarchical leadership and equally more organic expressions. It encompasses activity and character – in fact all anthropomorphic characteristics – and it is happening all around us all the time. For human beings in community, leadership is everywhere.

Figure 3: Influence between persons that leads to willing movement

If we define the essence of leadership in this way – as something amoral and intrinsic to shared human life – then helpfully it becomes freed from fundamentalist critique based on particular actualizations of leadership that are more obviously good or bad. Leadership is simply part of our social fabric, from which we cannot escape. Rather than rejecting the term because of caricatures, or because of our own emotional baggage, we need to have a theology for leadership – for the shape of our influence – or risk disengaging from reality. I think this is an important starting place from which to begin rethinking the essence of Christian leadership.

The teleology of leadership: exploring its purpose within the activity of God

So leadership is everywhere, whether we like it or not. To understand the distinctive attributes of *Christian* leadership, the next question is whether, buried somewhere beneath the lived-out experiences of leadership, and between the commentators' points and counterpoints about how leadership is exercised that we've skirted over already, there might exist a God-ordained intention for human influence. This takes us back to that question of purpose. What is the *teleology* of Christian leadership? This is another way of asking: what is the true teleology of human influence that the triune God, Father, Son and Spirit intends? Unavoidably in a fallen world, any expression of that *God-intended* leadership will be compromised to a certain extent. However, if we start with the bigger context of what God is doing in the world, if we understand what God is up to and how that becomes manifest through our human interactions, then perhaps we might begin to get to grips with what leadership is for.

To do this though, we need a bigger theological handle on what God's people, or perhaps we could say the Church, are meant to be doing in the world (we'll come back to the Church as a particular way of categorizing God's people later). It seems to me that since the start of human history, something is happening. Linked to our whole experience of time, events, activity and causation is this notion that God acts, people are invited to respond, and there are implications for others and for the rest of creation. Call it the story of God in and through God's people, perhaps. The important thing for us is that from the beginning of creation, God is up to something and humans are invited in.

And what is this thing that God is up to and within which we find ourselves? Well, at the beginning of all things we read about a good world that God creates, the zenith of which is the creation of us, humanity, as God's image bearers: stewards of the world, a people invited into fruitfulness and life and to exercise the delegated authority and activity of God in the world.[5] There are important things to say about how the world has changed since those first moments of creation, but at the outset we need to locate human purpose and activity as being about the actualization of the good life for which we were made. It's an idea that constantly bubbles up through the evolving story of God's people on earth. We come across it throughout the Torah, which in one sense was meant to reveal human sin and brokenness for what it was, but which in another offers a picture of that same good life through a rich and sustainable human society.

As the story of Scripture develops, we get the notion of the shalom of God: wide-open spaces, peaceful, restful places full of hope and possibility. We read of restored loving relationships between humankind and God and the wider creation. We read of worship, true religion, of the glory of God being reflected back through human beings who are truly alive. We read of humanitarian ideals in the Sermon on the Mount. Jesus' promise of having life to the full. A picture of heaven and earth united in intimate partnership. When the secular world speaks of well-being, of the conditions for human flourishing, they are absolutely rubbing up against one of the core reasons for which we were made. A collective, all-nations, universal kind of well-being – that is achieved through the sustainable governance of the wider world – is absolutely at the heart of human purpose. It's a foundational truth that we are not clear enough on within the contemporary Church and that sometimes we need reminding about by our secular neighbours. In the occasionally popularized words of Charlie Chaplin in *The Great Dictator*:

We want to live by each other's happiness, not by each other's misery. We don't want to hate and despise one another. In this world there is room for everyone, and the good earth is rich and can provide for everyone. The way of life can be free and beautiful, but we have lost the way ... The Kingdom of God is within man – not one man nor a group of men, but in all men! In you! You, the people have the power – the power to create machines. The power to create happiness! You, the people, have the power to make this life free and beautiful, to make this life a wonderful adventure.

Of course, as Chaplin acknowledged, these high ideals are not properly manifest in the world that we currently inhabit. Yes, we still carry God's image and hold God's mandate to care for one another and steward the rest of creation, but we find ourselves living in another narrative also; a narrative that locates humanity under perpetual temptation from forces opposed to God, struggling to be free from lives curved in on themselves. A narrative where in the beginning man and woman chose to try and usurp God's authority. A narrative where as a result God acted and the beautiful world was changed and we changed with it: God put walls around our activity and autonomy, painfully, but for our ultimate good.

To understand God's activity in the world, we need to understand both this darker narrative, of rebellion and decay, as well as the lighter narrative of God's original plans and purposes and God's very particular redeeming act that brings creation into renewal and rebirth. All the Abrahamic traditions see, wonderfully, God at work in the world to enact a plan of salvation; a movement that would ultimately draw in the whole of humanity. That movement started to take shape through the story of Israel. God called Abraham, Abraham listened, and we see a people responding in hope to a God who promises to sort things out. These promises take greater and more significant shapes, clarified and enlarged through prophets, angels, kings and an assortment of human stories, until, for the Christian, we arrive at Jesus: the embodied fulfilment of all that had been hoped for.

With the arrival of this long-awaited Messianic figure, the movement goes up a gear. Jesus is the fulfilment of the story of Israel, but also the birth of the age of the Church; a multi-ethnic people invited to respond to God under the influence of the Spirit. I should say of course that the story of Israel doesn't end historically with the person of Jesus, because much of Israel were still, and are still, waiting to come into the fullness of what God promised through God's Messiah.[6] But in a sense, the story of Israel ends spiritually with Jesus, because all of the hopes of Israel find their *Yes!* in Jesus. The main point for us here is that Jesus is both the fulfilment of the Israelite hope and also the author of the hope of the

Church, the new covenant people formed by the sending of the Spirit on Jesus' return to the Father.

And it is in this era that the followers of Jesus locate themselves today; here we are in the age of the Church, God takes action, people are invited to respond and the implications are spreading outwards, the movement growing. Breaking forth into the life of the believer is the Spirit: sanctifying, transforming and preparing the creation for the moment of final renewal and consummation. The Spirit enables the Kingdom to come, the lordship of Jesus becoming more manifest against the backdrop of God's fractured but originally good world. The promise, that wonderful promise, is that as creation finally, fully submits to the rule of the one good King, so the conditions for life as it was originally intended are restored – although perhaps I should also say renewed and amplified, as we will look at later.

As Christians, therefore, we are people of hope. We sense and see God's initiatives of redemption around us and we try to align ourselves with them, knowing that our participation marks the pathway of the journey homeward. We dream afresh about how our current life can more fully reflect life under the lordship of Jesus, in our families, workplaces and friendship groups, and we make changes to reflect that. We are blown along by the wind of the Spirit and respond to the Spirit's creative lead. It is within this full act of God's redemptive drama that we take our place, and it is this particular backdrop that begins to inform the shape of Christian influence. We rejoice at the cosmic movement of which we are part and we reach out to the world and creation with the invitation of love. Christian influence, therefore, needs to be located as a particular response of hope to the initiative and activity of God amid his people; hope that takes us on a journey, as Malcolm Guite put it in his poem:

> He calls us all to step aboard his ship,
> Take the adventure on this morning's wing,
> Raise sail with him, launch out into the deep,
> Whatever storms or floods are threatening.
> If faith gives way to doubt, or love to fear,
> Then, as on Galilee, we'll rouse the Lord,
> For he is always with us and will hear
> And make our peace with his creative Word,
> Who made us, loved us, formed us and has set
> All his beloved lovers in an ark;
> Borne upwards by his Spirit, we will float
> Above the rising waves, the falling dark,
> As fellow pilgrims, driven towards that haven,
> Where all will be redeemed, fulfilled, forgiven.[7]

The writer of Hebrews on hope

Hebrews is, in many ways, a book about hope. It begins by presenting the person of Jesus, and then offers a picture of the people of God journeying through time and history in response to particular promises and with particular hopes in mind. For the first few chapters the writer's focus is the superiority of Jesus over other agents in God's story of salvation, and the writer urges the readers to hold firmly to Christ in faith. Towards the end of chapter 5, the writer reveals his greatest concern for the readers and warns them not to fall away but instead to move forward in their faith beyond the 'elementary teachings'.[8] In urging them to grow, the writer then, in chapter 6, begins to speak of Christian hope and connects the realization of that hope to the Christian readers' faithful and patient diligence.[9] Hope has a vital purpose beyond just making us feel nice and elated. It is meant to do something. Specifically, it is meant to influence how we behave in the present. We don't earn it or even deserve it – hope comes to us as a promise based on the faithful work of Jesus; it is light, airy and sweet tuned and without forceful demands or oppression. But hope is a statement about an emerging future reality which we are invited to occupy, and we are meant to be moved to respond in faith. Without wanting to digress into the wider theological discussion about how we attain salvation, suffice to say this response in faith is both an internal movement of the heart and an external quality of life that evidences the internal movement. Hope finds expression in our response.

The writer goes on to outline God's promises to Abraham. Because of God's unchangeable nature, and God's promise to Abraham and to us as heirs of the same promise, the Christian's hope is a particular realization of those same promises made originally to Abraham. As such, Christian hope is far more concrete and certain than some of the vain or vague hopes that characterize much of our human experience. I suspect most people's thought lives are activated by things we want in the future, or of things that we would like if the world was somehow different. We dream of material possessions, better relationships and greater fulfilment, or perhaps of a very specific outcome in a situation. Unfortunately, we barely get guarantees on any specific outcomes, no matter how right or noble our desires, and for some of the other hopes we have, perhaps it's a good thing that many of them never come to pass. They almost certainly won't bring the satisfaction we think they will. Hope in general human terms is transitory, elusive, and that's possibly a good thing. But Christian hope, because it's founded on God's promises, is not vain or vague but instead has a concrete certainty about it. The really practical point here is that Christian hope is therefore something we can build our lives upon. We can make the difficult decisions because we *know* they are connected to that better future. As we journey, so the whole of our lives are meant to look different, and it's the certain and concrete quality of the hope we share that gives us the confidence to load everything on these foundations.

And hope looks forward. Perhaps it's stating the obvious, but hope is fundamentally about a person's expectation of something better to come. Hebrews makes it clear we share the same hope as Abraham: to be blessed and to have many descendants, at least spiritually speaking. But we also share the emerging hope of all the faithful down through history. The partially hidden but increasingly clear shape of our shared future pulls us forwards. Christian hope is the very specific expectation of the world as it is becoming the world as it should be.

At this point, let me summarize two really important points we need to take with us. The first, from our previous section, is that leadership has a sociological ontology; it is the exercise of influence from person(s) to person(s). There may be other qualities we can put around it, but the most basic definition of leadership is influence. Second, leadership becomes Christian leadership when human influence begins to be located in the activity of God. Christian leadership is an activity that enables a hopeful movement of others towards the kingdom of God; to bring renewal, transforming humanity and creation into their God-intended shape. It is within this activity – of God working in us – that we can begin to examine more closely the theological teleology of Christian leadership, such as by asking: how do we speak concisely and accurately about God's purposes for our influence on others?

Christian reality – life in the Kingdom – is eschatological/hopeful

So let us explore this teleology further, for we can now talk with a bit more confidence about what God is doing in the world through God's people and how our activity and embodiment of influence contribute to God's wider plans and purposes. We have a purpose within which we now fit. However, it is at this point that we run into a theological problem, or perhaps I should say a particularly Protestant theological problem. Most of the contemporary Protestant Church just hasn't been equipped to make theological sense of our role in the world, or how best to frame the Christian life.

For many Christians, and the watching masses of non-Christians in a post-Christian context, being a Christian doesn't hugely impact what we do, where we live and how we spend our money. The essence of our identity seems to be located in some vague notion of the future that says one day we will *go to heaven to be with God*. Becoming a Christian has been a bit like a full stop, where our new identity assures us of eternal happiness, which gives some nice feelings in the present, but doesn't necessarily require that much from us in this life. We can do the same jobs as people around us, spend our money in the same ways and call the shots in our life much like everyone else, or at least that is the false notion we have bought into.

A number of contemporary theologians have helpfully deconstructed this unfortunately inaccurate and ineffectual idea, and Tom Wright's *Surprised by Hope* is probably the easiest way to develop the discussion at this point. In the book, Wright argues that the ultimate Christian hope is very specifically not Christians *going to heaven to be with God*, but that the biblical picture is of God, and heaven with him, coming to earth in an act of re-creation. Very specifically, being a Christian means to theologically locate ourselves in this coming act of renewal, and to essentially align ourselves in our life and activity with the shape of a world that will one day be put right.

As Wright develops a more properly Christian hope for the world, there's plenty of meat on the bones, literally, and the bodily resurrection of Jesus is presented by Wright as a very specific affirmation by God of the physical; a promise that the physical will fully complement the spiritual in our eternal future. In a sense, Wright is arguing backwards from our ultimate destination, using this as a starting point to show how our lives in the present need to take shape. The new heavens and new earth will be physical places we can occupy, with physical bodies, that will be more perfectly human than anything we've known to date. Cats and dogs, trees and galaxies all topple into this re-created universe – such is its remarkable scope. There is a proviso that those who physically die before this re-creation happens will in some sense get to wait with Jesus in heaven for the final renewal, but that's simply an intermediary aspect of the Christian hope that fits within a much grander biblical scheme.

The really radical and life-changing idea that Wright and others are holding up is that this one and the same, eternal Kingdom is breaking into our current world right now. We can enter into this reality, at least in part, today, and it is this world that we are part of that will be renewed, not simply replaced by another. To be a Christian means, essentially, to be an active player in this movement towards the renewal of our world. Yes we are invited in by faith, which is an internalized movement of the heart, but that same internalized movement by definition, if it is real, then explodes outwards into our lives and the lives of others. A true follower of Jesus is called to constantly submit to Jesus' lordship in every facet of our humanity, which means to live as if this new reality were fully true, which it is, even if we don't see it perfectly yet over all aspects of creation. There are things we are invited to say no to. There are things we are invited to say yes to. The new horizon of our life demands a radically different set of life choices. Even more excitingly, or worryingly depending on your disposition, the things we do now can slow or hasten the Kingdom's advance and, to some extent, they can even influence the precise shape of that ultimate future. With this perspective, suddenly the things we do in this life matter; they matter in the sense of lasting for ever matters. It's worth including an extended snapshot of Wright's thinking, so we properly underline what's being said:

> Every act of love, gratitude, and kindness; every work of art or music inspired by the love of God and delight in the beauty of His creation; every minute spent teaching a severely handicapped child to read or to walk; every act of care and nurture, of comfort and support, for one's fellow human beings and for that matter one's fellow non-human creatures; and of course every prayer, all Spirit-led teaching, every deed which spreads the gospel, builds up the church, embraces and embodies holiness rather than corruption, and makes the name of Jesus honoured in the world – all of this will find its way, through the resurrecting power of God, into the new creation that God will one day make.[10]

Indeed, everything we do has the potential to last for ever in some way. When we live in ways aligned with Jesus' lordship, we become part of this bigger renewal of God. And importantly, when we step outside of Jesus' lordship, we fail to operate in this beautiful, eschatological reality and we start moving towards a different destination. Leaning back on the Church Fathers and on much of what seems to have been lost, Wright sets out a vision for discipleship that I think the contemporary Church is yet to properly unpack in our current context; everything we think, say and do as Christians, as well as the things we create and nurture, can carry forwards into eternity. This has massive implications for every Christian person in our family lives, in our jobs, in our communities and certainly in our churches. Equally, there are a whole host of things we think, say and do that have no proper connection to our ultimate future, and are essentially acting as blockers to the fullness of life God has for us now and, in some sense, perhaps limiting the shape of our ultimate future. I'm not saying of course that we can earn our way into blessings today or tomorrow, but I am saying that our faithfulness is connected to our experience of the Kingdom in this life and can carry forwards with implications for the shape of our ultimate future. Jesus' reference to the oversight of ten cities, five cities and none springs to mind at this point.[11]

The vital point for us here is that before we specifically define Christian leadership, we need to have a proper theological handle on Christian reality or life in the Kingdom. Christian reality functions eschatologically – or perhaps one could say *hopefully* – in that it is connected forwards to our ultimate future. This is the remarkable dualistic, now and not yet, quality of the advancing Kingdom of God, which is very important as we go on to think about the shape of truly *Christian* influence.

Jürgen Moltmann on eschatology

Of all contemporary theologians, Jürgen Moltmann is probably the one who has written most consistently and provocatively about the hopeful, eschatological reality within which we locate the Christian life. His literary work on eschatology began with the publication of *Theology of Hope* in 1964, and much of his writing since has built on this work as he's considered the implications of his approach to eschatology for politics, ethics and forms of ecclesiology.[12] Moltmann recognizes that eschatology was long called the doctrine of the last things.[13] He is harking way back, 1,500 years even, to the early life of the Roman institutional Church, and he argues that since this point eschatology has generally been limited to describing events at some final period of time before the end of things as we know them. One can certainly recognize this when one thinks of the contemporary use of eschatology and all the peculiar emphasis on rapture and millennialism and so on. Moltmann argues that this is a big mistake, that it reduces a vital biblical concept to something very narrow and dangerously ambiguous.[14] Instead, the first thing he wants to do is reposition eschatology as a movement that encompasses the whole of the Christian life, within which our experience of salvation and renewal is set. Eschatology, then, isn't a particular set of scenarios that we formulate from biblical texts reserved for some final hour; rather, it is a mainspring of many of our wider theological ideas. Moltmann states:

From first to last, and not merely in the epilogue, Christianity is eschatology, is hope, forward looking and forward moving, and therefore also revolutionizing and transforming the present. The eschatological is not one element of Christianity, but it is the medium of Christian Faith as such, the key in which everything in it is set, the glow that suffuses everything here in the dawn of an expected new day.[15]

Here he is underlining in the strongest terms what we've said already: eschatology is a characteristic of human reality; perhaps I should say a *potential* characteristic of all human reality, that connects the future reality of Jesus and his Kingdom with the present. It's worth mentioning that Moltmann sometimes suffers the scholarly critique that he doesn't have a well-informed enough Christology. By that I mean that some commentators think he doesn't root his understanding of eschatology in the person of Jesus sufficiently. However, for those who have the patience to read him, I'd argue that Moltmann does make it clear that 'Christian eschatology speaks of Jesus Christ and *his* future.'[16] The implication is that all our futures are dependent on, and will one day find reality in, the future of Jesus. Another way of saying it is that our hope is in Jesus and that Jesus is our hope. This is important, because if we stray too far from Jesus in our theological imaginings we can quickly become unstuck. In that sense, it would be appropriate to say that eschatology and Christology inform each other. Does the incarnate Jesus Christ, from whom we get our Christology, make sense to us without the original picture of creation, specifically with humankind in the *imago dei*, and most importantly, perhaps, the unfolding promises of God to redeem humanity and ultimately all of creation through the offspring of Adam? No. Jesus takes the shape he does, as a God-incarnate human being surrendering his life at the cross, because of humanity's past and future. And yet Jesus informs that past and future also. There at the beginning of creation. There in his life, death, resurrection and ascension at the defining moment of human history. There as Lord of our ultimate future. When Jesus says, 'I am the way and the truth and the life',[17] he encapsulates the Christian hope into himself.

In sketching the contours of this theology of hope and how it informs Christian influence, it would be inappropriate not to mention the foundations of promise. Throughout Christian theological reflection, and certainly within Scripture itself, underpinning this lively eschatological and Spirit-filled reality are the promises of God. Hope isn't something humanity dreamed up because we didn't like the taste of the day. Hope is given to us because promises have been made by one who is faithful, stretching back through the New Testament witness to Jesus' life, and going all the way back through the story of Israel. These beautiful promises are even found in the cursing of the serpent and among the escapades of Noah and the other early biblical accounts. Hope, Christian hope, true hope didn't begin when Jesus came out of the tomb on the Easter morn; it was always there, right from the beginning, although granted the resurrection of Jesus gave it the light and shape we now see.

The promise of human flourishing, the shalom of God if you like, develops through the story of Abraham and in it we see a picture of a people with a name and a home who will enjoy the blessings of God and then carry them into the wider world. This is a rough sketch of the Abrahamic covenant we touched on earlier, a foundational promise to the people of God. This promise is then taken up by prophets, priests and kings, repeated, re-emphasized, given fresh shape, and finally emerges out of the dusts of Galilee in the shape of a person. Without going into too much theological detail, which you can get in Tom Wright's *The Resurrection of the Son of God*[18] and elsewhere, Jesus took these promises, and gave them a much wider, literally cosmic dimension. All people are now invited in, Jew and Gentile alike. The promised land, their home, isn't a particular geographical area in the Middle East to be fought over by subsequent generations; it now extends to all creation, indeed the whole cosmos. The blessings are found first in restored relationship with God, the temple torn open and the spirit given, and extend outwards into all aspects of human life and flourishing.

Our future is not a future that we have to pull down through human strength. It's not a utopia that a minority dream up and then coerce the masses to join in with. Its advance is fundamentally not based on human forcefulness. The posture of our eschatological influence is activity in response to the promises of God, not activity based first on human effort. We do not work towards the utopian dreams of a strong minority. We respond to the initiatives of a personal and loving God who dwells among us. All authority of heaven and earth are in Jesus' hands, and we, the Church, are invited to fall in line with this good King, to kiss the Son if you like, and see his power at work among us. We don't invest our hope in our own abilities. But we still act. We respond with passion and energy to the promises God has given us, confident God will fulfil them, sometimes even in spite of us. Therefore, in relation to human influence, we can now say that God's activity in and through us is essentially hopeful. True influence, as God intends, is when we help others move towards and into the coming Kingdom of God; as we locate ourselves as agents of the emerging promises of God, we begin to partner with God on this communal journey forwards.

Richard Bauckham is a theologian who has critically engaged with Jürgen Moltmann's theology, and his take on the topic at this point is helpful. For Bauckham, the 'now' and 'not yet' tension of the Kingdom creates a constant possibility of renewal. In other words, it is when the human consciousness becomes aware of its habitation within a world in motion that the possibility and shape of involvement becomes manifest. As he puts it:

> In this way believers in the promise are liberated from accommodation to the present state of things and set critically against it. They suffer the contradiction between what is and what is promised. But this critical distance also enables them to seek and activate those present possibilities of world history which lead in the direction of the eschatological future. Thus, by arousing active hope the promise creates anticipations of the future kingdom within history.[19]

What is the gospel?

At the European Reformation the Protestant Church rightly emphasized that Christians are saved by faith in Jesus Christ rather than by works. This was the counterpoint to the totally unorthodox practices of a corrupt Roman Catholic Church offering assurance of forgiveness through financial indulgences and other forms of *works*. However many of the expressions of Church that have grown out of this Reformation movement have made the whole gospel equivalent to *justification by faith* and, very particularly, justification by a faith that is quiet, internalized and very unlike the kind of faith we read about in the New Testament in the wider sense. At its worst this reductionist gospel becomes like a passport ticket: say the sinner's prayer in faith and you're assured of eternal salvation regardless of the kind of life you decide to live as a supposedly *Christian* person.

In actual fact the Christian gospel is the proclamation that having lived, died, risen and ascended, the person of Jesus Christ is now Lord of all things and, which is another way of saying it, is now seated at the right hand of the Father. This remarkable truth explodes with a multitude of implications for the life of the Christian person, one of which is that following Christ has a very particular political

---

meaning. In fact, the very origins of the word *euangelion* find them-selves in the public proclamation of the inauguration of a new ruler. A new King has taken office and invites all of creation into freedom, through obedience to a new rule of love.

The offer of justification by faith is a vital part of this same gospel but it tells us specifically about the mechanism by which salvation becomes manifest in the lives of people. We are saved by grace alone through faith alone, as the Reformers liked to put it. There are multiple dangers with making this the whole gospel, though. First, it takes the focus of the gospel away from the enthronement of the one true King and puts it more centrally on the effective work in the life of the believer. The roots of individualism aren't hard to miss here. In addition, justification in itself is just one side of the coin of salvation.

On the other side, in contemporary times often in eroded or even scrubbed out detail, we find pictures of what life unavoidably looks like if that faith is truly real. The followers of Jesus are now called to live *as if Jesus were Lord* over our lives in every way; that is, in accordance with the new cosmic reality in which our lives are now located. In fact, our works are the evidence of how far we have plunged ourselves into that reality, and by implication the works themselves testify to the authenticity of that same saving faith. The works and the faith are intrinsically linked.

This emerging reality – or the Kingdom to give it its proper name – is the place where creation has submitted to Jesus' lordship, and is the place within which Christians locate themselves to the degree by which they have learned to faithfully follow Jesus. We inhabit the Kingdom all the greater the more we go on believing in Jesus, to give John 3.16 its proper emphasis. To take us back to Kroc and co, it is only when large numbers of Christians working in the corporate world think through what this means and choose to live faithfully to it that we will see the changes that we long for. Sadly, much of the Protestant Church has a long way to go to rework the imbalanced picture of the gospel that it has presented.

Christian leadership is Hopeful Influence

We can finally put our current ideas together. First we said that leadership is essentially our influence on each other where that influence initiates a willing and positive response. Second, that all Christian activity, and certainly influence, needs to be located within the activity of God before we can truly get to grips with it. Specifically then, as we've seen, the activity of Christian influence is something that enables others to move further into God's Kingdom. This influence is informed by our hope and rests on God's promises. At the core of this book I want to take this definition of leadership as influence and couple it to this eschatological, or hopeful, movement within which we locate the Christian life, and say very directly that the primary theological definition of Christian leadership is the exercise of eschatological, or hopeful, influence.

Christian leadership is *Hopeful Influence*.

So the central tenet of this book is that in Hopeful Influence we find a theologically robust, foundational motif for defining the true nature of Christian leadership and its distinctive qualities vis-à-vis leadership in general. In some ways it's a redefinition of terms. The term 'Christian leadership' just isn't precise enough, and dangerously ambiguous given the way we've used it. Redefining the kind of leadership Christians are meant to exercise as a form of eschatological, or *hopeful* influence moves the discussion on to more theologically robust foundations for marshalling our understanding. When we influence others in ways that enable them to move closer to the coming Kingdom, the place where Jesus is Lord, then it is at that point we can say we are enacting Christian leadership. True leadership, leadership as God intends, is the activity of influence from a person or group that enables others to take the appropriate next steps on their own eschatological journey. I believe this is the theologically robust key that can help marshal our thinking and enable the wider Church to find greater clarity and unity as we elucidate the practical distinctives of Christian leadership.

Theological implications of Hopeful Influence

As we have seen, Hopeful Influence happens within the wider activity of God. True Christian leadership therefore is best understood as the influence of Jesus through human agents. We aren't the ultimate leaders, we are following the leadership of Jesus, which then impacts on others. This is probably the main reason, as we observed earlier, that the early Christian writers deliberately avoided using the most obvious Greek word for leader, *archon*, in the New Testament. Not because positions of leadership were now redundant among the new community of believers (St Jerome just a couple of centuries later was clear about that[20]), but because they wanted to make it abundantly clear that being a Christian meant before anything else submission, deference and obedience to the one true leader of humanity – the ascended Jesus Christ. Any true Christian activity is in response to the activity of the human being who sits at the right hand of God. Of course I am not saying that Christians exercise Jesus' influence perfectly; we all do this with various degrees of imperfection. The important point though, the first theological implication, is that the truly good part of our influence is located somewhere beyond ourselves first. Our Hopeful Influence on others needs to be located in the ministry of Jesus before it is located in us. In that sense, Hopeful Influence is *an incarnational manifestation of the leadership of Jesus*, and the journey of a leader consistently takes us away from our agenda and towards the agenda of our Lord, as painful and existentially challenging as this will sometimes be.

If Hopeful Influence is a manifestation of the leadership of Jesus, then a second theological implication is that as an activity, *leadership isn't about us; it's principally about Jesus and about the good we can offer to others*. As we have seen, leadership's unavoidable collision with power and human significance carries this terribly destructive potential to curve in on itself and become more about the leader than the followers. St Augustine argued that the essence of sin is a life curved in on itself. If God is love, and love is an other-person centred posture, then however you like to put it – selfishness, self-centredness or the idolatry of the self – the root of all sin or disobedience to God is this elevation of the self. Perhaps this is the reason why leadership is so dangerous. When we build human structures where the many start to orbit a small number of highly capable, interesting or attractive people, then we start to play to the shadow side of the leader: the temptation to create a world that orbits around us. Because of this, sadly, failed leadership is what we should expect to find in this broken world, because without a God to meet our deepest needs, the strongest and smartest will elevate themselves at the expense of others to positions where those needs can be met.

Because of this, Hopeful Influence is a leadership *for others*. All of this is why Jesus deliberately chose to use the language of *servanthood* when he described both his own leadership and that of his followers:[21] Hopeful Influence is a leadership *for others*. Interestingly, the language of 'servant leaders' is quite popular in contemporary Christian circles, but it can become superficial parlance while not actually penetrating to the real meaning of the word 'servant'. Maybe we should drop the phrase altogether and replace it simply with *servant*. We are all servants, and this is why those of us in leadership should be more *servant* than others.

That said, *servanthood* in leadership isn't a licence for those invested with leadership responsibility to abdicate that responsibility either. At the moment in our church we're discussing how many children's groups to have at our two services; one service at 10.30 on a Sunday morning and one at 4.00 in the afternoon. There is a sense in which the church leadership is trying to discern the best provision for the new people who might walk through the door over the coming months, as well as the best provision for those currently within the church community. There is a delicate balance between gearing our children's provision around the perception of our immediate needs, versus how we make the Sunday church experience as good as it can be for those we are looking to invite in. As an ordained leader, I have to balance these pictures and try and help us work out the compromise solutions that work best for the ongoing life of the church. Being a servant leader doesn't mean doing what the mums and dads with the loudest voices want me to, or even saying yes to what a majority of parents think is best for them and their children at the current moment in time. There is wisdom and authority that leaders need to exercise that might not always sit well with the majority; but still, Hopeful Influence is always *for others*.

The theological picture we have drawn is one of a disconnected humanity, redeemed by the saving work of Jesus, following Jesus on creation's journey towards the new world where everything is right. A third implication, therefore, of Hopeful Influence is that it is *made manifest to us by the Holy Spirit*, given to God's people to define a new quality of life in the current age. There is an open heaven to resource us on the journey, which, as with servanthood, almost certainly means more for our demotion than promotion. For those who have welcomed this same Jesus into our hearts, who have chosen a life of repentance, of perpetual turning back to God, who, as those early Christians did, have found our identity first in the phrase *Jesus is Lord*; for those of us who have accepted God's invitation by faith, so we have the very Spirit of Jesus living within us. This certainly doesn't mean we get it right all the time. It doesn't mean we have a hotline to God. It certainly doesn't give us licence to elevate all of our own subjective thoughts and inclinations to the realm of *so God has said*. It doesn't mean a whole host of things which we'll unpack as we continue our exploration. But for now, it does mean that we have the potential to access everything we need to be fruitful and effective and, more importantly for our current discussion, fruitful and effective in the lives of others.

If we locate our influence/leadership as an act of servanthood for others, shown as beneath them in Figure 4 below this leads to willing movement forwards. We can therefore visualize this as follows.

Figure 4: Influence, willing movement and servant leadership

Graham Tomlin on pneumatology within eschatology

In his 2011 book *The Prodigal Spirit*, the now Bishop of Kensington, Graham Tomlin, explores the connection between heaven and earth, the spiritual and physical, in the emerging reality of the Christian hope. For Tomlin, eschatology isn't a vague dimension of Christian theology, it is a reality into which we step when we are energized by the presence of the Spirit. It's the now and the not yet again: two characteristics of the same reality. He summarizes, 'as this eschatological dualism present in the New Testament makes clear. The Spirit brings the future into the present ... this new dimension of reality has within it a new way of being, a new rationality and a new order.'[22] Like Moltmann, Tomlin recognizes that the work of the Spirit is central to this developing eschatological reality which we occupy. To enter the life God has for us we need the Spirit, and so it helps to know more about how God works among us and how we align ourselves with the Spirit's work.

Theologically, we need these pneumatological underpinnings if you like, and elsewhere in *The Prodigal Spirit* Tomlin develops a

contemporary theology of the Spirit in which he locates human vocation in God's wider movement of redemption and renewal in the
world. This pneumatology is lively and vivid, a constant listening
out and following the movement of God, the wind and the whispers,
and vital for our understanding of what God is doing and how God
is doing it.

For Tomlin, authentic Christianity emerges out of God's pneumatological initiative in human life, giving shape to our Christological
identity and eschatological purpose. As he puts it, 'being in Christ
by the Spirit means becoming caught up in His work to prepare
for the new creation';[23] humanity has always been on this wider
journey: from the garden of Eden to the heavenly city, from self-
centredness to Godly love, from separation from God to union and
a place with Christ at the right hand of the Father. And our role
in this transformation is as participants as well as beneficiaries.[24]
Tomlin argues that to be Christian is to locate ourselves, and our
activity, in this pneumatologically inspired eschatological narrative:
seeing the future Kingdom of God breaking into the present by the
Spirit. Encouragingly, Tomlin continually roots this understanding
in Scripture and in the creative imaginings of a host of respected
theologians, and it is unsurprising to find the likes of Karl Barth,
C. S. Lewis, Dante and Bunyan referenced as Tomlin develops his
thinking.[25]

So there are some primary theological implications of Hopeful Influence
as we've defined it. For now we've said that true leadership is the leadership of Christ exercised through us as his agents on earth; that we
understand any leadership activity as an act of *servanthood* for others;
and that Christian leadership finds its most complete expression under
the influence of the Holy Spirit and it is the Spirit who is the means by
which Jesus' lordship becomes manifest. We can now extend our understanding of Hopeful Influence to incorporate these implications. As an
aside, it's important to recognize the limits to the scope of leadership
also. We have located Christian leadership within discipleship: when we
refer to influence we are just talking about one aspect of our discipleship.
Following Jesus, being a disciple, means lots of things. Principally it's
about entering into a loving relationship with God through Jesus Christ
and by the power of the Spirit. It's also about our personal growth and
holiness. It's about the quality of life we enjoy within Christian community. It's also about serving others beyond the life of the Church and

building the Kingdom of the God in the widest sense within the created world that we live in. It's all of those things and more. Defining Christian leadership as we've done is a bit like looking at discipleship through a lens – the lens of influence. We lift the lens up and we look at human life and behaviour, and the lens immediately helps us see the moments of influence happening in all the social interactions around us; within the scope of this book that is what we are interested in, nothing more.

Towards a theology of Christian leadership

Through our exploration of leadership, influence and the theology of hope, it would appear that we have now said something a bit more definitive about what is happening theologically in the activity of leadership – certainly more than most contemporary Christian commentators have wanted to say. We have redefined the essence of Christian leadership and presented a particular theological lens which we can apply to our thinking. At the heart of this is a controlling idea that gives shape to what God is doing in and through our leadership. The idea that there is a Christ-shaped and Spirit-led teleology to our human activity: we journey forwards, together, within an emerging eschatological reality. Moltmann, Wright and Tomlin are essentially painting a picture of a growing community of hopeful people, moving forwards into God's renewal of the world, inviting humanity and the rest of creation in. This is the robust, theological underpinnings I have sought, which will lead to greater clarity around the realization of Christian leadership. I would like to think that despite some technical theological language, a picture has emerged of true leadership being about the expectation of exciting possibilities, of a trustfulness that God is at work, of a positive, optimistic sense of *let's go for it*, and a maturing awareness that the journey is far bigger than any one of us. Our shared future will be shaped by the effectiveness of our Hopeful Influence, and this is central to any exploration of Christian leadership.

And despite the terrible corruptions of leadership that are often found in all spheres of life, and the muddled failings and confusion of the Church, the strands of God's true purposes still find their way through. Reality is inescapable even if we fail to recognize and articulate its true form. What church isn't wrestling with the call to proclaim a hopeful vision of what will be, as a motivator to transform our current allegiances? What business doesn't have a vision statement to align its present behaviour with its future goals? What political leader or charity worker isn't engaged with moulding things that are into what they think things should be? What counselling session doesn't run on the premise that the human soul is on a journey of change? Even the former Manchester United manager Sir Alex Ferguson, when reflecting back on his 26-year journey in charge of one of the world's biggest football clubs, makes a statement about his role as leader that shows an extraordinary level of eschatological awareness; 'my job ... was to make everyone understand that the impossible was possible. That's the difference between leadership and management.'[26] As leaders we help others move into a new future that many cannot currently see.

In the positions of leadership that we formalize in our different communities, the world does seem to understand enough to know that these roles are fundamentally about helping others journey into a different kind of future. It is certainly true that the lack of understanding of eschatology, of what life is meant to look like under the lordship of Jesus, impoverishes our clarity of the shape of the future to come. It is certainly also true that this in turn impoverishes our clarity around what the appropriate next steps are in realizing that future, to say nothing of the required embodiment of leadership to enable that change most effectively. But even with this lack of understanding we are still unknowingly acting and thinking eschatologically, or *hopefully*, because that is the nature of things. Eternity has indeed been written into the hearts of humankind.[27] We all get glimpses of the deeper truths in front of us, even if we struggle to hold them together clearly.

Having skirted the theological contours, what we need to do now is try and flesh out this theology of leadership and begin to explore what it means to apply these ideas to particular applications of leadership: we need to elaborate a clearer shape of Hopeful Influence. We have what we need in the realm of God's promises, in the story of Jesus, in the gift of the Spirit, in the hope of our own bodily resurrection and in the location of Christian people as active participants in the story of redemption. In all these things and more, we have identified some of the essential theological furniture to build a model for informing the true shape of Christian leadership. I'm excited about how this could change my own life and ministry. I'm excited for how this can unify some of the divergent strands within contemporary discussion on Christian leadership. I'm excited about how this can resource every Christian person as they exercise influence, and even appeal to those who haven't, as yet, embraced a Christian identity. While this particular book will only offer a small beginning, let us now turn our attention to how we might begin to develop our theological understanding of Hopeful Influence further.

Comment
Ian Parkinson, Leadership Specialist, CPAS

As noted earlier, Bishop Steven Croft suggests that the Christian Church is the inheritor of the longest continuous tradition of reflection on leadership in communities that the human culture has ever seen.[28] Far from being alien to the work of the Church, leadership is, on this account, integral to its healthy functioning.

Perhaps some of the disagreements around the appropriateness for the Church of embracing leadership discourse arise from a failure to discern the diversity of different leadership discourses and a failure to acknowledge the impact of context upon specific forms of leadership. The word 'leadership', though used indiscriminately to describe responsible people in a variety of contexts, may well admit to a variety of subtly different, and even conflicting, definitions. Its legitimate use to describe those exercising responsibility in the Church does not imply an endorsement of every other use of the term, nor an embrace of all that is understood by such uses.

Leadership is ultimately shaped by the ends, purposes and values associated with the specific organizations in which it finds its locus. Thus, leadership that arises from commercial or similar sectors in which the drive for profit and the satisfaction of shareholders is paramount, may well be inappropriate as a blueprint for those engaged in leadership in the Church. By the same token, given that leadership is generally concerned with the oversight of people, and with their motivation and enabling, it may well be the case that wisdom may be found in leadership traditions that emerge from other sectors, and that to overlook such insights will ultimately impoverish our own exercise of leadership. Perhaps fuller and more considered reflection on the Christian tradition and its core theological motifs might not only give us the tools to discern what might be borrowed from other sources but, more importantly, allow us to discern what the precise form and ethos of a distinctively Christian leadership might be.

By contrast with some secular understandings which present leadership as *instrumental* and as the *creative* work of the leader, the Christian tradition sees leadership as ultimately belonging to and conducted by God in the first instance, and then shared with those whom he calls. Thus, leadership is seen in Scripture as a stewardship exercised on behalf of another. This is reflected not only in the self-understanding of leaders but also in the titles used to describe those exercising positional leadership.[29]

As we have seen, leaders who understand this will see their task as not only to be stewards of a received past (often the default mindset of church leaders) but equally to be curators of an anticipated future. They will be transformational people. In addition, Christian leaders will take seriously the present work of the Spirit in every member of the body of Christ, gifting each one for service, and they will understand their own role to be that of *animating*[30] the Church and its members, bringing to life and creating space for the exercise of the ministries of every believer. This is an activity that is best described as leadership, but a leadership that is richer and fuller, and subtly distinct from, many other practices bearing the same name.

Notes

1 Václav Havel, *Disturbing the Peace: A Conversation with Karel Hvížd'ala*, trans. Paul Wilson (London: Faber and Faber, 1990).

2 Bernard M. Bass, *The Bass Handbook of Leadership: Theory, Research and Managerial Applications* (New York: Free Press, 2008), p. 7.

3 Simon Western, *Leadership: A Critical Text* (London: SAGE, 2008), p. 40.

4 James Lawrence, *Growing Leaders: Reflections on Leadership, Life and Jesus* (Abingdon: CPAS and The Bible Reading Fellowship, 2004), pp. 23–4.

5 Genesis 1.26–31.

6 Romans 11.11–12.

7 Malcolm Guite, 'The Call of the Disciples', in *Sounding the Seasons* (Norwich: Canterbury Press, 2012), p. 21.

8 Hebrews 6.1.

9 Hebrews 6.9–12.

10 Tom Wright, *Surprised by Hope* (London: SPCK, 2007), p. 219.

11 Luke 19.16–24.

12 Jürgen Moltmann, *Theology of Hope* (London: SCM, 1967).

13 Moltmann, *Hope*, p. 15.

14 Moltmann, *Hope*, pp. 15–19.

15 Moltmann, *Hope*, p. 16.

16 Moltmann, *Hope*, p. 17.

17 John 14.6.

18 N. T. Wright, *The Resurrection of the Son of God* (London: SPCK, 2003).

19 Richard Bauckham, *The Theology of Jürgen Moltmann* (London: T&T Clark, 1995), p. 38.

20 Saint Jerome, *Dialogus contra Ludiferianos*, chapter 21, in Roger Heuser and Norman Shawchuck, *Leading the Congregation: Caring for Yourself While Serving Others* (Nashville, TN: Abingdon Press, 2010), p. 182.

21 Matthew 20.25–28.

22 Graham Tomlin, *The Prodigal Spirit: The Trinity, the Church and the Future of the World* (London: Alpha International, 2011), p. 46.

23 Tomlin, *Prodigal*, p. 54.

24 Tomlin, *Prodigal*, p. 58.

25 Tomlin, *Prodigal*, pp. 43–7.

26 Alex Ferguson, *Leading* (London: Hodder & Stoughton, 2015), p. 239.

27 Ecclesiastes 3.11.

28 Steven Croft, *The Gift of Leadership* (Norwich: Canterbury Press, 2016), p. vii.

29 Cf. John N. Collins, *Diakonia: Re-interpreting the Ancient Sources* (Oxford: OUP, 1990).

30 Cf. Stephen Pickard, *Theological Foundations for Collaborative Ministry* (Abingdon: Ashgate, 2009).

Reflection

Now and Not Yet

Revelation 21.1–5a

Then I saw 'a new heaven and a new earth,' for the first heaven and the first earth had passed away, and there was no longer any sea. I saw the Holy City, the new Jerusalem, coming down out of heaven from God, prepared as a bride beautifully dressed for her husband. And I heard a loud voice from the throne saying, 'Look! God's dwelling place is now among the people, and he will dwell with them. They will be his people, and God himself will be with them and be their God. "He will wipe every tear from their eyes. There will be no more death" or mourning or crying or pain, for the old order of things has passed away.'

He who was seated on the throne said, 'I am making everything new!'

Questions

1 Do you have hope for leadership? Why?
2 Are there different ways you would describe leadership? What are they?
3 Is leadership influence? Why?
4 What do you think God is doing through our leadership?
5 What does Jesus teach us about hope?
6 What is your understanding of eschatology, and is it true to say that all of Christian life is eschatological?
7 Is Christian leadership Hopeful Influence? Why?

Prayer

Father God, thank you that our ultimate future is wonderful. Thank you that the perfection of the world is something you have promised. Thank you that you are making all things new and that victory over the darkness is something you have already won through the faithfulness of Jesus. We acknowledge that you are seated on the throne over all heaven and earth right now, and we ask that you would send the Holy Spirit to us afresh, to empower us to live for you. Help us today to be people of Hopeful Influence; serving the advance of your Kingdom in the lives of others. In Jesus' name, amen.

PART TWO

What is Hopeful Influence?

4

Movement

It was one of those early winter days, when the temperature drops and the weather alternates rapidly. Dark clouds with rain and the occasional hail. Then – all change, brilliant sunshine with cool, fresh and clear air. It was a retreat day for Church of England ministers, and a colleague and I had cycled the seven miles or so from our church to the Aintree racecourse, fortunately missing most of the wet weather. We ended up seated in a large suite overlooking the racecourse, listening to an address on the subject of Advent. Waiting in hope.

Despite the beauty of the morning, my mind drifted critically back to my cycle ride there. Cycling through tough Liverpool estates, half-eight in the morning, the smell of strong cannabis, skunk weed, drifting from a group of school children. Roads full of potholes. Glass on the pavements, on the side of the road. The thick, noxious smell of heavy morning traffic. My mind wandering to the levels of pollutants, of dangerous diesel particulates floating in the air as I breathed deeply, cycling hard, sweat running from my brow. *I want to see this brokenness changed*, had lifted as a cry from my heart. This *can* be changed.

One critical thought can lead to another, and my mind then went back to the conversation the night before with a group of students I was mentoring that year. One of them shared some of the challenges of being in a local cricket club. This lad loved cricket, was a really good player. But at the club, beneath the joy of the sport and the team camaraderie, there was a broken subculture. An expectation of heavy drinking. Sexual promiscuity. Of regular trips away fuelled by excess. This lad, with so much ability and future potential, felt hugely isolated within the club. 'A different world', was the phrase he kept using. As I'd cycled past the

Liverpool billboards advertising provocative dress-ware, expensive jewellery and myriad commercial messages proclaiming their own form of Christmas, I just felt overwhelmed. A sense of exploitation. Of desperate escapism. Of deeply unsatisfying forms of culture. Of people the length and breadth of the country smothered, suffocated, drowning under the weight of unfettered commercialism and moral confusion. My heart ached for the lad in the cricket team. For the school kids. For the young mother navigating the heavy traffic at the zebra crossing.

One wall in the conference suite was floor-to-ceiling windows. I was sitting on the other side of the room, but even from where I was I could see the blue of the sky so clear, sharp, piercing. The speaker was talking about hope. Hope for a better world. The invitation at Advent to see the first shoots of future life breaking into the current world. As I reflected back on the morning cycle ride and listened to the message of hope washing over me, I knew that I needed to look out of the window. To see life more clearly – as it could be. Fortunately, the speaker caught the mood of the room, because they wrapped up the message with unusual promptness and invited us to take half an hour or so to respond in whatever means felt right.

I moved across the room, the light pulling me across with the great promise of beauty. As I looked out, the green of the racetrack, lush, rich, vast, almost impossibly green as each blade of grass reflected the bright low sunlight. In the distance, low hills, a scattering of white cloud, the occasional cry of seagulls overhead. Like the hope of the Kingdom to come. Like the impossible beauty in C. S. Lewis's *The Great Divorce*; the grass was more like grass than any earthly grass, the sky was more perfectly sky than any earthly sky, the call of the gulls like the tug to a distant shoreline. And there I understood, in a fresh way, why we all need regular signposts towards the Kingdom. In that moment I felt energized, inspired, enflamed for what was possible. Here it was, the new creation life breaking through, the taste, the feeling, the sense of what it really will be like in the new creation: beautiful and wonderful. As I gazed at this signpost of beauty, that brilliant image of pure sunshine over the Aintree racetrack, so I felt fresh desire, fresh rage even, in a pure, clear-minded sense, to see the world transformed. A fresh calling, a fresh ordination, to work for the Kingdom in this city. How could I help others to see the Kingdom in similar ways? How could I help others to be energized by that same promise of beauty and goodness for all? How could our wonderful city become more aligned to the shape of God's future, even amid our inherited brokenness and decay?

These are the kinds of questions we take into this next part of our exploration on leadership. While they emerge here from one particular experience of my own, in some ways these questions are common to all people. At different points in life we get a sense of how life could be. To greater and lesser extents, we are energized by the possibilities to move towards a better future. What we need help on, abundant help, is how to translate our desires for something better into influence on others that is properly aligned with God's plans and purposes. With that aim in mind, we now have arrived at a theological definition of Christian leadership that moves the discussion forwards and that seems to have unifying potential amid the diversity of ideas around Christian leadership. In an important redefinition of terms, we have said that Christian leadership is eschatological, or Hopeful Influence. We're now in a different place to where we started.

The next challenge is to flesh out a more precise shape of this Hopeful Influence. How does Hopeful Influence authentically manifest itself and how do we help others into the movement God has for them? We can then explore how Hopeful Influence works in positional leadership roles, and see how it plays off against other leadership models. As we do this, we'll need to see whether the thinking stands up, and whether it is enriched or requires any modification from what others have learned. We need to do all this before we can begin to talk concretely about how we can apply Hopeful Influence in different spheres of life, which comes from the final part of this book.

Hopeful Influence through our personhood

First, let's say a bit more at a foundational level about how Hopeful Influence takes shape within our personhood and within the world we live in. We have said that Hopeful Influence helps people to take particular steps towards the Kingdom: to move towards the world as it should be where life is found under the lordship of Christ. However, we need to be a bit careful here that we don't equate our influence with a person's response. Things are more complex than that, and people are also more complex. For influence to be influence, we've said there needs to be a willing response on the part of the follower. However, our activity of leadership travels through the context of another person's personhood and therefore the actual movement of response is as much a function of their personhood as it is a function of a leader's leadership. Again, this might feel like stating the obvious, but it's important to be clear about it. We might exercise tremendous leadership but nothing happens. Or awful leadership, and people go on to do great things. The quality of our leadership isn't coupled directly to a person's response; responsibility for that lies with the follower.

The potential for such varied response to our influence is of course linked to the fact that leadership happens between persons. The act of leadership gets worked out through our humanity, and therefore has the potential to be affected by our physical, emotional and spiritual states as well as by our character and personality and other factors such as our language, cultural background, intellect and values. In addition, we can still influence people when parts of our personhood are hidden. Over the telephone or via a letter. On television or in a newspaper. Online or through social media. In all these forms, parts of our personhood become limited, and there is an important work, which is beyond the scope of this book, to explore how our Hopeful Influence is well marshalled when our relationships are presented in virtual forms – that is, less than fully human.

For our purposes, there are three theological points we need to make about personhood that affect how Hopeful Influence gets worked out in practice. The first is our need for *significance*, activated primarily through purpose and activity. As we looked at earlier, at the birth of humanity God gave men and women together a role of the most extraordinary significance: we were asked to steward creation. As such, we have a longing for purpose and activity and we desire to fulfil this need. In a sense this is a good thing. It's a longing for what we were made for. It's also a longing that can get powerfully activated as we participate in the renewal of the world. However, within the world as it is, the longing can also quickly become a broken thing. I once had the opportunity to see a mechanical digger for a bore hole. It had the potential to be a very significant piece of kit. It was automated, and once you put it in the right place and set it running, it essentially hammered its way down into the ground until the hole was the required depth. Brilliant if the digger is located in the right place and used the right way. But imagine if it was to be taken out of the environment for which it was made, and left to hammer its way arbitrarily through buildings, or down through our tunnels and mains supplies of electricity, water, gas and all those underground fibre optic cables we enjoy the use of. Taken out of the environment for which we were made, we no longer know where to dig, and our pursuit of significance is often highly destructive. We don't know what significance is good, we don't know what significance is sustainable and we don't know what significance is just our desperate desire to shore up our transient identity by influencing events, activities and people. I need purpose, and I will often pursue it blindly, and there go the vain, misguided efforts of millions of *leaders* down through history. You may well recognize those among you who just have to voice an opinion, who just have to have their say, who just have to get a sense of having been significant in someone else's life. The truth is, we've all got that desire to some degree.

In addition, as human beings we need *security*. The world isn't the safe place it was at its beginning. The expulsion from the garden took us into a chaotic and messy world where bad things happen; it is an often dangerous and hostile place. Deep in our psyche, learned in our early years and reinforced as we grow older, we know we have to play this world a certain way to assuage the negative consequences of the forces beyond us: parents, teachers, siblings, not to mention that deeply annoying child in the year above us at primary school. We have a huge need for security, and this is part of the birthplace of our desires for power and control. We develop defence mechanisms to handle the independence of others – those who are different from us, but who can hugely affect the quality of our life experience. Simon Walker is brilliant on this point, and essentially maps out the way people gravitate towards positional leadership and other forms of influence as tactics to defend the self.[2] We will connect with his findings later in the book, and especially how the particularly Christian possibility of *undefended* leadership connects with Hopeful Influence, but our business for now is just to recognize some particularly relevant aspects of our personhood.

A third aspect of our personhood that needs to be recognized is our need for *relationship*. Before the birth of human community, God said, 'It is not good for the man to be alone.'[3] We were made for relationship with one another; to relate and to be related to. To be seen and known and to see and know. We need these connections; with God and with one another. Unfortunately though, as with our needs for significance and security, our need for good relationship is shot through with experiences of bad relationship. We need each other, yet we hurt each other. We need each other, but we disappoint each other. We need each other and, in a sense, we need others to need us. But they often don't need us, at least not in ways that are easy for us to fulfil. Again, our early life experience is formative. We develop complex ways to build and maintain relationships; to give and exchange affirmation, interest and friendship. Unavoidably colouring any relationship where influence is exchanged is our basic need to be accepted, liked and valued. In all sorts of ways these needs creep to the surface, shaping our tone, our willingness to listen, the extent of what we are willing to ask of others.

Much more will need to be said of course about how the nature of personhood affects our influence, but these three needs, and particularly the ways they manifest themselves, have to be recognized early in the formation of our understanding of Hopeful Influence. Essentially they all relate to our need for identity, or clarified existence if you like. All the major religions agree that there is something wrong with the world, something wrong deep within our personhood as well as in the surrounding world, and the Judeo-Christian-Islamic traditions all locate this within the narrative of the Fall. Our personhood has been compromised, and specifically our identity as commissioned, secure people in good relationship with God and with each other has been shattered. Hence our needs for significance, security and relationship consciously and unconsciously dominate our interactions. We crave these things and in this life we will always be living with a measure of frustration. John Calvin did most of the hard work on this, building on Church Fathers like Augustine and the Cappadocians, and the likes of Neil Anderson's 'Freedom in Christ' ministries have popularized it today. I don't offer solutions at this stage, just a summary awareness of what we are dealing with.

Because our leadership and the response of others travel through this complex terrain of personhood, we also have to say that Hopeful Influence is unavoidably hard. Finding truly *hopeful* ways of influencing others is difficult, because our own baggage so often gets in the way, and even when we lead well there is an intrinsic resistance from others because of their own baggage too. As persons we are fallen, and the world around us is fallen, and the turning of that which has rebelled is not an easy task. Even if our influence is largely free from the artificial projections of significance, security and relationship; even if it is pointing in an appropriate eschatological direction; even if it is presented through Christlike character, full of the Spirit's anointing – it may still fail. The world after all is a broken place; the lives of those who respond to our influence are broken, the structures of our society are broken, the natural fabric of the world around us is broken. Steven Croft framed it as a vital insight when reflecting on the three millennia of Judeo-Christian leadership tradition:

> The entire tradition is built around the truth that leadership in communities, in business, in political life, in the Church is very, very, very difficult. If we understand this then we have made a good beginning. Unless we grasp this, then we will continually struggle and fall.[4]

Hopeful Influence through positional leadership

So Hopeful Influence is expressed through our personhood, which means it is affected by the deep complexities therein and is therefore, among other things, hard. An interesting extra dimension to this is how the positional leadership positions we occupy can impact the effectiveness of a person's influence. Within communities we broker relationships around particular goals towards which we want to move; we do this especially with leadership. Forms of influence become manifest that will enable us to realize our shared goals. As I've argued earlier, that is the way of things in our shared human experience: we were made for movement.

Depending on the organization or community of which we are part, and most of us are members of multiple groups, our shared goals will be different. These formalized positions of leadership, and within that definition I am including the more organic, bottom-up forms as well as those tightly defined from the top down, are meant to allow influence to be channelled more effectively. Of course there are no guarantees of that, but for the person exercising a form of positional leadership, there will be a higher degree of potential to exert influence and therefore generally a higher degree in which we can realize truly Hopeful Influence. Having said that, our influence in these organizations won't necessarily be *hopeful*; it requires careful discernment to know how to align our influence eschatologically in our complex organizational webs when often an organization wants to move in a different direction. But either way, positional leadership is a very powerful dynamic. You could say that positional leadership is a way of structuring the innate relational power that exists within an organization, or even a way to limit and give shape to our influence. This is visualized in Figure 5.

Figure 5: Influence through positional leadership

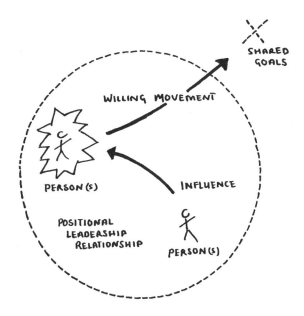

So we have these ideas about a better world, and we want to do things that will take us there, therefore we formalize positions of leadership to hardwire the kind of influence we think will be most effective in our institutions or social structures. But if the positional leader begins to operate in ways that essentially imply they are not open to Hopeful Influence from others, then their leadership begins to manifest like an eschatological full stop. This can occur when a leader uses excessive authoritarianism, or when they play up their role as the lone expert in an organization (as I suspect Nouwen did at Harvard before he rethought the leadership paradigm). In these instances the fully communal eschatological influence that needs to happen in any healthy organization stagnates, and the whole notion of every person playing a shared role in an organization's development is undermined. This is what Nouwen was picking up on, brought into particular focus through his own life story. As a vicar, every time I give the impression that I'm beyond critique or the teaching of others, then I fall into this trap too.

The real point here is that we have a general definition of Christian leadership as Hopeful Influence, which describes the true nature and purpose of our leadership, but then we find ourselves in forms of positional leadership that are formally written into the structures of our institutions or social groups. Sometimes these forms will help our expression of Hopeful Influence and sometimes they will hinder it, but there is tremendous potential, if we get the scope of these roles right, for Hopeful Influence to really take off in the organizations of which we are part. As we explore this further, there will be times when we will need to talk about leadership within an organization as a formalized set of relationships to enable particular goals to become better realized. In the main, I'll tend to refer to leadership in the theological sense as I've defined it, simply as Hopeful Influence, but when it is important to differentiate between leadership in that sense and when it is expressed in a particular way through positional leadership, then I will highlight this.

Our movement is not protological

Behind the beauty of creation that we read about in the first two chapters of Genesis lies an unavoidable question when we get to chapter 3. Where did the snake come from that came to inhabit the garden and deceive humanity? Clearly something had happened before human beings entered the scene that gave rise to the presence of evil in the world. Things were not quite so perfect and, as many scholars on the subject of theodicy have speculated, it is perhaps the very presence of evil in creation that led God to create fragile persons in God's own image who would eventually participate in the overthrowing of that same evil. Indeed, things may have taken a particular shape because of that very purpose.

It's worth reading Jacques Ellul on this. Ellul is a brilliant theologian who carefully deconstructs the notion that the Christian journey is protological, like a return to Eden, but who invites Christians to creatively imagine the new city of God, and to use this imagining as a key resource for how Christians are to live today.[5] God's future isn't static and Ellul invites us to dream. There's very little that is new in the discussion of theology, just older ideas applied to new contexts, and in some ways the notion of Hopeful Influence is an application of Ellul's thought within the specific context of leadership. For Ellul, this way of thinking is essential to Christian progress. He argues that if the people of God, in fact all of humanity and creation, are doing anything then we are on a journey from what has been and what is, to what can be and will be. He sees the same underlying eschatological movement beneath our created order, which he frames as a movement towards a city, the place where transformed creation resides, consummated in a new, perfected relationship with its creator. The end goal is markedly richer from that original garden.

Enabling others to see, participate and experience the Kingdom

So Hopeful Influence operates through our personhood, is unavoidably hard and can be facilitated through the positional leadership structures we humans inevitably create. What we need to consider now are the particular ways Hopeful Influence takes shape as we seek to enable others towards the Kingdom. To help us with this, we now turn to a theologian who, without majoring on leadership, has grappled significantly with the underlying purpose of the Church and how Jesus' ministry to the world is expressed through his body. In his book *The Household of God*, Lesslie Newbigin makes particular effort to define the Church as a people on the move, reaching out to all humanity with a message of reconciliation as we go, but very specifically journeying towards a God who promises to meet and transform us.[6] Newbigin's picture of the Church goes beyond any particular institutional or localized expression and tries to express something of the corporate identity and purpose of every Christian. His contribution on this point perhaps reaches its high point when he articulates through the language of *sign, instrument* and *foretaste* the essentially eschatological nature of the Church, and by extension every Christian person.[7] This was adopted when an ecumenical group of churches came together in 2001 to express their unity in the Reuilly statement of faith, with the minor yet helpful modification to read, 'the Church is sent into the world as a sign, instrument and foretaste of a reality which comes from beyond history – the kingdom, or reign of God.'[8]

What is being said here is that there is a wider movement of redemption and transformation which is becoming increasingly manifest through the lordship of Jesus and which every Christian person is called to enter into and, most importantly for leadership, also enable others to enter into. It is the proclamation of the gospel – Jesus is Lord – now come and enter this reality. Show others what it's like. Help other people to join in. Enable others to experience the goodness of it with increasing measure. This illuminates the heart of a very particular form of Christian activity, and sharpens how our influence as Christians fits into the overarching story and purpose we've already explored. In other words, we can now see how Hopeful Influence manifests itself within the underlying teleological framework of the Church's activity.

Going a little deeper, if we rephrase Newbigin's language of sign, instrument and foretaste within the activity of leadership, then we can say that eschatological influence finds expression when we enable others to see, participate in and experience the coming Kingdom; see, participate and experience being practical translations of how we act as signs, instruments and foretastes respectively. If this is right, then enabling others to see, participate and experience their families, political structures, businesses, charities and communities, as well as their churches, in closer alignment to their God-given potential is therefore theologically at the heart of Christian leadership. And as we saw in the last chapter, these activities are founded on, and are in response to, the promises of God, and they become truly and appropriately manifest as we allow the Spirit of God to move within us. And all of these things are beautifully birthed out of a theology of hope. With these thoughts in mind, we are much closer to understanding how our definition of Christian leadership translates into genuine movement towards the Kingdom.

Enabling others to see

First, let us consider influence that acts as a sign of the Kingdom. As an example, take the giving of an engagement ring. A peculiar act of influence I know. An engagement ring is meant to be beautiful, and beautiful things have a value in and of themselves. But the beauty the engagement ring contains is also meant to point to something even more beautiful than itself, and that is the faithful promises of the marriage covenant to come; of the beauty of a loving and committed life together. In fact, even more than that the engagement ring points, via the marriage covenant, to the unbreakable faithfulness of God and the assurance of the kind of loving relationships we will enjoy, with God and with each other, into eternity. When I gave my wife her engagement ring, as well as simply an expression of love, it was also an act of influence. I was basically saying: let's dive in. Let's throw ourselves into a relationship of absolute, 100 per cent, committed, passionate, selfless love for one another. And it's safe to do it because the whole wonderful wild romance points towards something far bigger than itself. In giving you this ring, I want to express my unique hope for us as a couple and help us prepare to enter into a commitment that extends far beyond itself. That bigger picture is awesome and the giving of the engagement ring a helpful act of influence along the way. Of course, with our tendency to think smaller rather than larger, there's always the danger that we get obsessed by the superficial beauty of that gorgeous ring with its shining mounted gemstone and fail to see the true beauty behind. Even my wonderful wife is a sucker for that one! But Jesus invites us to make the connections between the present and the future, and to seek out acts of influence that help people understand the hope to which we are called. Our Christian activities, for our specific purposes the expressions of Christian influence, are meant to point people forwards towards the world as it is meant to be. When the council puts up 'no litter' signs, it's not just for the preservation of this current world but, for those who are listening, it acts as a signpost towards a world where there will be no litter, because one day every person who occupies it will be passionate about the world's care.

Enabling others to participate

Second, let's consider how we help others to participate in the Kingdom of God. It may seem an unlikely example to some, but let's consider the sphere of business. All the world over, people are working endless hours to design more efficient cars, faster computers, tastier food, more durable clothing – at least that's what companies should be doing when they aren't fettered by short-term commercialism. We struggle and strain to make the world a better place, and one of the principal ways we do that is through the production of goods and the delivery of services. Now I'm sure that the exchange of money as we know it, and the often painful experience of work, will be thoroughly renewed in the world to come, but the improvements we make today are in some sense an instrument, or a participation with God, in God's work of renewal in the universe. We are God's image bearers in God's world, invited into God's work of sustainment and transformation. We are meant to produce things that will improve our experience of life and we are meant to build them and use them in ways that are sustainable, and we are meant to help people to join in in this very physical transformation of the world, even via employment. This is the proper role of business, and helping other people participate in the advance of the Kingdom is an activity that we are invited into in every other sphere of life too. Theologically speaking, this is also why Martin Luther, when asked what he'd do if he knew the world was ending tomorrow, said he'd plant a tree. We do things that make the world a better place. It's not that the tree lasts for eternity in its current form, or that the thoroughly improved toothbrush does either, but both are a participation in the Kingdom that is breaking in. When we influence others in ways that enable them to join in with this movement of the Kingdom, so we are exercising truly Hopeful Influence.

Enabling others to experience

We signpost the Kingdom, we help others participate in its advance, and we also help others experience it. Don't just help someone to make that improved toothbrush, give it to someone to try out. Get out there and market it so people can experience it for themselves. Improved experience matters. In increasing measure, God wills it that we should experience something of the quality of life when Jesus is Lord. This experience of true human flourishing matters to God; that is God's will for us because God loves us so, and we should expect our journey into the true future to include regular foretastes of Kingdom life breaking through. More widely, as the world increasingly aligns itself with Jesus' lordship, so we should expect to find an improved quality of life for all, albeit that quality doesn't always neatly fit with the individualistic or particular subjective qualities we might want to impose on it. When I lead a church service, I am trying to help people experience the goodness of God in ways that will overflow into the rest of their lives. In part, when I exercise political leadership, it's people's experience of life that I am wanting to improve; same for leadership within a company or third sector organization. When I exercise influence among my family, at my best I want them to experience the goodness of loving relationships as God would have them. In ways we are often ignorant of, God deeply cares about our experience of life and our future is shot through with a form of godly hedonism. As a contemporary observation, for all the criticism of millennials and their sometimes excessive attention to personal experience, they have something important to teach the rest of us about the value God puts on pleasure. God calls us to help others to experience true and lasting sources of that today and, when pursued properly, it has the remarkably cathartic effect of helping hearts grow colder towards the present world's false claims about fulfilment and satisfaction. As Thomas Browne in the seventeenth century put it:

> And if any hath been so happy as personally to understand Christian annihilation, ecstasy, exaltation, transformation, the kiss of the spouse, and ingression into the divine shadow, according to mystical theology, they have already had an handsome anticipation of heaven: the world is in a manner over, and the earth in ashes unto them.[9]

Leaders enable people to move

Signposting the Kingdom for others, helping others become instruments within it, and enabling others to gain a foretaste of what is to come are all examples of what it means to engage in Hopeful Influence. This is where our theology comes to life in beautiful movement. However, this isn't perhaps as revolutionary as I might make out. In a sense, all Newbigin was doing was identifying the forms by which we travel into the future together. The fact that they take a very particular eschatological shape in true Christian influence, doesn't mean that there aren't all sorts of counterfeit attempts to lead into the future in ways that aren't Christian. In a sense every person of influence operates this way; they just help others see, participate and experience different futures. Despite the fact that Newbigin was talking about the missional *telos* of the Church, in some ways he's also talking much more generally about how humanity collaborates together – he's just giving it the very specific direction towards God's Kingdom.

What I mean by all this is that leaders essentially enable other people to move towards a different future, and that happens through the process of helping others see, participate and experience a different future from the reality that they currently inhabit. The world as it could be against the world as it is. That is the essential work of a leader: to help people move towards that different future – and movement is activated as people grasp the vision, get stuck in or begin to feel the benefits of that better future for themselves. One way of looking at it is to say that this threefold movement essentially relates to the different elements of our personhood. When we see the future, there is a movement of the mind. When we participate in the future, there is a movement of the will. When we experience the future, there is a movement of the heart. We would need to qualify will, mind and heart a little to make full sense of this, and no doubt there might be more to say philosophically here, but these different types of movements help anchor the activity of leadership. We will use these aspects of our humanity to help visualize the different forms of Hopeful Influence as this book develops.

Figure 6: Hopeful Influence enables others to see, participate in and experience the Kingdom

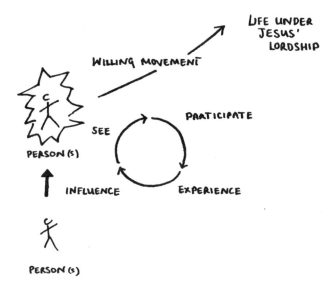

Zooming in on our ability to help others see, participate in and experience God's Kingdom brings into sharper focus the moments of influence that are connected with the ultimate future God is inviting us into. To help us understand this better, let's consider the example of someone preaching the good news about Jesus in church. Is this an act of Hopeful Influence? And if so, how? Well, to begin with, one would hope that preaching the good news would somehow involve proclaiming that Jesus is Lord and talking about the kind of life God wants to invite us into. If the preaching is good, then hopefully people will see the unconditional love of God more clearly, hear the personal invitation to redemption and catch a glimpse of the call to live as a new community of people under the lordship of Jesus. One could say, and it will help us in our definitions of terms, that in seeing the Kingdom, listeners to the sermon will have experienced a movement of the mind.

Having seen something of the Kingdom, having experienced this movement of the mind, let's assume that a person new to church hears the sermon and decides to pray a prayer of Christian commitment for the first time. In a sense, the person is choosing to participate in the Kingdom by making a faith response in prayer. For our definition of terms, let's say that at this point they have experienced a movement of the will. They have chosen to participate in this Kingdom; in this example, in a sense, they have stepped deeper into it.

What happens then? Well, every conversion experience is different, but let's assume that as the person prays a prayer of commitment, they begin to experience something of the love, grace and goodness of God breaking into their subjective experience. It is at that moment that we can say they are beginning to experience the Kingdom. Again, it might be helpful to think of this as a movement of the heart. Hopefully, long after the sermon has been preached, and through myriad different ways, this movement of mind, will and heart will begin to work like a cycle in the person's life. Their imagination has been caught, they've responded, felt something within, and hopefully will now seek out a Christian community where this cycle of movement becomes a regular and sustaining part of life.

This example is of course artificially neat and overly simple and I don't think there is necessarily any order to how the movements of mind, will and heart take shape within a person. When hearing the Christian gospel a person may feel a response of the heart long before their mind consciously grasps what they are hearing. The very decision to listen may in itself be a movement of the will irrespective of any movement of mind or heart. However, what we can see is that the lens of Hopeful Influence shows the connection between the present and the future, through signs, instruments and foretastes, or through movements of mind, will and heart. Connecting the present with the future is the way Hopeful Influence operates.

The example of preaching is deliberate because of its simplicity. For clarity's sake I want to illustrate the picture of *see*, *participate* and *experience* with a movement that is unambiguously towards the Kingdom. Other examples of Christian leadership function the same, but have a degree of ambiguity sometimes about the level of movement forwards into the Kingdom. I help my son with his homework. It's an act of kindness. It enables him to mentally grow and contributes towards his future potential. It also helps fulfil my God-given responsibilities. It feels hopeful, eschatological even, but to what extent is it located in Jesus' story and to what extent does it connect with my son's ultimate future? I don't precisely know. The answer to those kinds of questions are less certain, although, as we'll see, there are tools we can use to help gauge this better.

Movement to renewal

If Christian leadership is best understood theologically as Hopeful Influence, then we need to understand more about how Hopeful Influence creates movement towards the Kingdom and how that movement brings the renewal God seeks. We know there can be a better world, and in this chapter we have seen that Hopeful Influence is a major part of God's plan for how that better world advances. More than that, with Newbigin's help, we've seen that our Hopeful Influence takes shape in three distinct forms: helping others to see, participate and experience the Kingdom of God. At its core is the activation of the mind, will and heart of those who follow us. As we help others see, participate and experience the Kingdom of God in increasing measure, then it is at that point that we can say that we are applying Hopeful Influence or true Christian leadership.

We've set these processes very intentionally within human personhood, with all its inherent complexity and difficulty, and clearly getting traction on effective Hopeful Influence will require significant reflection on what is happening within the personhood of leader and follower alike. Equally, we've recognized the power within positional leadership and the way that enables our influence to stick. There is very significant potential for Hopeful Influence to be harnessed and channelled through our roles of positional leadership within organizations, although decoupling the potential for truly Hopeful Influence from the potential for other forms of influence isn't entirely straightforward, as we will continue to explore.

Our next task is to begin the process of exploring some of the tools we can use to help others see, participate and experience the Kingdom of God. No doubt these activities can take a variety of shapes, but are there things from the theological journey we've been on that help inform how these different activities become more manifest in our lives? Can we get to grips with the idea of Hopeful Influence in a more practical way? And as we understand Christian leadership better, can we find ways of unifying some of the leadership discourse and equipping Christians everywhere to be more effective in their God-given role as co-workers in the Kingdom? It is this final question that I believe God wants the Church, and indeed all of humanity, to give significantly more attention to – so let us explore it further.

Comment
Revd Dr Michael Leyden, Director,
St Mellitus College, North West

Christianity has never been a static religion. From its earliest days it has been a movement. Jesus' call to the first disciples was to follow, journey with, copy, imitate, and obey all that he taught and did. It was a whole-life commitment that embodied in every detail their relationship with him and their commitment to his Kingdom. They left things behind to go where he went and do what he did. At Antioch they got the nickname 'followers of the Way' because their faith in Jesus was a way of life: active, dynamic and transformational.[10] The New Testament is alive with this Spirit-inspired energy and verve!

Hope is the context for this way of life. Hope footed and grounded in the resurrection of Jesus from the dead, and energized by the on-going Spirit-mediated presence of the living Lord.[11] Christian hope is never retrospective. Remember Paul's words to the Corinthians, 'If only for this life we have hope in Christ, we are of all people most to be pitied.'[12] If hope is only about the present and for the present, then it is powerless. But Christian hope is prospective, look-ing beyond the present to what lies ahead, imagining what could be within the economy of God. Hope's well-spring is the event of the resurrection, but its orientation is the coming Kingdom. We live for that day of Christ's return, when the Kingdom is fully realized and the topsy-turvy world is turned upside down and therefore the right way up. For this reason the Swiss Reformed theologian Karl Barth referred to hope as 'a confident, joyful active looking to the future'.[13] Hope is proleptic, meaning that it anticipates what will be in the Kingdom of God. As has been said, we live under Christ's lordship now. In choosing to live *hopefully*, Christians call the future into the present; living today in the light of what is to come, discern-ing what matters to the Kingdom's King and setting about doing it now. Reframing leadership as Hopeful Influence means leadership that moves people towards a Kingdom-shaped future in resurrection power. This is central to the Church's mission. It's our *raison d'être*, our USP, our purpose and goal.

One example of how this plays out can be seen in a New Year's Day sermon,[14] in which St Augustine of Hippo described hope as a 'sentiment of the soul' that reveals itself in our outward choices and actions. Those who hope in God live differently from those who do not; they move throughout the world differently. But nothing of this is for the sake of being different. Christians live a particular kind of life because they have chosen 'to follow [their] Redeemer'. Augustine is clear that simply because Christianity is the movement that grew up around Jesus the Christ it cannot be the case that the Church exists for itself. On the contrary, he encouraged the congregation to seek the well-being of their neighbours, in particular the poor, through acts of giving and service. Because they were under Christ's lordship, they should take practical steps that would make a difference to others as Christ also sought to bless his enemies. For Augustine, this should manifest itself in Christians stopping wasting money on trivialities such as good-luck presents and using it instead to feed the poor and hungry. It's a very concrete example of the kinds of signposts of the Kingdom of God that this chapter has considered. Their Christ-centred, Kingdom-orientated lives were to have present-day, community impact. Through it, people – in this case the poor and hungry – could see and participate and experience something of the Kingdom through redistribution of wealth and resources. Augustine's congregation had no wriggle room to exempt themselves from obedience to Christ. Instead they were to obey him, to move themselves and their neighbours with them in a Kingdom direction by living out Kingdom values.

Hopeful influencers will take people on the same sort of journey; they'll bring their Jesus-centred, resurrection-powered, Spirit-energized, Kingdom-orientated lives into contact with others at work or school or church, and ask questions about what matters most. What present actions and decisions are setting up for the future now, and what could be if we were shaped by a Kingdom vision?

Notes

1 Greg Wells, Benj Pasek and Justin Paul, 'A Million Drams', *The Greatest Showman*, sung by Ziv Zaifman, Hugh Jackman (New York: Atlantic Records, 2017).

2 Simon P. Walker, *The Undefended Leader* (Carlisle: Piquant, 2010). See in particular Book 1, Part II, pp. 67–121.

3 Genesis 2.18.

4 Steven Croft, 'Adventurous and Courageous Leadership', 14 May 2018, https://blogs.oxford.anglican.org/adventurous-and-courageous-leadership/ (accessed 20 August 2019).

5 Jacques Ellul, *The Meaning of the City* (Grand Rapids, MI: Eerdmans, 1970), pp. 188–96.

6 Lesslie Newbigin, *The Household of God: Lectures on the Nature of the Church* (Carlisle: Paternoster, 1998), p. 18.

7 Lesslie Newbigin, *The Open Secret: An Introduction to the Theology of Mission* (Grand Rapids, MI: Eerdmans, 1995), p. 110.

8 *Called to Witness and Service: The Reuilly Common Statement* (London: Church House Publishing, 1999), p. 18.

9 Sir Thomas Browne, *Hydriotaphia* (London: Cressnet Press, 1961), p. xiii.

10 Acts 11.19–26.

11 John 20.22.

12 1 Corinthians 15.13–19.

13 Karl Barth, *Church Dogmatics*, Vol. II.1 (Peabody, MA: Hendrickson, 2010).

14 Augustine, Sermon 198, commonly called *Against the Pagans*.

Reflection

Going from A to B

Hebrews 11.8–12

By faith Abraham, when called to go to a place he would later receive as his inheritance, obeyed and went, even though he did not know where he was going. By faith he made his home in the promised land like a stranger in a foreign country; he lived in tents, as did Isaac and Jacob, who were heirs with him of the same promise. For he was looking forward to the city with foundations, whose architect and builder is God. And by faith even Sarah, who was past childbearing age, was enabled to bear children because she considered him faithful who had made the promise. And so from this one man, and he as good as dead, came descendants as numerous as the stars in the sky and as countless as the sand on the seashore.

Questions

1 What changes do you long for in the world around you? Why?
2 What particular things come to mind when you think about Hopeful Influence expressed through personhood? Are there things in your life formation that make leadership particularly hard for you?
3 How is Hopeful Influence expressed currently in the positional leadership you occupy or sit under?
4 Can you give examples of how yours or others' influence can help people see the Kingdom of God more clearly?
5 Can you give examples of how yours or others' influence can help people participate in the advance of the Kingdom of God?
6 Can you give examples of how yours or others' influence can help people experience the Kingdom of God more fully?
7 What new opportunities for Hopeful Influence are there in your life?

Prayer

Father God, thank you that we get to share in your compassionate concern for a fallen world. Thank you that you invite us to join in with the redemption and transformation of that world. We offer you our personhoods, in all their damage and fragility, as vessels for you to inhabit and work the renewal that you desire. We offer you the positions that we hold and responsibilities we carry. Use us to help others see, participate in and experience your Kingdom in increasing measure. Give us fresh revelation for how we might do this, and the courage and obedience to follow you as you lead others through us. In Jesus' name, amen.

5

Renewal

Few will have the greatness to bend history itself; but each of us can work to change a small portion of events, and in the total of all those acts will be written the history of this generation ... It is from number-less diverse acts of courage and belief that human history is shaped. Each time a man stands up for an ideal, or acts to improve the lot of others, or strikes out against injustice, he sends forth a tiny ripple of hope, and crossing each other from a million different centers of energy and daring, those ripples build a current that can sweep down the mightiest walls of oppression and resistance.

Robert F. Kennedy (1925–68)[1]

I once worked as a business consultant for a large information company, focusing on fraud prevention. The team I was part of had responsibility for working with different clients. I was fortunate to work with a number of the big banks in the UK. They weren't always the quickest to innovate, but the people I worked with were fantastic: highly professional and at the top of their game. I worked with one particular client quite a lot, and it was clear from the off that a number of their fraud prevention systems were too antiquated, and the different systems they employed across the bank were disparate and inadequately joined up. Mine was an interesting role, because I engaged with different divisions across their business, many of whom didn't know what the other divisions did. I had a helicopter view, but I also understood the detail, not least because I'd helped implement a chunk of it. In a sense, I could see what no one else could see. The longer I worked with the client, the more I could see that our business could help them bring together a number of their different systems and provide a more streamlined, joined up, and ultimately more effective, fraud-prevention solution.

The problem was that it was going to require quite a lot of expensive work to upgrade and migrate systems, retrain people, modify communication links, build and install new software applications, test, validate and all the other procedures that goes with a project of this kind. And before all this, I had to convince both people within the bank and people within my own business that this was an appropriate step to take at that point. In truth, I didn't have all the answers. I could see the technical advantages, but I didn't fully understand the financial implications of such an upgrade to the bank, or the impact on staff. I knew enough, however, to be sure that the case was strong. There then began a period of about twelve months where I tried to communicate this vision to people within both businesses. As is my style, I drew lots of pictures and talked quite a lot but, I won't gloss it up, some of my communication and vision casting could have been better, and the initial take-up was slow. Eventually, after a long process, we got to a place where people in a variety of roles within both businesses understood the cost-benefits of the project as well as the technical and staffing challenges to implement it. It became one of my most significant pieces of work. It took another couple of years to fully implement, during which time I had the opportunity to work with teams on various detail challenges that always arise when you get into making something happen. But eventually we had a platform that leveraged the best of what we had and that was properly expandable to incorporate additional services. Again, after we'd built the solution, I was able to work with teams from the bank to fine-tune things and help them get the most from the system we had developed. As you might imagine, the company I worked for was more enthusiastic about the build phase and getting paid than it was about partnering with the client to maximize value over the long term. That was an unfortunate short-term reality of how our business was structured, which we've touched on already. But we delivered real value. It wasn't a perfect solution, but it was a good step forward.

I share this at the outset of this chapter, because it hopefully shows in part why I am so interested in influence. I had the privilege of looking in detail at the way a business worked, and essentially being employed to imagine a better way of doing things. Not only that, but I then had opportunity to help others see the future as I imagined it. The power holders were brought together to help others participate together in making that future a reality and they then worked together to ensure the best possible experience of that new reality and really make life better for folks. What I didn't realize when I did that piece of work, is that this was a good example of the way in which Hopeful Influence works in the world. In fact, I would say that at the time I only loosely connected my faith with my activity at work. I did have some sense of the value of making the world better, and I'm personally glad that my efforts were directed at preventing fraud rather than simply improving the bank's trading potential, as important as that is also. What I've said is that having caught a glimpse of the future, of a better world in whatever sphere of life we find ourselves, then helping others see that world, participate in its coming and experience it more fully is right at the heart of what we are meant to be doing as Christians. What we need to reflect more on now is how to do these activities well.

Using imagination to help people see the Kingdom

So if Hopeful Influence, Christian leadership, is all about enabling eschatological movement into a God-shaped future, then the first question of course is: 'Where we are headed?' We need to know the goal towards which we move – our direction of travel, the vision ahead of us, if you like. And because we are talking about the activity of influence, this social transaction that happens between people, then we have to recognize that there are two elements to this vision: there is the perception of the vision of the person exercising influence and the perception of the vision of the person who is following or responding. To better understand the activity of Hopeful Influence, we need to consider how we see the future in the general sense, but also specifically how this perception takes root in the leader and the follower, if I can use those terms.

Well, the theological underpinnings we've already laid out are informative here. First, we are talking about a movement into the future. We are talking about the world as it could be: more fully under the lordship of Jesus. Or more simply even, we are discerning the will of Christ for a particular situation. At the risk of stating the obvious, because we are talking about something that is yet to be, the place where this discernment happens is in the mind. Right at the heart of the exercise of Hopeful Influence is a godly form of imagination, which will need to happen within both the leader and the follower.

Jürgen Moltmann actually locates imagination as the birthplace of eschatological movement when he explores the possibility of human beings responding to the promises of God under the influence of the Holy Spirit, although he never applied it directly to leadership. As we understand more about the shape of the world to come and more about the kind of world implicit under Jesus' lordship, so our imaginations are stirred to see the world as it could be in any situation, rather than the world as it is. Moltmann frames this in terms of *spes quaerens intellectum*: 'hope seeking understanding'.[2] For him, eschatology could be restored to its controlling role in theological thought, but still remain ineffective as a tool for discipleship, unless we grasp that it is first a posture of enquiry before God. In leadership terms, we have to ask 'What is Jesus' will for this situation?', 'What is God already doing here by the Spirit?' and 'How can I help others to see this potential movement in alignment with God's will?' Exploration of this kind of enquiry is something to which Moltmann devotes significant attention in his 2012 book, *Ethics of Hope*,[3] and that necessitates a leader's exercise of godly imagination and of course discernment.

Godly imagination and discernment aren't necessarily at the top of the requirements on a typical job advert for a leadership position. They don't get a mention in the Church of England's nine criteria for ordained ministry.[4] Admittedly they are held up as leadership attributes by wider commentators, although the reasons commentators make reference to imagination and discernment tend to be via a collection of anecdotes and assertions.[5] James Lawrence implies this when he says that 'the heart of Christian leadership is paying attention to God and where He is leading His people.'[6] However, because Christian leadership properly understood is a response to God's promises about the future, and how those promises might impact our current reality, we now have robust theological under-pinnings about why the execution of imagination and discernment is so important to a properly eschatological and therefore properly Christian form of influence.

Right at the heart of a Christian's purpose is a God-given mandate to dream. To desirously consider, to picture and imagine the world as it could be rather than as it is. To allow the possibilities of our future to take shape in the forefront of our minds. To reimagine our families, well connected with others, and with rhythms of life conducive to the formation of the very best kind of relationships. To reimagine our workplaces, and the kind of contribution we can make that will lead to the most significant and sustainable betterment of the world. To reimagine our communities as places where the common good is understood and pursued and where the good stewardship of our resources is a goal we all share. To reimagine our churches as places of the greatest sustenance, the deepest friendship and the highest forms of equipping and mobility for shared mission. At the birthplace of Hopeful Influence, God invites us to dream.

If Hopeful Influence starts with imagining the future, and then moves towards discerning and implementing the next appropriate steps for a body of people on the journey towards that future, it is vital that the long-term vision and the discernible next steps are appropriately eschato-logically informed. In essence, we need to know what to do and how to do it in our specific contexts, without aiming too high or too low. Build-ing dozens of churches in an area with very few church-going Christians (as was once the practice in East London) is an over-realized form of eschatology. If legislation were passed today banning the sale of diesel and petrol cars, that would be an equally over-realized eschatology, when the market hasn't been given time to generate the new models required. However, failing to plant a new church in an unreached area or failing to work with the automotive industry to ensure medium- and long-term environmental changes are equally examples of under-realized eschatology. To that latter point, why governments haven't set more aggressive targets to remove diesel and petrol cars from our roads, given our advances in technology, is a massively eschatologically under-realized expression of leadership, to the great cost of many. It is in the navigation of over- and under-realized forms of eschatology that we find the cut and thrust of whether leadership will work, and I contend that it is imagination and discernment properly executed that leads to the sweet spot of appropriate eschatological activity: marking out the truest forms of Christian leadership.

Over the past few years, the church I'm part of has been working on a project to develop our building. It's an odd situation: an eighteenth-century building, closed for 40 years, reopened for use by a new worshipping congregation. No running water, no proper toilets or sanitation, no kitchen, very limited heating, but a tent inside the building which we initially constructed to prevent things from falling on our heads. This might sound a bit ridiculous in twenty-first-century Britain, but such is the nature of rebuilding the Christian landscape after a period of decline. In the UK context, there's money available to restore historic buildings like these through English Heritage grants, generally funded by the National Lottery. As the years have gone by, we've made three large and high-quality applications to restore the church building, all of which have failed. To me, the main reason is fairly obvious: until recently we haven't used the building much for wider community and heritage-related events. When you go to the funders and present speculative future use of a building without a track record, quite rightly there is a degree of scepticism. Now of course there are others reasons – points of detail like the level of match-funding we offered – which led to the failure of our applications, but at its heart we were attempting an over-realized form of eschatology. We wanted Heritage money to develop a building before we had even developed a worshipping community (with all the natural links into wider community life) to make it viable. We should have parked the building project, poured our efforts into growing the church congregation and engaged creatively with the community and with Heritage only where that served our focus on growth. Together, and I'm culpable in this process as a key leader, we failed to discern the appropriate eschatological steps for our shared journey. We wanted to build certain physical foundations before they could be laid. I have little doubt that one day our building will be restored fully, but that day will only come once we're able to evidence the required engagement and sustainability to prevent the construction of yet another white elephant paid for by public money. The fact that secular institutions, like our Heritage partners, understand this even better than the Church is one of the interesting paradoxes of a Christianized society.

It is also interesting to reflect on the process of discernment. I think we confused the priority of our calling to develop the church family with our calling to develop the building, and as leaders we should have steered our folks through that confusion. Many in our Church spoke out in support of the project, but my sense is that they were affirming the call to build a Church rather than a building. I also think, personally, that we missed some of the Spirit-led signs of being on the right track. I often find myself drawing others' attention to the signs of the Spirit in their own discernment, but I think we lacked them on this project. Finding a sense of peace. Experiencing a strong gut feel, ka-ching moment, particularly after corporate discernment. Praying together and then being fully clear as a group about a way forward. I think we ignored the absence of some of these signs, and brushed over uncertainties and disagreements because of a false sense of haste and urgency. Knowing when to back off and breathe for a bit before trying a different path wasn't something that came easily to us. Thankfully we did change tack eventually but there is much we could have done differently. The point is, we could see the eschatological goal in the future, but we failed to see that there were more immediate steps to be taken before that could be realized. We lacked the wisdom and sufficient attention to the Holy Spirit to see what steps we should have focused on, and I know I have learned much personally from this failure.

I should say at this point that if I'm implying that all influence is pre-planned and the result of long hours of imagination then of course that's a nonsense. Most of our influence just happens. We're in situations and stuff gets said and done. We ask questions and point things out. It is ludicrous to suggest that we can fore-plan most of our influence in a neatly eschatological way. However, some of our influence *can* be planned like this. More typically, we can step back from situations and use our imagination afresh. We can certainly reflect back on our influence and assess whether it is indeed sufficiently Christian and *hopeful*. The approach I'm commending is about how we set ourselves up to make the most of our opportunities to exercise influence, and how we change and improve the influence we realize we've made. We'll get to a few caveats and boundaries on the use of imagination and discernment shortly, but for now let's celebrate that in our imagination we've theologically located a wellspring of life in the activity of the leader.

Imaginative leadership

I suspect many readers will, by intuition and experience, sympathize with the notion that imagination is at the heart of leadership, but it gives me much added confidence to see it emerge from theological first principles. When I was a boy of probably six or seven years old, we were fortunate enough to have a large garden, and ours progressed over three levels. There was the upper level which was a bit more neat and tidy and the predominant concern of my parents and our tortoise. There was the middle tier, which was an open grassy space ideal for football and other games. At the bottom the garden extended into a small wood, and this tier was a series of earthy mounds and slopes where predominantly pines, but other trees as well, were often quite densely packed together. At least, that is my memory of it all, no doubt size and shape exaggerated in my recollections from childhood.

One of my strongest memories is of playing with my brother, George, and my next-door neighbour James. James was a year older than me, and George a couple of years younger, but despite the years between the three of us we enjoyed a brilliant camaraderie. In this particular memory, and there are many like them, the three of us were on a mission as daredevil pilots to fly as a team into enemy territory. We fired up the engines, our vocal cords tested by the engines' power, our arms and legs energized with an unnatural strength, and we soared in formation from the middle tier of the garden, deep behind enemy lines among the trees to implement whatever the strategic bombing operation was that we were tasked with. In many ways, I was the leader of our little tripartite, yet I don't think I've understood until now exactly why this was so. Admittedly I was the elder to my brother, but James was older than me and hardly a wallflower, and we were all robust enough to resist overbearing influence from any of the others. No, the reason I was the assumed leader is because I was the one who was most often coming up with the ideas for our games. It was my imagination that was the source of much of our play. The others were willing to defer to my ideas, because by and large mine were the ones that came quickest and were most fun. Fortunately I also wasn't the kind of child to insist on my own way, and there were plenty of times when George or James led the way, but the predominant influence was mine. On reflection, I'm increasingly convinced that our propensity to lead is birthed in our imagination.

As I think about it now and look back on the 35 years since those wonderfully childish games took place, I can see why I have always tended towards leadership in the social contexts in which I've operated. Yes, there have been occasions when I have exerted influence because of shadow sides craving the fulfilment of significance, security and relationship, and all the phoney self-realization therein. Yes, there have been occasions when I have exerted influence simply as a result of positional leadership which I happened to occupy. Yes, there have been occasions when I have exerted influence because of the misguided notion that only I had the right answers or appropriate vision of the future. All of those things have been true on occasion. But I can see now that the root of the healthy leadership that I've exercised, the real reason why I self-identify with leadership so much, is that God has blessed me with a particularly active imagination, which all too readily gets expressed in the form: *I've been thinking about how life could be better* ... Beyond the realms of leadership, this is what Samuel Taylor Coleridge was writing about when he positioned imagination as the wellspring of human change: 'Imagination that compares and contrasts with what is around as well as what is better and worse is the living power and prime agent of all human perception judgement and emotional reaction.'

Given this elevation of the role of imagination in the life of the leader, it's worth thinking a little about how our imagination functions. I remember a South African friend of mine, years before the malaise of the banking crisis and Brexit and all that, remarking on the effect of football in the thought life of the British. His opinion was that football was acting a bit like a narcotic, particularly on the working-class male. So many young men spending hours of their thought life pondering team selection and the relative attributes of various footballers or teams. Instead of railing against lack of opportunity and the widening social inequality, or perhaps channelling their frustrations towards personal opportunity, their mental energy is hijacked by fruitless football fantasies. To say nothing of how much time is spent in front of television screens and mobile devices gathering information, and maybe even watching a game or two. It's an extreme opinion, but my friend essentially claimed that society would be at a violent tipping point if it weren't for the narcotic of football. Include in those sources of wasteful imagination the likes of gaming, gambling, pornography and all the rest.

Now, whether his conclusions about violent uprisings are even remotely accurate is less the point than the fact that our imaginations are easily distracted by things beyond us, and marshalling our imaginations is vital to realizing our human potential. I confess it now. For most of my life, I've dreamed of owning a nice motorbike. And for most of my adult life I could have afforded one; but I've never quite had the peace of mind to make a purchase. When I'm tired and bored my mind will often wander to the image of a sleek machine from Triumph or BMW; and of course the sun always shines in my imagination. When you've thought enough about these kind of things, wasted enough time perhaps, you do get particular insights into your own sense of motivation. I reckon that at least 90 per cent of the time when I'm inclined to think about owning a motorbike, I'm essentially just trying to make myself feel better. I'm picturing the nice lines of the bike, the feel and the sound, and there's an emotional massaging happening; pure escapism. If I bought one on those grounds I know I'd be hugely disappointed, those promises of worldly satisfaction never measuring up. I know enough about life to know that. However, perhaps ten per cent of the time, often when I'm outside, the air is fresh and the sun does happen to be shining, I find myself thinking about riding a motorbike in a different way. In those moments it is a genuine desire to experience life in a richer, more intoxicating way. To feel the summer air rush over my face, the smell, the excitement as speed builds and the bike begins to exercise its technical excellence for which I paid all that money. That is something different. It's when the promise of the nice lines and the look and feel of the bike become manifest in a genuine human experience of life in greater fullness. This isn't a bad thing; this is a good thing – even a God thing. Desiring richness, pleasure, beauty in a joyful, celebratory, intensified experience of life. That's imagination well used, and it's the reason why one day I might actually buy a motorbike.

We want a better world. When we imagine a better world, when we locate ourselves in scenarios where our deepest needs are being met, we get an emotional payback; our fantasy about a future life makes us feel better. In a sense, that is how the gift of imagination is meant to work: we dream the future, we feel its potential and we take steps towards it. Imagination is meant to inform and direct our influence. Although of course that is not how much of our imagination works because a lot of it is disconnected from any reality that would actually be good for us and we've simply developed a habitual misuse of imagination as a tool to lift our emotional state. It's why people wake up in mid-life and realize that so many of the things that have mattered have passed them by. We've lived life in our minds somewhere else, and the realization of it can occasionally be catastrophic. Marshalling our imagination to enable movement into genuine renewal is key to effective Hopeful Influence, and to that we will now turn.

Marshalling imagination

So we've recognized that there are forms of influence that are birthed from imagination per se, connected to all sorts of longings and desires, and there are forms of influence that come from imagination that have been intentionally marshalled in a Christian way. We are particularly interested in the latter, because we're trying to identify the resources God gives us to discern the right vision of our Hopeful Influence. Our imagination can take us anywhere, but there is a sense in which we need to know what God's future looks like, the steps to get there and how to travel well together. Taking each of these in turn we can say that the process of marshalling godly imagination therefore applies three particularly Christian practices, which often overlap in their activity.

There is a task of theological reflection on how the context we are in can become more shaped by the lordship of Jesus. What does this situation look like where the lordship of Jesus is increasingly manifest? How do I apply the Bible to inform this particular hope? As we'll see, it is important that our contextual imaginings don't stray from the biblical sketches of the Christian hope, and we will continually need to sense-check our ideas against the wider imagery of renewal that we read of in *Scripture*. There is also a task to invite Holy Spirit-led discernment to identify the most appropriate steps that are neither over- nor under-realized eschatologically. The ultimate future may be clear, but the specific steps on the journey towards it almost certainly will not be. Some might call it wisdom, or even *reason*, which helps us discern how far to step forward. The final task is to take this theological reflection and Holy Spirit discernment and bring it into conversation with other leaders and followers, perhaps even leaders and followers of a different age from our own, and see how our shared understanding informs what we think is appropriate. This might be called corporate engagement with culture, or even our *tradition*, as we try not to run too far ahead of where others have been willing to go. And of course, God sends the Spirit to God's people, and therefore the assumption is that some measure of corporate discernment is required to hear God's voice most clearly, and certainly it is foolish to suggest that the leader will have a unique hotline to God's plans and purpose.

These three practices nicely overlay onto the three sources of authority that the Anglican Church and most mainline denominations would recognize: *Scripture*, *reason* and *tradition*. It's worth saying, as we seek unifying theology and language, that they also neatly overlay onto the ways denominations tend to organize themselves: evangelical, charismatic and catholic. All three sources of authority are vital, and to emphasize one to the exclusion of the others represents an imbalance. Even if we agree with the Anglican Reformer Richard Hooker, as I do, in saying that Scripture takes precedence, it is actually quite difficult most of the time to draw fast lines between the three or to consider Scripture without the inherited bias of our particular ways of reasoning or our inherited church tradition. There's more to say about all this of course, but the main point is that the foundations of how to apply Hopeful Influence are already rolled up within the wider Church; we just need help to notice it from time to time.

It's therefore the process of using these tools to marshal our imagination that differentiates Hopeful Influence from other things we might call leadership. As a Christian exercising some influence in the world, you might not necessarily have as active or vibrantly creative an imagination as your non-Christian peers, but you do have a way of marshalling your imagination, of locating your ideas within the real and true story of humanity, in the Jesus story, that gives far greater potential for your imagination to be realized in a sustainable and properly life-enhancing way. This isn't a licence to assume that because you're a Christian your ideas are right – that's a disaster waiting to happen. But it is licence to have confidence in biblically based reflection, the Holy Spirit's promptings and to have confidence in the council of other Christians. Too often we limit creative imaginings to a select few, and there is a very important releasing of imagination within the wider Christian community that needs to happen. Scripture, reason and tradition are the essential tools to marshal it.

Communicating from our imagination

Up to this point, we've explored imagination in the general sense and considered it particularly from the perspective of the leader. Of course, for Hopeful Influence to happen, a leader has to be able to stir the imagination of others, to help others see what life could be like by joining further into the Kingdom of God. It was with this in mind, I suspect, that Walter Wright said, 'Articulating the vision may be the single most important responsibility that a leader has.'[7] We picture the future that God is calling us into and we try to communicate that to others. But once we see the vision, how do we communicate it well so that others will see it too? Well, the simple answer is that Christian leaders need good communication skills, but in particular, one important aspect of communication comes into its own when we think about leadership in these terms: the use of story and pictures as tools to envision those we influence.

A few weeks ago I was with a group of students from our church. We'd gathered together towards the end of the academic year, and we were looking ahead to the following year. One of the things I was trying to do was to get our students excited about what God might have in store for them in the year to come, and to begin to imagine the role God might be calling them to within our student community; hopefully in a way that honoured all the other communities they are part of and responsibilities they carried. Now, having been a leader in our church for a few years, I was at a significant advantage over our students when it came to picturing the future, because I knew our past. We put a lot of energy and resources into growing and strengthening our student ministry in church, and I've seen how God has grown a handful of students six years ago into the best part of a hundred students today. I began to talk about my hopes for the year to come, and some of the things that a number of our leaders, students and others, were discerning. After I'd prattled on for five minutes or so, I realized that the team weren't quite as gripped by the vision as I clearly was, and so we changed tack slightly, got people into discussion groups and moved towards a time of sharing and prayer. There were all sorts of reasons why my vision talk wasn't quite as effective as it could have been, but the biggest one, I think, was that while I shared a picture of the future, I failed to locate this within the wider story of what God was doing in our church, in our city and in the world, and specifically in the lives of the students who were in the room.

The ideas for the future I was trying to share hadn't just been birthed out of nowhere. They had emerged out of our journey, our story if you like, over the past few years. A story that had seen the student community grow in spiritual depth and in numbers every year. A story that was located within the wider story of our church building being reopened eight years before with a new commission after 40 years of closure. A story that included the fresh, contemporary style of church that we, as a church, enjoy, intentionally structured to connect with young adults who may have walked away from more traditional expressions. A story that linked in with countless stories like it across our nation; of churches flexing their ecclesiological forms to connect with a changed and changing culture. A story of young adults being invited to lead and shape the Church for the next generation. A story echoed down through history by churches shaping themselves for mission in their context and then experiencing growth and being able to make the difference in their communities that God intends. A story of God on the move within the world, and a story into which many of these students had been invited. These are some of the contours of the wider story within which our own story is located – the very things that give us confidence for the future and inspire imagination – and I sadly realized after my little pep talk that I hadn't framed the future in this bigger story at all. Instead of helping our students create a picture in their minds of how what had been might grow into what might be, I'd simply resorted to some didactic proposals about what I, and a few others, had been thinking.

Jesus used stories and pictures in his leadership all the time. It is true that first-century Israel had more of an aural, story-telling focus than most contemporary cultures, so let's keep that context in mind. It is also true that Jesus used story, or at least certain types of stories, to deliberately hide the truth of his mission from those opposed to him.[8] The apostle Paul, and others, resorted to more didactic forms of teaching, and clearly non-story forms have great value too. However, even with these provisos, it is still remarkable how much of Jesus' communication was done through stories. When Jesus presents the gospel, his own story if you like, he starts with the story of Moses and the prophets and locates himself within the wider promises of the Scriptures.[9] Through parables, by analogy and even allegory, Jesus presents the truth of the King and the life of the Kingdom to his followers, both then and now. He wants to create pictures in our minds to activate our will and stir our hearts.

Most preachers will tell you that a sermon without a story isn't going to spark anyone's imagination; teachers and parents across the world take it for granted that children's mental learning revolves around their engagement with stories, and even politicians and business leaders know the power of stories to evoke a response. When I started working as a software developer, we drove our software design through numbered requirements. It took a certain personality type to find meaning and joy in a system's behaviour being reduced to hundreds of single sentence statements. By the end of my time in that field, we'd progressed to using cases and user stories, which were much more descriptive requirements that focused in on processes and interactions within the system – storyboards of activity – and some of them were actually worth reading. The best politicians have always appealed to the most positive national narratives: the stories that make us feel good about ourselves and optimistic about the future – Tony Blair's rise to office being a good example. Sadly, what happens in politics all too often is that the power of stories is used to ferment fear; unless we do such and such then all manner of economic, social or military distress will result, or so the story goes. Stories are powerful in every sphere of life, for good or ill.

One of the members of our church works for the Home Office in the UK, and they employ an interesting method of process and policy transformation that revolves around story-telling. Instead of trying to pin down all the factors and requirements in a more traditional form, they tell the stories of citizens' experiences and try and bring to light the successes and failures of the systems employed to serve people resident in the UK. It's a novel approach, not without its critics, but the tremendous strength is in its humanity and the innate ability of stories to convey a huge palette of truth and meaning within fairly time-limited constraints. What they've found is that they have historically articulated purpose and function within the Home Office's processes in ways that simply aren't rich enough to describe and serve people's needs effectively. Within the huge complexity of that organization, the activity of story-telling has become a vital part of the leaders' communication strategy and they are making very significant strides towards a government as it should be in the rapidly changing times in which we live.

A really helpful recent book on the use of story within church leadership is *Leading by Story*.[10] In it, Vaughan Roberts and David Sims argue that one of the principal tasks of the ordained leader is to remind God's people of the story they inhabit and to steward an environment where stories of God's advancing Kingdom can be shared. Locating the story of a particular expression of Church within the wider story of the context within which it operates is essential for healthy mission and discipleship. People of Hopeful Influence need to be able to tell stories well. Stories help us understand where we've come from and stir imagination for where we might go.

Using power to help others participate in the Kingdom

As well as helping people see the future, we help people do things to make that future a reality. In other words, when we see the future together we then have to ask, 'What must we do to get there?' To help others participate in the coming Kingdom, that second strand of Hopeful Influence if you like, we essentially have to enable them to do something – and at the heart of the ability to do anything lies the unavoidable question of power. The power we exert to help them take action as well as the power they exercise to fulfil that action, which is often power we give, share or help them to find. We had to arrive at the contentious subject of power at some point in our exploration of leadership and this is the place to explore it.

At the outset it is important to acknowledge that power divides opinion. We understand it in different ways and, like the subject of leadership, we load things onto it that have as much to do with our past experiences of particular types of power as any fundamental definition of the word. Before we get swallowed up in subjectivity, let's define power first in an amoral sense: as simply the ability to do something. In this sense, Jesus used power all the time.[11] We use power when we walk out of the house, or help someone across the road. It is power that ensures criminals get caught and that people less privileged in our society are able to enjoy life and make a contribution that their fully human identity demands.

Unfortunately, many Christians, while they may embrace this amoral definition, get a bit tied up in knots when it comes to applying power or advocating the application of power in the contexts we find ourselves in. Somehow it's only God's power and work that really matters, as if that was an ethereal force independent from us worldly people, and that any attempt by Christians to harness power and control is simply a vain effort to act in isolation from the God whom we serve. The very notion that our human efforts might advance God's Kingdom might almost be described as blasphemous. You may not recognize this, but it does sadly linger. At its heart, as we've looked at already, it stems from a misunderstanding of how God has ordered the world and our role in its renewal. Tom Wright summarizes it nicely:

> God has ordered his world in such a way that his own work within that world would take place through ... human beings who reflect his image.[12]

So we are invited to use power, which is the application of our resources, human and material, to achieve things. Everything we do requires power of one form or another, so – as with leadership – power is an unavoidable part of our human reality, which unfortunately means there are also many and damaging abuses of power. The challenge at this point is how to reflect on the kind of power that is birthed out of a proper understanding of Hopeful Influence, both in ourselves and those we lead, and how the application of that enables the most effective movement towards God's renewal.

The God–human partnership

I was in a broadly liberal eucharistic service the other day, and, in an interesting liturgical twist, the traditional movement of confession and absolution was reversed so that the absolution was declared first. The absolution started in fact with the words, 'in the Gospels, forgiveness always precedes repentance.' In many ways, the authors of this particular liturgy are right. Jesus came to die for the sins of the world through a plan dreamed up before the human story had even begun. He was in some sense, as the book of Revelation picks up, 'slain from the creation of the world'.[13] The forgiveness he offers is there for all and for any, even before we ask for it.

However, it is perhaps truer still to say that in the Gospels it is *the offer* of forgiveness that always precedes repentance. In Jesus' earthly ministry, whenever we see the imparting of forgiveness it is always linked to a response of faith or a person's willingness to turn around and begin again. Our response of repentance and faith and the impartation of forgiveness seem to go hand in hand. Perhaps another way of putting it, more simply, is that forgiveness is there for those who would turn to Jesus. Forgiveness, as a spiritual dynamic, if you like, can't be activated by a hard and selfish heart; it requires a recognition that what has happened is wrong and a desire to do things better. That was why Jesus got so cross with the Pharisees of the day,[14] his words of judgement on them so harsh, and why he grieved so much over the city of Jerusalem for its unwillingness to recognize the work of God, even when it was happening right there among it.[15] To say that forgiveness always precedes repentance misses this fundamental truth and, at its worst, can lull us into a false sense of harmony with God without adequate inspection of our own hearts.

I say all this because at the kernel of all human movement back to God, even at the point of forgiveness, is this remarkable God–human duality. There is a Gospel *transaction* between God and man (if I can use a word like that to describe something so profound and beautiful). God invites and we accept. God reveals a better path and we take it. God offers forgiveness and we repent. God promises the renewal of creation, invites our submission and we then partner in the most extraordinary work. It is from this kernel that all human activity, and certainly Hopeful Influence, is understood. We do it *with* God.

Aspirational kenosis as an expression of our power

Given the abuses of power, and the speed with which it often becomes self-serving, no doubt debates will always rage about the appropriateness or otherwise of power as a tool for Christians to use. We've seen helpful contribution from the likes of Henri Nouwen and Leonard Sweet already, and Sarah Coakley is a contemporary theologian who has pursued the theological underpinnings of the Christian application of power. Her particular contribution is that human relations, and by implication this includes expressions of Christian leadership, should eschew power in its worldly forms and instead embrace a form of power that is fundamentally kenotic[16] – or self-emptying – much like Jesus' use of power seen perfected on the cross. Coakley herself describes kenosis as 'power-in-vulnerability',[17] which she elaborates upon to mean the creation of space for people around us to make good and godly decisions; enabling, preferment of others and leading from beneath would all be typical of this. Essentially it's power that honours and facilitates the choice of another, but that does so in a way that reveals our humanity and appeals to the best aspects therein. This sounds good and is certainly in line with some of the language that we tend to associate with more progressive forms of leadership. However, standing against the idea that all our expressions of power can really be like this are practitioners who want to argue that leaders need the capacity for hard power to really get things done; they need to direct, determine activity, shape culture, hire and fire, to put people *on the bus* and take them off it as needed. We've looked at some of these contributors already, and while the concern about shadow sides remains, there's no doubting that this harder power can facilitate the action required to grow and develop organizations significantly.[18]

It would be easy to polarize these two positions and to play them off against each other. However, taking an eschatological view, thinking *hopefully* about power, may give us the theological resource to unite these two ways of thinking and show that both are appropriate in different circumstances. Eschatologically, we can say that we are moving towards a world where all of our relationships will be kenotic; that's what power expressed through relationships of love is meant to look like. As such we should be constantly looking for opportunities to express our leadership to others in these kinds of ways. In fact, the best kind of movement forwards, perhaps the truest kind of movement, is kenotic movement. We point to a God-shaped future and invite others to step into it. However, we are also trying to discern to what extent this pursuit may be an over-realized form of eschatology in different circumstances. It may not be best to give a person complete freedom to define their own actions and behaviour as they may need firm challenge in their own character development or they may need more forceful help to find the best fit for their talents; ultimately, for the wider eschatological movement of an organization, they may need to leave. Jesus didn't invite every person into his team of disciples; there was control over who was in and who wasn't. He hung round in a place for a few days, and when he decided to move the team on he did just that. He was focused on his particular mission, often to the exclusion of the wishes and desires of those closest to him – however well-meaning Peter's advice sometimes was. Jesus drove the money changers from the temple with a whip and a cord, such was his zeal to protect the God-given purposes for which it was made. And the apostle Paul even commended a very final application of hard power within a Christian community in an extreme pastoral case.[19] In short, I am suggesting that both kenotic power and hard forms of power are legitimate within the eschatological movement towards the Kingdom. Kenotic power creates space for our movement forwards and hard power protects the ground that has already been gained.

Now, a comprehensive study of power is far beyond the scope of this book, but what I am highlighting is that legitimate forms of Christian power are linked to what is happening eschatologically in our relational contexts; Hopeful Influence gives us the lens with which to clarify our use of that power. In an extreme example, if my son were to run into the road I would use hard power to protect the continuation of his own eschatological journey – in other words, his life. Hard power isn't always a bad thing. In a more nuanced example, a broad-based group of British citizens, mobilized for power, walk into the flagship branch of HSBC and take over each and every deposit desk during peak period, alongside a flurry of publicity, as a negotiating tactic to force the HSBC board into a dialogue over the living wage. They haven't blown anything up, but they have forced a very wealthy organization to take a proper look at the injustice they were perpetuating, instead inviting them to take a different path. In a sense they wanted to protect the eschatological journey into human flourishing of the lowest-paid service workers. To do this they chose a form of power that provoked the strong power holder out of its lethargy and inertia and into very real steps towards a better world. It worked, and because of the organizational genius of Citizens UK, HSBC become the first of the big UK banks to implement a living wage across all their staff, including the cleaners. I am arguing that Hopeful Influence requires a recognition of the power we hold and the power structures that exist around us, and ensures that our context, and our eschatological journey within that context, inform the best use of power to enable genuine movement forwards. To say that Christians eschew power in all its forms is a big theological mistake, but so is missing the necessity to constantly aspire to kenosis as the form of power to best move people forwards.

Should Christians hold power?

For much of the history of the Church, Christians have experienced some form of oppression. We think back to the early Christian martyrs, humbly submitting themselves to the worst possible deaths in the Colosseum, and we wonder whether Christians are ever meant to exercise strong power at all. Didn't Jesus say 'Turn the other cheek'? The police, just wars, even directive parenting; can we make a theological case for these things as Christians?

Well, the uncertainty I think arises from applying particular expressions of power to every situation without thoughtful application. 'Turn the other cheek' invites an aggressor to consider the validity of their actions. It's a particular kenotic response in a particular moment. What happens after that initial slap, and how we go on to respond to an aggressor, particularly when others are threatened, lies beyond Jesus' initial statement. In addition, the particular case of martyrs, down through history, has generally been to preserve life, escape if you can and then find the best ways to confront the injustice at a later date. The fact that God is able, through a remarkable counter-play, to use the witness of martyrs to radically advance God's Kingdom, isn't a call for people to queue up in passive submission to evil oppressors.

The power of that witness is the reason why within a few hundred years, the Roman emperor Constantine, the ultimate power holder, bowed on his knees before the feet of Jesus, and the Western world has never been the same again. Admittedly, the positive and negative implications of that are argued over, but that doesn't mean we shouldn't long for the highest office holders to become Christians.

In short, it seems to me that Christians get to hold all sorts of power positions within society and within our social structures, and this is absolutely what God wills. Yes, we have an aspiration for a world where these forms of power can be exercised in ways that are genuinely kenotic, and we should long for a time, and seek opportunity today, to use our power to create space for others to choose and shape their futures in ways that recognize their human autonomy and that are aligned with the person of Jesus. However, we are called to steward the power that we have, and very specifically there are occasions when we need to exercise stronger forms of power to protect, nudge and sometimes even agitate for advancement on society's wider eschatological journey. If we abdicate power because of a misguided notion that Christians should never exercise it, then we passively accept vacuous situations where power will become misused by others.

An emphasis on mutuality, equipping and empowerment

Implicit, I think, in this aspiration for kenotic forms of power, is a recognition that our future is a future of mutuality. In the Kingdom where Christ is King, we need each other to fulfil our God-given purposes. The apostle Paul used the different parts of the body as the best analogy for illustrating our mutual interdependence. In a sense, we should expect collaboration and mutual activity as markers of the pathway back to God, and this is the kind of shape that Hopeful Influence takes as we help others join in. As a vicar with an interest in the health of my local community, I think this gives added weight to the importance of working with and alongside other stakeholders in my community, regardless of their particularities of faith. As a parent, it is within the interconnected web of family, friends, school and locality that my children's formation will occur, and my vision for parenting should include my influence towards these wider structures. Healthy businesses should understand the supply chains that they are part of, and the social and environmental impact of their activity, and should also seek to foster partnerships that ensure the whole lifecycle of their operations are geared towards human flourishing. We need to be mindful that we are travelling together, even if we don't see people necessarily making Christian commitments in the timeframes we would like. As Christians influence others towards the Kingdom, we must do this in as open-handed and generously inclusive a manner as possible, trusting that as more people share the journey so all the boats will rise.

Alongside this, connected to what we've already said about mutuality, is the necessity to equip and empower others to continue the cycles and processes of change beyond us. We do, we help others do, we help others help others do, and the baton of leadership is passed successfully to the generations to come. This is what John Maxwell calls the level-five leaders. You can find it neatly summarized in Paul's advice to Timothy in his second letter: 'the things you have heard me say ... entrust to reliable people who will also be qualified to teach others.'[20] Paul passed it on to Timothy, and Timothy needs to pass it on to people who will be able to pass it on to others. Four generations right there. In a very positive sense, baton-passing and empowerment of others is self-evident when we understand what we are doing as leaders and how our influence connects into the ongoing work of God within the much wider human story. We are seeking transformational steps forward that won't just evaporate, but will become part of first one person's, then another's, shared future. It is certainly true that no generation can be accountable for the conscience of the next, but we can certainly fulfil our duty in giving them the best possible start.

Within the church that I'm currently part of, and I suspect it is true of many churches, we have a particularly influential and servant-hearted couple, who, needless to say, are a little older than most of the rest of us. We met as a leadership team recently to discuss some of the new initiatives that we felt God was calling us to, the most significant of which was the formation of a new worshipping congregation. As we explored the vision together it became clear that one of the primary things God was doing through the proposed birth of this congregation was creating space for new, younger leaders to set the direction of that ministry. Consistently, the sense we had was the need for us to put down our leadership roles and create space, supportive space, for others to lead in the creation of something new. Right at the heart of this conversation were our older, wiser couple. With tears in their eyes they shared their joy at seeing new leadership released; not entirely, I suspect, because of deficiencies in the current leadership, but with a seasoned awareness that this was right at the heart of what we were called to do. Enabling others to take a more significant place in the bigger movement of God was more important to them than any personal sense of involvement or achievement; their leadership truly was for others.

Help others experience the Kingdom by living well

I've made the case at a few different points in this book that God wants us to enjoy life. There are all sorts of caveats and important things to say to help us make the best sense of that, but living under the lordship of Jesus means living in a world where we matter; where we have a strong sense of personal identity and where we experience life in a very positive way. For all sorts of reasons, this important truth can get lost on the Christian journey, and if we aren't careful our expressions of leadership can become dangerously task-focused and fail to pay adequate attention to the present and the importance of our Christian experience. This is particularly essential to how we work with and alongside those towards whom we exercise influence, and an illustration from my own leadership experience should help at this point.

A few years into my career, some while before I'd moved into consultancy, the firm I was working for was taken over by a much larger, international company. During the takeover, some of the more senior folks would occasionally travel to the larger company's HQ for various discussions around the integration of our smaller business into the wider whole. On one such visit I remember our team being very struck by the behaviour of the CEO of the business unit we were becoming part of. Midway through a meeting, the CEO's phone rang. It was a personal call from his wife, but the CEO took it and started to chat in the middle of the meeting. As a group, there was some initial surprise, but as the call developed it became clear that the CEO's wife had recently given birth and she was phoning to update her husband on the developments from their little bundle of joy and, presumably, to get some adult interaction in the middle of a very demanding day. Soon the CEO had the gurgling of his tiny infant coming through on speaker phone, while the meeting room purred appreciatively at his willingness to bring some very definite humanity into the discussion. It was a surprising experience for many of the team. Not only were personal phone calls not really the 'done thing' during working hours, but the CEO shattered the expectation of someone who would be totally caught up in the business of the day to the exclusion of everything else.

In some ways it was an insightful picture that also shed light on some of my own particular failings as a leader in that time of my employment. I'd grown up in the south of England, and my first working experience was with a defence contractor a short journey outside of London. The environment was highly professional, there was a degree of secrecy and security around the work I was involved in, and I got used to a fairly functionary existence as a software developer. We had our weekly team meetings. We chatted at lunchtimes. There were occasional design conversations and training activities. A few of us played football together once a week. Apart from that we just turned up and did the job. And we worked hard and long hours.

A couple of years after this first job I started working with a different company; I'd moved to the north of England and culturally things were a bit different. I'd been recruited to oversee a group of software developers and analysts working on a new project. Without realizing it, I took with me some of the cultural assumptions from my previous employment – namely long hours and fairly limited interaction; I thought this was normal in all working offices. It wasn't. Many of the team at the new company had young families to attend to, so getting out the door by 5 p.m. or earlier was really good for them. Equally, as well as doing the job, it was really important to these folks to enjoy their time in the office, to have a good chat and, in a sense, to be understood and respected on the basis of their wider humanity and not just whatever contribution they happened to be offering within the company. How wonderfully human, you might think. Well, it wasn't to me, at least not initially. I wasn't used to people knocking off on time. I wasn't used to people standing around chatting. I wasn't used to people bringing their family issues into the workplace as if they warranted as much air time as the discussions around our products' requirements and design. I simply hadn't reflected enough on the importance of employees having a good experience of their workplace, and I'd failed to see how the 'professional' practices I'd learned down south were often less human than the ways of these predominantly northern lads.

Fortunately, even if my understanding of Christianity hadn't developed sufficiently to see the goodness within that different working culture, it had done so enough to realize that any challenges I faced in the office were just as likely to originate from my own brokenness as that of others. So began a process of self-reflection through which I began to see a much happier medium, which held together the commercial needs of the business with the human needs of the workforce. I am certain, and the quality of relationships I enjoyed gave testimony to it, that when I eventually left that organization I had changed for the better.

In our pursuit of Hopeful Influence, there needs to be this attention to the present: we need to live well. If I'd worked the team mercilessly, we might have achieved our business objectives, we might have helped move the company eschatologically forwards on its outer journey, but on our inner journey we would have been shattered. I would almost certainly have faced some kind of social coup within the office and, even if I'd survived it, the team would have voted with their feet and been out the door – all their experience and knowledge base having gone with them. As we'll go on to explore in the different spheres of life, enabling a particularly biblical vision of living well is a vital aspect of helping others experience the Kingdom as we move forwards.

Nurture a theology of play to step into life

One of Jürgen Moltmann's lesser known works is *Theology of Play*, in which he explores how Jesus' teaching to 'become like little children'[21] might take better shape among our very adult, purpose-driven lifestyles. I personally find it very encouraging that a theologian who has reflected so much on the eschatological reality that Christians inhabit should unavoidably find himself writing about fun and the quality of life we are meant to enjoy. The book wasn't consistently appreciated though, and it may have been that Moltmann, in a desire to make a point, made too much of a polemical argument against structure, order and purpose, and ended up pitching the notion of play against much of what we know also makes for good life and human well-being. However, he makes some important points, not least that an over-emphasis on particular forms of achievement proves ultimately destructive, as he summarizes:

> Our social and political tasks, if we take them seriously, loom larger than life. Yet infinite responsibility destroys a human being because he is only a man and not god.[22]

God wants this increasing quality of life for each one of us, which, as we've noted, can seem slightly at odds with some aspects of the Christian faith. To be clear, I am not talking about increased self-indulgence, or promoting a view of the world that says the Christian faith is a pathway to our prosperity in worldly or even in purely individualistic terms. What I am saying is that the closer we get to God, the more we experience the fulfilling measure of God's presence and the existential rewards of finding our true identity in relationship to the one in whom all identities are found; that this is a fountain of well-being that overflows into all aspects of life.

As people of influence, as leaders, we need to understand this. It's no good flogging the horse until it drops. It's no good harvesting the fields without periods of fallow. It's no good denying time and space to celebrate what's been achieved and to enjoy the benefits that come with that. We are meant to have fun together, and we are meant to theologically nurture our understanding of this. Our shared future is characterized by God's playfulness, and if we aren't able to carry that with us and make space for it among those we lead, then we are just as liable to veer off track as if our moral compass was offset. So many times in my own leadership I've been too focused on the plan and the action and missed the joy that was happening around me. Certainly, in our current cultural moment at least, there is a great need to move our eyes off the activity at times and towards the relationships and the shared experiences that are happening around us. For Christians the adage should be true, that 'those who were seen dancing were thought to be insane by those who could not hear the music.'[23]

We'll explore the implications of all this later on, but for the moment I will share how deeply freeing this has been for me as a church leader. At most of the churches I've been part of, in the Sunday services the ordained leader either sat at the back keeping an eye on things or was fulfilling some specific duty from the front. I think that's sad. It gives the impression of not being able to switch off from responsibility, unable to join in and participate just as a regular member of the church. One of the most healthy moments in my development in ministry was seeing this for what it was. Hopefully, if you were a guest at one of our services, you wouldn't necessarily know I was a leader because I'd be messing about with the kids at the front or lost in worship like everyone else.

In some ways my own journey of change has coincided with what has happened in the wider society around me. As I write, there is a lot of comment about the cultural identity of the 'millennials', and how their social values are sometimes at odds with those of the generations above them. One thing millennials are criticized for is their 'flakiness'; their emphasis on the experiential value of the present set against any particular plans or purposes they may have agreed to yesterday or even five minutes ago. There is a certain irony here though. Every generation is a product of another, and many of the cultural values of a particular generation emerge in response, either positively or negatively, from what has gone before. While as a Generation X person I might think I understand the need for a quality of life, actually I'd inherited quite a bit of the austerity and social conservatism of the baby-boomers who went before me. While it is appropriate to give millennials a bit of a kick from time to time, I have actually found that I've learned hugely from them; particularly in their value and appreciation of the moment. For all the critique, I suspect it will be millennial leaders who are able to inhabit the moment and thrive off a theology of play the best, and I'm thankful for what I've learned from them.

Living well requires peace for what cannot be changed now

So living well requires regular nurturing of a theology of play to help us inhabit the moment and enable others to experience the Kingdom as it comes to life around us. When much of our influence is future focused, this is a vital balancer to the only place we can ever meet God, which is the ever-present now. Equally, as leaders, as people, we become vulnerable to disappointment and forms of depression when we experience blockers to our hopes and dreams of a better future; when we live with strong attachments only to the future we risk entering a danger zone. While we long and work for a better future, because the movement forwards of Hopeful Influence has this kenotic emphasis, we are constantly living with the possibility that our efforts to help others see, participate and experience the Kingdom are not taken up or responded to positively. The danger zone, with particular attention to how we help others experience the Kingdom, is that when we don't see the movement that we hope for, there can be an adverse reaction within us – anger, frustration, disappointment – which we can all too easily project back on others and undermine the actual movements forwards that are happening.

I was watching an interview recently with a successful football manager. The backstory was that some of the team hadn't fulfilled their potential that season, the star player was carrying a bit of an injury and been below their usual standard, and that, while the manager clearly had a vision for where the club could go, the team were clearly still in a transition moment. However, the whole posture of the manager was one of celebration and commendation for the team. Even if it might have sounded overly positive to fans with a more critical eye, what extraordinary resilience on the manager's part. To go into the club every day. To train and to coach and to see your efforts only partially rewarded, mostly because of factors outside your control, yet maintain that enthusiasm. And what fantastic messaging to the players: 'Even if things aren't quite going our way, come on, I believe in you, let's keep pushing on!' It took me back to different experiences of leadership that I'd had and my own propensity to allow negativity and failure of movement to discolour my whole posture as a leader. I remember in a corporate environment, on a busy stressful project, how quickly I let my frustrations boil to the surface and how disaffecting that was to some of the team I was overseeing. Equally, in the charity sector, working with volunteers, wanting so much more from people and getting annoyed that there wasn't more commitment and that people hadn't bought into the vision of the organization adequately. How my dissatisfaction was expressed in subtle forms that probably acted more like a parking brake for some of these volunteers' own quality of experience. This chimes well with the prayer for serenity, in its modern form attributed to Reinhold Niebuhr, which reads:

> God grant me the serenity
> To accept the things I cannot change;
> Courage to change the things I can;
> And wisdom to know the difference.[24]

This prayer has been popularized particularly through the Alcoholics Anonymous movement, which, in many ways, is a movement about leadership of the self. At team level we need to watch how our dissatisfaction gets expressed and be careful about its damaging potential. Even more so, perhaps, at a personal level, the disappointment of wanting more from ourselves and seeing consistent forms of failure can keep us locked in a spiral of defeatism and self-loathing. Hopeful Influence wants to point out and recognize the reality of the Kingdom in our present lives; it wants to draw attention to the presence and work of God, even when there is a whole load of stuff that isn't as it should be. As leaders, a huge part of our vitality and sangfroid comes out of this deep acceptance, and the wisdom to refrain from expending energy on battles that cannot be won today.

There are some interesting tensions here, and it is certainly true that a healthy *Christian* spirituality embraces emotional honesty and moments of lament, in the same way that we see the psalmist walking in and through the broken and painful moments of life. An authentic spirituality isn't always expressed through happiness and smiles and continually looking on the bright side, and some people can find leaders who only put on a positive persona off-putting because of a narrowness in their humanity. Sometimes life is rubbish and we need to make room for that.

However, the emphasis of Hopeful Influence is that a vital ingredient of any leadership is helping others inhabit the reality of God's presence today. Disproportionate attention to the perceived absence of God in some areas pulls us back from recognizing and living with the remarkable presence of God in the areas where God clearly is at work. We want our *influence* to be positive, and that often requires compassion, restraint and an intentional turning of our posture towards all that is good.

As a final reflection, let's return to our football manager example. A premier league manager once remarked that the worst part of their job was match day. What they were expressing, I think, was that match day was the one part of the week that they couldn't control. The one part of the week when frustration at the team's inability to execute the plans and intentions that they had practised became too acute to bear. How sad for a leader to acknowledge that. To be so consumed by inadequacy that you can't enjoy the moment that all of your leadership efforts are geared towards. Hopeful Influence demands that we inhabit the present with a peace towards that which is beyond our control, which, in the context of leaders who facilitate the imagination, activity and playfulness of others, is just about everything.

Applying Hopeful Influence to positional leadership

What we're now interested in is how to apply our thinking about eschatological influence to positional leadership. Everything we've said so far is applicable, and hopefully will be applied, in interactions that happen between anybody, anytime and anywhere. However, as we considered in Chapter 4, because we organize ourselves socially around shared, future goals, helping the people who have positional leadership roles to exercise more faithful forms of eschatological influence has a particular urgency. Whether it's a defined role within an organization, or something more organic that has just emerged within a set of relationships, we create positional leadership within our communities. When Christian leadership is exercised as faithful, well-informed eschatological influence by these positional leaders, then we are on the fastest, most sustainable journey towards the proper renewal of the world.

However, having said that, there is immediately a tension which every positional leader has to navigate: the tension between agreed future goals intrinsic to their function as leader within a particular organization, and the much wider potential eschatological movement which the Holy Spirit is wanting to exercise in and through them. As an example, consider the team leader in a business. Their positional leadership has been shaped around the realization of particular goals. For simplicity, let's say their role requires them to exercise influence on the team to achieve four goals: timely completion of tasks, contribution to process improvement, adherence to company values and ensuring they have a good workplace experience. Of course, in many organizations each of those goals will be fleshed out so it is clear what they mean in the dynamic working environment, but the point is that the role of the positional leader is shaped around the realization of specific goals. Where the tension comes from, is that in a Christian person occupying this role they will also begin to get insights into broader ways in which the Holy Spirit wants to exercise influence through them. They begin to dream. And of course those dreams might not necessarily overlap neatly with the agreed organizational goals. In fact, sometimes they might be at odds with them.

I've experienced this at least once. I was once asked to do some work with a third-party consultancy firm, to help us understand more about our competition. I was a bit green to things. As you might guess, the project eventually involved the third-party group going to our competitor and *pretending* to be a prospective client, so they could hoover up as much information about the products that competed with our own. It was a method of lies and deception that was birthed out of excessive fear and inadequate engagement with our own customer base to understand what they really wanted. When I challenged our leadership on the project, it was justified by the rules of the playground: 'They've done it to us, so we'll do it to them.' Now it was certainly true that every business in our sector was behaving badly, but that was hardly an excuse to propagate the same errors. It was a very unpleasant experience for me as a positional leader to try and reconcile what I felt were God-inspired objectives within my role against ones that clearly weren't. If I had my time again, I would have asked to not be involved in the project at an earlier stage. To the credit of the leaders around me, I don't think it would have counted heavily against me, although in many businesses it might have.

Those are the worst of the tensions. Most tensions are thankfully less polarized than that, and probably revolve more around the questions, 'How could I fulfil my goals in a way that more fully reflects the lordship of Jesus?', or 'Are there other things I could do in my role that are eschatologically important but that haven't been written down as agreed objectives?' Typically we will need to broker variation from agreed roles and responsibilities with those around us in our positional role, and we'll need to show the benefits of doing things a different way.

An example of this is the classroom. If you walked into a classroom in Britain in the 1950s, then you'd probably be greeted with complete silence and a certain deference from the children. The tightly controlled reign of the teacher enforced by the threat of corporal punishment. Walk into a British classroom today, and you'll probably see a more relaxed atmosphere, the application of softer power more prevalent, and the voice and needs of the children shaping the environment more. At its best, an eschatological development with a wider scope for the pupils' enjoyment and contribution. I did say at its best, as there are scenarios when all this use of soft power towards people in the early stages of life gets abused, as many a teacher will tell you. In both contexts though, the teacher is there to fulfil multiple roles, one of which is the academic oversight of the class and another is having some responsibility for the wider personal developmental of each pupil. As we've said, these roles have been brokered around a set of goals to which the class, individually and corporately, will move. Back in the 1950s, the focus was more on the academic goals. Really great teachers were also recognized by their ability to help pupils in their personal development, but this was rarely written into the role back then. I imagine there were a whole host of teachers who could see that they needed to complement the academic learning with wider character development, and who fundamentally mistrusted the ability of corporal punishment to shape true character; they lived with huge tensions between the agreed goals and what they sensed to be better.

Nowadays, we've moved forwards. Teachers' goals will certainly include some measure of academic progress and, depending on the school, will also factor in additional goals around development of character, social skills, non-academic competencies and a measure of health and well-being. The setting of these goals is done by the school, but hopefully this is carried out with helpful and creative input from other stakeholders like parents, governors and local and national government. Of course, they probably won't use the language of eschatology in setting these goals, but I want to suggest that it is in the increasing life of the Kingdom in the widest sense that we see the best terms for planning, executing and evaluating the children's learning and development. The world is able to sense what is right and good, and often it's ahead of the institutional Church on some of this stuff, but as Christians we have the best tools to get at these questions. We just don't always use them.

However it plays out, all of the stakeholders we've recognized are therefore able to exercise Hopeful Influence on the class; they are all leaders in that sense, even if it is the teacher who will principally realize that *influence*. To enable them to fulfil their role, there is a sense in which the teacher is given a level of authority and power to ensure that the classroom is a healthy learning environment for every pupil; that is – to give every pupil the best chance for movement towards the agreed goals. They can do things to ensure the environment is the best, but only within the agreed boundaries put around the methodology of leadership, which are then linked back to the realization of the goals. In both the realization of the academic and developmental goals and the methodology of leadership, the teacher will still have a fair amount of flexibility, although in many schools they will be highly accountable on both fronts because the goals are measurable and the methods of influence have clear boundaries.

Obviously in many positional leadership roles the goals are less measurable and the methods of influence have fewer boundaries; as a result the leadership becomes less accountable. We'll look at how some of this plays out in the final section of this book. For now, there is a whole realm of social complexity around how a positional leader carries out their role, but the essential point is that they have a very high potential for influencing individual and corporate movement, but more often than not the goals and method of leadership need to be brokered with other leaders. This is a vital process to ensure the leadership involves as much Hopeful Influence as possible.

Hopeful Influence that enables movement into renewal

In starting this chapter we asked questions about the tools required to implement Hopeful Influence and the kind of shape that it takes in practice. We want traction on how to influence others *hopefully*, and we've identified imagination, appropriate forms of power and living well as vital resources and practices to make this a reality. These emerge from our theological focus on helping others see, participate and experience the Kingdom of God, and the utilization of each takes specific forms, the outline shape of which we have begun to explore.

Imagination is hugely powerful, a gift, it seems, to find our way forward into different kinds of futures. Yet marshalling our imagination requires the whole gamut of Christian authority, specifically Scripture, reason and tradition. As they do elsewhere in church life, these different sources function as filters to keep us on the narrow path to the Kingdom. Embracing this kind of leadership takes us deeper into the realm of pictures, imagery, narrative and stories, and communicating the vision as Hopeful Influence unavoidably draws on these forms when we encourage imagination that connects with life as it could be.

Power is at heart of our ability to do anything, and Hopeful Influence demands continued theological reflection on the use of power in leadership. Hopeful Influencers aspire to kenotic forms of power, creating space and understanding for others to choose their own paths back to God. However, harder forms of power are also necessary, particularly when it comes to protecting the eschatological journey of others and ensuring that we don't move backwards on our collective movement into renewal. In addition, our shared future is a collaborative one, where mutuality and shared equipping and empowerment are normal strands of communal life.

Living well is a potentially ambiguous phrase that deserves an equally central place in the armoury of a Christian leader. Ambiguous because we can load things onto it, but absolutely central because life in the Kingdom has a *now* component as well as a *not yet*. When we influence without an adequately developed theology of play or when we hold tightly in frustration to things that are not yet what they could be, we can become drag weights for the wider eschatological journey of others. Hopeful Influence requires an attention to the present and a persistent enabling of others to experience the life that God has for them today.

And finally, for those of us who occupy roles of positional leadership in the different community structures that we create, there is huge potential for us to exercise Hopeful Influence, but also huge tensions to navigate as we try to discern its true forms and properly manifest it. In all this, we are starting to see the kinds of leadership activity that God wants every person to be involved in, and the particular aspects of leadership activity that we need to pay special attention to. The movement into renewal that God desires for us is accessed in part through particular attention to these kinds of activities, and they are the foundations of forms of leadership in different spheres of life that will bring the kinds of changes that we long for. Before we move to specific questions about what Hopeful Influence looks like in those different spheres of life, let us revisit the potential our theology has for unity amid the often confused leadership discourse.

Comment

Selina Stone, Tutor and Lecturer in Political Theology, St Mellitus College

I think it is important to begin by recognizing that to be a Christian leader is in fact to be a disciple of Christ first, and then as one who finds themselves in a position of leadership and influence among others in the world. The life and service of the Christian leader is centred not on self-centred agendas and motivations but on Christ, his gospel and the Kingdom he came to proclaim. The vision we are looking for and longing to see fulfilled is for ourselves as well as other women, men and children: to be liberated by Christ and formed in his image. Our hope is to see signs of the work of the Spirit among us, and to see the ultimate fulfilment of the Kingdom through Christ's return. These hopes are not attained through striving but through surrender. Any notion that we can pull down the Kingdom for ourselves, or through our human agency move towards these hopes, is false; this is the work of the Spirit of God who opens eyes and makes straight the paths to the Kingdom, according to his ways and his timing.

As a lecturer who is committed to theological reflection and practice through engagement in church and public life, the question of hope is crucial. Theologies of the Kingdom and eschatological hope are some of the core foundation stones to a theology and practice of Christian leadership that impacts within and also beyond the walls of the church. It is particularly relevant today as technology and globalization give unprecedented access to information which forces us to confront the social and political realities that are the opposite of what Christ calls us towards as the human family. The task for the Church, at least in social and political terms, is to discern what, in the light of the timeless gospel and our contemporary realities, God is calling us to be and declare in our context and in our time. This, then, has to be a primary concern for those called to be leaders of the Church.

Jesus tells us very explicitly through his words and his actions, not to lead in the way the world does; that the way to participate in the Kingdom is through service not dominance. Yet one of the biggest temptations for leaders in our current time is to ignore these words of Jesus and to insist (subconsciously if not explicitly) on what we believe to be more effective means. What we seem to want is to have a Kingdom that allows us to hold on to power, to dominate others and maintain control, in order that we might establish justice, see the Kingdom come and see people come to faith. However, ironically, the means can be the biggest stumbling block to those noble ends. I think one of the most important ways of avoiding these traps is by being open to listening; not to the people at 'the top' but to those on the fringes and at the bottom of the pile. If the Kingdom truly belongs to children, to the poor and the meek, then why do we trust so much in the methods of the experienced, the wealthy and the bold?

Leadership can only be hope-filled when nurtured by prayer, worship and the study of the Scriptures. I have been fortunate in my work as a community organizer to belong to a team which practised rhythms of prayer, worship and reflection alongside action. Prayer is a discipline that ultimately leads to a sustainable and peace-filled participation in God's work. It gives God room to show us himself, and to reveal ourselves to us including our impatience and ego. It is not in isolation, but through attentiveness to Christ in worship and through shared communion and action with other believers, that we experience something of this Kingdom that is at hand. As we are willing to love God and our neighbours as ourselves, not sentimentally but through sacrificial action and the bearing of one another's burdens, we see glimmers of these hopes for our formation and the work of God in the world.

Notes

1 Robert F. Kennedy, Day of Affirmation Address, University of Cape Town, South Africa, 6 June 1966.

2 Jürgen Moltmann, *Theology of Hope* (London: SCM Press, 1967), p. 33.

3 Jürgen Moltmann, *Ethics of Hope* (Minneapolis, MN: Fortress Press, 2012).

4 www.churchofengland.org/sites/default/files/201710/selection_criteria_for_ordained_ministry.pdf (accessed 23 August 2019).

5 James Lawrence, *Growing Leaders: Reflections on Leadership, Life and Jesus* (Abingdon: CPAS and The Bible Reading Fellowship, 2004), pp. 192–9.

6 Lawrence, *Growing Leaders*, p. 192.

7 Walter C. Wright, *Relationship Leadership: A Biblical Model for Influence and Service* (Downers Grover, IL: Inter-Varsity Press, 2012), p. 108.

8 Mark 4.11–12.

9 Luke 24.27.

10 Vaughan S. Roberts and David Sims, *Leading by Story: Rethinking Church Leadership* (London: SCM Press, 2017).

11 Luke 6.19.

12 Tom Wright, *Surprised by Hope* (London: SPCK, 2007), p. 218.

13 Revelation 13.8.

14 Matthew 23–25.

15 Luke 13.34–35.

16 The term deriving from Philippians 2.7: 'rather, he made himself nothing [*heauton ekenosen*]'.

17 Sarah Coakley, *Powers and Submissions: Spirituality, Philosophy and Gender* (Oxford: Blackwell, 2002), p. 4.

18 Bill Hybels, *Courageous Leadership: Field-Tested Strategy for the 360° Leader* (Human Ecology Partners, 2011), pp. 64–6.

19 1 Corinthians 5.13.

20 2 Timothy 2.2.

21 Matthew 18.3.

22 Jürgen Moltmann, *Theology of Play* (New York: Harper & Row, 1972), p. 23.

23 Anonymous.

24 Reinhold Niebuhr (1892–1971).

Reflection

The World as it Could Be

Ephesians 2.4–10

But because of his great love for us, God, who is rich in mercy, made us alive with Christ even when we were dead in transgressions – it is by grace you have been saved. And God raised us up with Christ and seated us with him in the heavenly realms in Christ Jesus, in order that in the coming ages he might show the incomparable riches of his grace, expressed in his kindness to us in Christ Jesus. For it is by grace you have been saved, through faith – and this is not from yourselves, it is the gift of God – not by works, so that no one can boast. For we are God's handiwork, created in Christ Jesus to do good works, which God prepared in advance for us to do.

Questions

1 What areas of renewal, which you have contributed to, are you most pleased about?
2 What dreams of a better world do you have?
3 How might you marshal and communicate your imagination better?
4 How might you use power to advance the Kingdom?
5 How might your own uses of power be more kenotic and what opportunities do you have for greater mutuality, equipping and empowerment?
6 What does it mean to help those around you live well?
7 How might you nurture a theology of play and a peace for what cannot be changed now?

Prayer

Father God, thank you for the saving work of Jesus. Thank you that in Christ we have been raised up and seated in the heavenly realms, right now. Thank you for the ways in which we have already helped others to move towards and into your Kingdom. Thank you for the gift of imagination. Help us to marshal and communicate our imaginations well, so that others can see the world as it could be. Thank you for the ability to do things. Help us to seek softer forms of power and to share our power with others, so that they might contribute to the world as it could be. Thank you for life and life in abundance. Help us to promote an understanding of that life, a peaceful acceptance when change doesn't happen quickly; grow a desire in us for others to inhabit the world as it could be. In Jesus' name, amen.

6

Clarity

The task of a leader is to get people from
where they are to where they have not yet been.
Henry Kissinger (b. 1923)[1]

If you rewind a decade or two in the Church of England, there were two camps who understood the role of ordained church leadership in very different ways. There were the traditionalists, who wanted to think about ordination in terms of the priesthood. Ordained church leaders were priests: that was their primary identity and function. Admittedly there has always been the intermediary step of ordination as deacon but the emphasis, for this camp at least, was around a very particular category of priesthood. People spoke of an ontological change at the moment of ordination within this theologically high view of priesthood, with the ordained person as a unique kind of intermediary with particular spiritual authority to pronounce absolutions, blessings and oversee particular sacramental rituals like the Eucharist. A priest was entrusted with the cure of souls for their parish, holding spiritual authority within a particular patch.

In the other camp were those who would probably self-identify as reformers or more modernist thinkers. They didn't like the language of priest as the overriding model for thinking about ordination. They were much more comfortable using the general terminology of minister within a church, which could then take different shapes in different contexts. They had reservations about the way the Church of England had tied particular functions to the role of the ordained priest, and there was occasional mirth at all that talk of ontological change. Alongside all that, they wanted to stress that every Christian person had a priestly identity, and that using a term like priest for a church leader undermined the sense in which every Christian shared that identity.

However, if you scratched beneath the surface, there was sympathy on both sides for what the other camp was saying. The modernists often recognized that the traditionalists were 'on to something' in their insistence of a high view of priesthood. They could see that church leaders were set apart for their particular ministry, and there was no escaping some of the significant personal, practical and spiritual implications of this. While they might not have had much of a theology for it, many ministers from the modernist camp eventually came to recognize that a lot of the strange things traditionalists said about priestly ministry were indeed true as they got more miles under the belt. On the other side, some of the traditionalists developed sympathy for what the modernists had been saying. They lamented their lack of training in basic leadership skills, and sometimes felt pigeon-holed into a particular type of ministry that might not have been the best fit for their particular gifting. They could see that their role was manifest, and that investing all their ministerial eggs in the basket of priesthood, at least in a particular form of priestly ministry, was going to significantly limit what God could do through them. They also got frustrated at the implicit disempowerment of the laity that the trappings of their office often played into. Of course exceptions abounded, but these are broad brushstrokes of the lie of the land.

What has happened since then, is that various theological thinkers have tried to unify some of the divergent thinking about priesthood, and tried to show that deeper theology can overcome more superficial disagreements. John Pritchard, in his seminal work on ordained Anglican ministry, began this in some ways by arguing that the office of priesthood only made sense because all Christians were priests.[2] That the ordained office of priest was a particular grouping of Christians, set apart to exercise their priestly ministry to other Christians, who in turn would exercise their priestly ministry to the world. As we've touched on, and will return to later, Graham Tomlin took this argument forward by looking at the whole theme of priesthood running through the Judeo-Christian story. Tomlin locates the office of priesthood at the centre of concentric circles of blessing, flowing out from those priestly church leaders to the wider Church, then from the Church to all of humanity, and finally from humanity to creation itself. This priestly model emphasizes the servant nature of church leaders, the priestly nature of all Christians and the wider movement of renewal that God is working in the world.

Using this model, many of the old divisions between the two camps have been deconstructed. The modernists, or reformers, now have a compelling theology for why the role of church leader has a 'higher' dimension to it, and this theological understanding helps to keep them focused on their own ministry to the Church, acting as a parking brake to them spending too much of their own time doing the job of the whole Church, such as ministering to humanity and the world. They are primarily there to equip the Church for this activity. As such, reformers can relax a bit in the knowledge that this 'higher' theology of priesthood doesn't undermine the priesthood held by the rest of the Church, but is simply an extension of it. In addition, reformers can locate a lot of what they have been saying about the need for good leadership and plurality of expressions of ministry within this grander theology of ordained priest-hood. Suddenly a 'higher' form of priestly ministry doesn't have to look so one dimensional. Equally, traditionalists, now that their core con-victions have secure theological underpinnings and are safe from some of the modernist critique, can make more room in their ministry for other aspects of church leadership without losing their understanding of the priestly function. There is a softening to the modernist stance and trad-itionalists don't feel attacked in quite the same way. Traditionalists can celebrate good theology that supports some of what they know to be true, and this same theology protects against some of the most extreme forms of a 'high' priestly ministry, which most of the traditionalists would reject anyway.

The real point here is that with theological depth we often find theo-logical congruency. When we press into the essence of things, we often find that superficial differences can be reconciled. The important things that we shouted at one another find fresh meaning when absorbed into higher ideas, and we gain sympathy and understanding for opposing ideas when we see them in the light of deeper truths.

We can, therefore, with a high degree of optimism, revisit some of the pain and confusion of leadership briefly touched on in the first two chapters of this book, with an expectation that many of the disagree-ments and conflicting viewpoints can be resolved with our renewed grasp of Hopeful Influence. In fact, as we'll begin to explore in the final part of this book, an even greater prize awaits. By applying Hopeful Influence to the contemporary challenges of leadership around us, can we avoid some of the pain of the past and build a world that is truly good for all?

A clear reality gives us freedom to lead

Before we explore how Hopeful Influence brings clarity to the theological debate on leadership, it's helpful to revisit the underlying eschatological, or hopeful, reality in which the Christian life is located. If we are going to really get to grips with how Hopeful Influence works in different contexts, then we need to recognize that there are some fundamental problems with the way we tend to think about life and reality. In a British, Ameri-can or European context, with all our particular histories of thought, why doesn't all this talk of eschatology sound more natural to us? Let's remind ourselves where we've come from, both in terms of our history as well as the arguments we've framed in this book so far.

Eschatology essentially presents a view of reality that says the only truly human future is located under the lordship of Jesus in a fully redeemed new heaven and earth. In a European and North American context, our inherited Greek thought has wanted to give us permission to create our own reality, to give us the notion that through cause and effect we can be masters of our destiny. The eschatology of Hebrew thinking says that, on the contrary, the things of today only have value and meaning to the extent that they are connected to the ultimate future in which the Messiah reigns. This marks an important divergence in thinking. Western or Greek thought says that we are essentially free to decide our futures, and invites us to forcefully strive for personal and/or collective utopias which the human spirit working collaboratively has the power to create. Hebrew thinking says that true freedom isn't some innate human quality, but actually only comes within very specific boundaries that connect with the world to come. A classic analogy for helping us think about freedom is the goldfish bowl. The goldfish is free to swim wherever it likes in the bowl, but if it jumps out of the bowl it will die. Is it free? Yes, the goldfish is free as long as it stays in the water. The very nature of freedom is defined as freedom within limitations.

For human beings, we find freedom when we choose to align our lives with, to live within the boundaries of, if you like, this slowly, and sometimes quickly, advancing Kingdom of God. Some people are able to do this with acumen for the period of their earthly lives, either by common grace, a Christianized society, good parenting, the legacy of their inherited image of God or some combination of all that. However, most are not. And even for those who are, there are questions about how the trajectory of their lives runs into eternity if they haven't at a deeper level bowed before the feet of Jesus. The wonderful Christian invitation, though, is for every person to experience an increased vitality and ability to live within these boundaries through the Holy Spirit when we make a choice in this life to turn to Jesus.

There are two very important implications therefore of this particularly Hebrew, eschatological, way of thinking. The first is that our experience of freedom is related to our pursuit of and submission to a God-shaped life. If we repeatedly and unrepentantly engage in sexual promiscuity, then the power of sex and intimacy will ultimately master our desires and destroy our freedom. If we build up financial gain predominantly for ourselves to the exclusion of others, then obsessive greed and financial anxiety will overcome us. If we live with the underlying assumption that we are in control of our own destiny and we don't broker life through healthy relationships with God and other people, then despite our wealth and myriad technological resources we will end up lonely, dissatisfied and deeply unhappy.

The second implication is that there is a very real sense of freedom still permitted within these eschatological boundaries – in fact the truest form of freedom that there is. In a sense, Greek thought was right, but it only got half the story. It was right in the sense that God does give us freedom to shape our own destiny. God doesn't want robots who will build a future in a pre-programmed way. That's the awesomeness of it all. God wants us to grow up. To choose a future, independent in a sense from any detailed designs that God forces us to adhere to. Yes, the Spirit plays notes that we can follow, but within the unlimited, cosmic variety of that we have tremendous scope to build a world of our own design. Up to a point. Up to a point, in that the only future for humanity is a future under the lordship of Jesus. We can dream, create and party as much as we like, as long as it is within the boundaries that lead to life. The life that we find in Jesus.

We get beautiful pictures of this, not just in the Bible, but drawn out through our human history. If I had lived in England 250 years ago, and had a certain amount of personal wealth, then I would probably have owned slaves who would have helped do the chores required so that I could seemingly enjoy the greater pleasures in life. Who enjoys dusting or washing the dishes? If I tried the same approach today, I would have all personal liberty stripped from me and I would be thrown in jail. Such extreme self-centredness is simply not allowed. We have shaped the structures of our society to reflect this increasing eschatological reality. It's beautiful; for in the Kingdom where Jesus rules there are no slaves. In the establishment of our laws, as a society we have passed through a particular eschatological boundary in relation to legalized slavery.

As we now synthesize some of our thinking and point forward to how Hopeful Influence gets expressed, we need to do this with an awareness that Jesus is drawing us into a God-shaped future where we all still get to play. We need to straighten out some of the seemingly opposed perspectives that we looked at in Chapter 2, but we do this with a posture of leaning into the Spirit's lead with an expectation of being surprised and changed. That means for everyone, on all sides of the leadership conversation, there will be things we need to rethink, assumptions we need to challenge, prejudices we need to drop. At our best, that's hugely exciting; we don't know exactly where it will take us, but we know that if we stay close to Jesus, in the fullness of all that means, then we are heading towards a world that is better for all. With that in mind we can now revisit some of the earlier confusion.

Leadership clarity – seeking unity

Let's begin by revisiting the confusion around whether leaders lead, or whether leaders follow. We have looked at Henri Nouwen and Leonard Sweet as advocates of *followership*. In a sense, they said, if we find ourselves in positions of formalized leadership in the world, then the best resource to us is having a theology of our role as a follower. A follower of Jesus first, but also a follower of others as we help communities of people move together in the world. So let's use the paradigm of Hopeful Influence to help us marshal this idea.

First, we have to say that they are right. As we've seen, a Christian leader is doing nothing if they aren't following Jesus first – both in their own life and heart – but also only if their influence on others is aligned with the influence Jesus is wanting to exert through them. Equally, if a leader develops a self-understanding in which they are always leading, or always have to lead, then they have misunderstood how leadership works. We are meant to be a teachable people, learning from one another on the journey home, yet there is a dangerous propensity to retreat into impenetrable bubbles of presumed authority. Leaders – people of Hopeful Influence – are followers first. A quick glimpse at the contexts out of which Nouwen and Sweet speak is helpful in understanding why they want to emphasize these important points so much.

Nouwen moved to a L'Arche community and was surrounded by people who had experienced their own leadership potential crushed by a world unsympathetic to their own particular needs and wiring. Within this context, enabling a group of deeply disempowered people to take the first steps of self-leadership was absolutely vital. Equally, Sweet, writing as he does from a contemporary North American context, seeing a great deal of *archon*-style leadership where the charismatic and financially or intellectually powerful dictate the way, wants to push back hard on our overemphasis on this kind of leadership. Nouwen and Sweet are both saying important things which resonate with aspects of Hopeful Influence. In a sense, part of their critique is shared by the historical Anglican reticence to talk about leadership that we explored in Chapter 2 also. However, there is more to Hopeful Influence than that particular lens, and that is where some of the other commentators on leadership are required. If we push all the leadership energy into forms of followership, then we risk missing the essential purpose of Christian leadership, which is to intentionally help people move towards the Kingdom of God through the mechanisms of seeing, participating and experiencing that we explored earlier. We should anchor leadership in followership, but we don't reduce its definition to that or we lose its essence. Intentional Hopeful Influence, as we have seen, has to lead to movement and renewal.

This begins to take us towards the confusing question of how much leadership practice Christians can legitimately borrow from the world. One of the things I'm struck by when I look at the landscape of secular leadership, is how often much of the wisdom is actually biblical, Christian leadership. My colleague Neil in my current church tells the story of when he first served, as a fresh teenager, in a ministry context. He was young, had bags of energy, and had a schedule involving a lot of room set-up for visiting groups. At 11 o'clock in the morning, there was a cup of tea and biscuits. Neil looked forward to his tea and biscuits. But of course, when 11 o'clock came, he was instructed to go and get the next room ready for the groups after their break. 'But what about my cup of tea and biscuits?' asked Neil. 'You don't get to have those now, Neil', came the response. 'You're a leader, and you'll have to wait until everyone else has had theirs.' As Neil, slightly begrudgingly, got on with his jobs, he was very aware that the leaders' eyes were on him. Had he understood? Had he grasped the servant nature of leadership? He was only a fresh teenager, but if he hadn't got the basics right then he wasn't ready to lead. Fast-forward 30 years and we find Simon Sinek writing a bestselling book entitled *Leaders Eat Last.*[3] He took some of the servanthood and people-focused practices he saw in the US military, themselves strongly influenced by the New Testament, and constructed a picture of a leader as someone who prioritizes the well-being of those around them first. His book sold millions of copies to a secular audience, hungry for more effective and sustainable forms of leadership, and was lauded as a new and radical way of thinking that could transform the culture of business leadership. For the current generation of Christians growing up, sadly they are perhaps more likely to learn this beautiful, godly truth about leadership from a world that has realized it, than from a Church that has retreated from the leadership discourse.

This is hopefully informative when we revisit the more confrontational aspects of Sweet's analysis on stronger church leadership styles and par-ticularly his provocative question about whether Hybels' propensity to borrow wisdom from the world is actually a way of putting our trust in something other than God. Well of course it might be, but if we frame all wisdom borrowed from the world as a sell-out of our dependence on God, then we're making a mistake. The mistake lies in equating life in the institutional Church as good and life found elsewhere in the world as bad – in assuming, essentially, that there are no forms of Hopeful Influence apart from those applied by us Christians. Consider Figure 7.

The reason there is so much potential for good wisdom beyond the Church is because the world operates within God's domain and is able to draw conclusions about how things work best. When an intelligent, experienced business-person with no Christian conviction realizes that encouraging people, helping them develop their skills and empowering them to make decisions leads to a fruitfulness of activity, they're not coming up with some independent ideas about the world. What they're seeing is God's good design for leadership amid humanity becoming realized. When church culture lags behind some of the good things the

Figure 7: Wisdom within God's domain

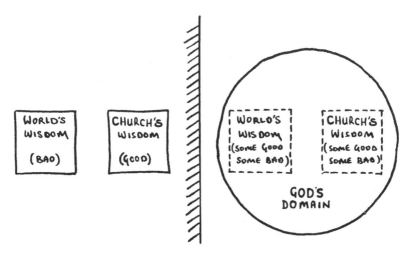

world has observed, then Christian leaders are right to call it out. Even more so because in a post-Christian environment the world may have learned things from the Church that the Church has now forgotten. Of course, if Christians embrace worldly wisdom simply because it seems to be effective in a particular context, without looking for nuances in how that wisdom translates into appropriate *life in the Kingdom*, then they should be critiqued and sometimes forcefully. But the problem is not intrinsic to borrowing wisdom from the world; the challenge is simply discerning what is godly and what is not. In that sense, Sweet has applied the wrong hermeneutic. For Christian leadership, I would suggest that the hermeneutic isn't about where the wisdom is coming from, but whether that wisdom is aligned with the picture of Hopeful Influence that we've explored in this book.

This is helpful when we return to the current debate about the best means to train and resource senior leaders within the Church of England. On the one hand we have Archbishop Justin Welby overseeing a trans-formational programme to invest in leadership development after what is perceived to be decades of inadequate resourcing, particularly for senior leaders. On the other hand there are those, like Martyn Percy, who argue that the Anglican Church is uncritically embracing forms of managerialism without sufficient theological foundations for them or the wider picture of leadership within which they sit. Into this confrontation, Hopeful Influence helps us see where the theological foundations actually are and helps us recognize more clearly vital things that both sides want to say. We've seen that Hopeful Influence revolves around the activity of helping others see, participate and experience the Kingdom. We know that leadership is hard, and that movement and renewal require forms of imagination, power and shared life that need careful attention, often trained and developed attention, to be got right. We've also seen that leadership within a team or organization sometimes requires harder structures to facilitate the right speed and direction of travel. It is clear that the world understands some of this. In large, successful institutions, we often see well-formed mechanisms to enable effective corporate travel into an agreed future. In many ways, this is bread-and-butter leadership development that the Church has ignored for too long. The danger of Percy's critique is that managerialism, or borrowing managerial practices from the world, gets thrown out on principle without assessing the tremendous good that they can bring. On the flip side, Hopeful Influence helps us identify a kernel of leadership activity that is genuinely Christian, and provides a filter to how much we might borrow from the world. There is a tranche of emerging senior leaders who have been successful within a particular expression of the Church of England. For them to exercise and marshal imagination for the Church's future requires dialogue with and immersion within the full range of expressions in the Church. This is obviously essential if we are to travel well together. Equally, for the more forceful or impatient types, a strong reminder of the kenotic power, to which our leadership activity should aspire, and a reminder of how this has been held and nurtured within our historic formularies, will be important. Building impenetrably hard power structures, creating a culture of preferment and replicating ministry emphasis without deep contextual and historical reflection will rightly set alarm bells ringing in the wider Church. The danger of the 2014 Green report, and initiatives like it, is that they become carte blanche for adopting practices without the application of a filter like Hopeful Influence, and that is the kind of work that Percy and others seem to be advocating.

Leadership clarity – we don't merely synthesize

What we are rubbing up against here, again, is how to apply a motif like Hopeful Influence to existing leadership practices to help straighten us out. As such, it would seem like a good time to return to the writings of John Maxwell. In one sense, Maxwell's pursuit of the effective methodologies of leadership isn't wrong. When he used the example of Kroc's expansion of the McDonald's franchise, he was making the point that, within a particular commercial paradigm, the method of leadership can be taken up a level to enable massively increased output and revenue. However, we just have to be clear that he has offered no resource for thinking in a Christian way about the purpose of the leadership in that context. The unfortunate truth is that vast numbers of Christians from around the world, and plenty of others besides, have picked up his material and become much more effective leaders at collectively moving the world backwards on its eschatological journey. Such is the crisis of leadership that we need to be clear about what has happened and what is happening. This isn't discipleship at all. This is simply methods of behaviour harnessed for the worsening of the quality of our shared life together, driven by the predominantly self-centred needs of a few. I believe God is saying enough is enough. It's worth noting that these same leadership methods of lifting the lid led to the growth of chains like Primark, empires historically built on exploitative labour practices, or the mass proliferation of arms like the AK-47: used to maximize the killing potential in genocides, tribal feuds, terrorist attacks and wars the world over for decades.

So what's the solution? Well, Kroc was a Christian. Understanding brand identity, economies of scale and methods of business multiplication aren't bad skills; they aren't by definition ungodly, nor will they unavoidably lead to unfettered capitalist destruction. However, it seems to me that, as the business grew and expanded, Kroc wasn't resourced in his discipleship sufficiently to theologically reflect on the eschatological purpose of his influence, and to create space for Holy Spirit-led imagination on improved qualities as well as quantities. He didn't understand the world to which he was heading and his participation in that movement. There was a slow seduction towards bottom-line profit, no doubt fear around emerging competition, and ultimately there was complete submission towards profiteering. Kroc says it himself with his often-quoted reflection: 'I believe in God, family and McDonald's – and in the office, that order is reversed.' It wouldn't have been easy, but McDonald's had the opportunity to trail-blaze scalable quality and win hearts and minds around ethical and sustainable production; and they blew it. Our challenge is to resource the next generation to do differently.

We might benefit from locating ourselves in a bigger picture for a moment. In a sense, I would argue that the momentum behind the Western world's slippage into unbridled capitalism can be attributed in significant part to the proliferation of the reductionist gospel we explored earlier and a deep misunderstanding of the Christian hope. The myth of human progress, the false confidence in the market, the deprivation of our social services and the disintegration of community can all be connected back to the failure to apply Hopeful Influence, and other paradigms like it, to the realization of our leadership. The Western Church lost the plot and the Western economy, and large swathes of society, was subsequently hijacked by the powerful and greedy.

Perhaps more significantly still, the poverty of our contemporary life together might be affecting the shape of our place in that ultimate future.

As we saw in Chapter 3, this isn't the same as saying we earn our salvation, certainly. But we affect aspects of our ultimate future by the extent to which we align ourselves with Jesus today. In this life we set the trajectory of our character and the extent of our stewardship over the world as they will be realized, in some sense at least, in the life to come. Of course, in the world to come there will be no sin; it is a place where only righteousness dwells.[4] We will all inhabit the future world perfectly in that sense. However, even in God's perfection there will be variation. I am fairly certain that the apostle Paul will exercise greater influence than I in that place of re-creation and adventure, just as the star of a sports team offers more than the reserve player; we are both welcome, important, and will find eternal joy as we fulfil our different roles. There is more at stake than we realize, and our discipleship needs to reflect Jesus' call to be a faithful servant.

Only God truly knows, but it seems to me that Kroc and the like are behaving in the very opposite way to the faithful servant. They clearly had a great gifting for organization, for stewardship, for oversight, and yet rather than putting these gifts to use for true Kingdom goals, they settled for worldly returns; returns that looked bright and fulfilling but that were ultimately spiritually empty because they evidenced lives curved in on themselves. Admittedly, they did create a significant employment base, which certainly counts for something. But hardly the broader Kingdom goals that could have been reached. The institutional Church has nurtured a multitude of *Christian* people with misguided spiritual courage and confidence, who have led businesses that have ended up pioneering the world's journey away from God. No doubt many will still find eternal salvation but, as the Bible suggests, their works run the risk of being consumed by fire and their ultimate reward may be less.[5]

I was at a conference recently where John Maxwell spoke, and I had the privilege of being part of an open-forum discussion session. Given his prestige, pretty much all the questions asked were of the type: 'Tell us, John, how to lead better in this area of detail or that.' As an audience we were pretty captive and I won't pretend he didn't answer his questions well. However, as I sat in the audience I found myself trying to formulate a different question, with a bit more agitation. There was no doubt that John had clearly managed to identify some very powerful truisms about the methods of leadership, and he'd also helped teach the world more effective methods of leading, rooted in his engagement with Christian Scripture and history. However, wasn't there a danger that he was just helping humanity drive off the cliff a little bit more quickly? If we don't couple the methods of our leadership to a clear understanding of where we are leading and what the ultimate direction and purpose of our leadership is, then aren't we actually doing something dangerously anti-God?

There has to come a point when we Christians stop teaching people how to do things unless we are willing to locate our activity in God's overriding purposes and show people these also. Now, it is true that Maxwell does touch on purpose when he engages with the idea of *adding value* which, while a bit popularist and not theologically clear, is probably the closest he gets to the notion that God has an intention for our leadership that sits over our methodology.[6] There is also certainly no doubt that he has chosen personally, in some of the different leadership roles he has taken up, to pursue goals that are Kingdom-shaped. However, I would say that because Maxwell hasn't wired God's true purposes into his understanding of leadership, the vast bulk of his contribution looks like a synthesis of what the world already knows about leadership and how to make it more effective. And, importantly, the Church's role isn't to synthesize the world's voice, but rather to present a clear picture of what Christian life looks like and, in the leadership case, why that is a distinctly different and better form of influence than any other. I suggest that it is in the theological resources of this book, and other material that goes beyond it, that we will find the discipleship resources for the next generation of Christian leaders.

Leadership clarity – developing a common framework

As we saw in Chapter 2, the lack of a theological definition of leadership has created the vacuum into which far too much inadequate projection and subjective reflection has been spilled. We have seen how Hopeful Influence can be used to unify arguments and to see through and beyond some of the limited or imbalanced contributions to Christian leadership. Let us now apply Hopeful Influence to more mature material on leadership, and look for the theological resonance that we would expect to find. A good case study to consider, which we've looked at already, is James Lawrence and his material on *Growing Leaders*. Lawrence's primary concern is to help us think about the qualities that make successful leadership within the church community.[7] As we've seen, he is less interested in explaining what is happening theologically through our leadership, but more focused on drawing our attention to how we identify and nurture the leadership qualities we have; interestingly though, many of the elements of Hopeful Influence are still there.

Lawrence starts with the idea that leaders are *chosen* by God. What he means by this is that our primary identity as Christian leaders isn't in our role as leaders but is in our loving relationship with God – our *first love* as he puts it. As he goes on to illustrate, if we lose sight of this then we can quickly become burned-out, task-focused people. As a context for the Christian life, any Christian life, this is essential, and as we've seen in our exploration of Hopeful Influence, this finds its root in the location of the leader as a follower of Jesus on their own eschatological journey into the Kingdom. 'Come, follow me,' says Jesus, 'and help others to follow me too.'

Lawrence's model then outlines a leader's *call*. Rightly, Lawrence differentiates between the general call of every Christian to be a disciple and the specifics of our calling based on the shape of our gifts, abilities and opportunities. However, he doesn't take the larger theological step in asking what a call to leadership looks like in the context of God's renewal of the world. Leadership is something that we do, but it isn't presented specifically in terms of another's journey into the Kingdom. Because Lawrence doesn't draw on that larger picture, he ends up focusing on more individualistic understandings of calling – like SHAPE profiling, current responsibilities and the development of a personal life statement[8] – and the spectrum of leadership he presents isn't as wide as it could be at this point.

Lawrence adds *character* to his model. He emphasizes the essential importance of godly character for a leader, encourages us to be self-aware in our deficiencies and offers a variety of helpful and appropriate ways we can grow and develop into more Christlike characters. This is a vital fit within Hopeful Influence, because of a leader's own journey towards the eschaton. But again, godly character presented on its own like this can feel like an individualistic pursuit, when actually it is bound up with our communal journey: we grow as we lead, at least that is the great potential when viewed through a wider theological lens.

The next component of the model is *competency*. For this Lawrence selects a passage from the book of Timothy[9] on the attributes of the church leader that Paul commends, which he draws together under the tag line *leaders lead themselves*. He then adds three further competencies: embodying Kingdom values, handling vision and developing others. All good and really helpful stuff, but hopefully we can begin to see past the slightly arbitrary way Lawrence selects them and start to locate them in their proper theological place. Leaders lead themselves because they are also on the journey of eschatological renewal. They embody Kingdom values because in their leadership they help us see what increasing life under the lordship of Christ looks like. They handle vision, because their role is in helping us know where to go, eschatologically speaking. They develop others, because we're all on a journey together and the movement forwards that God seeks is far wider and greater than that which we ourselves can influence. Throughout his development of the model, Lawrence's assertions all echo strongly with Hopeful Influence, but our exploration now gives them a wider picture within which they can be located with coherence. A common framework for Christian leadership takes us away from assertions and conflicting language and gives us greater confidence in the excellent material that already exists. When we position Lawrence's ideas within Hopeful Influence they seem less arbitrary, and more like the appropriate theological building blocks that fit together properly to construct an actualization of what is happening in true Christian leadership.

Can only Christians exercise Christian leadership?

Our focus in this book has been on Christians and their expressions of leadership. However, an important question as we come towards the end of our theological discussion is whether people who haven't chosen to follow Jesus, who aren't Christians, can lead in ways that we might call *Christian*. This is a big question that could be answered in different ways depending on the definition of terms. In the context of this book, there are two important things that need to be said that take us to one particular answer.

First, in any situation we need to be careful about saying who is and who isn't a Christian. At its core, Christian identity is found in the heart, which no one can see but God. This is particularly relevant in the post-Christian Western context, where many people may have heard the gospel, turned to Jesus in the deep waters of the human heart, but then found expressions of Christian community so unconvincing, so off-putting or simply downright unwelcoming, that they have rejected Christian identity in any cognitive sense. A person may not embrace a Christian identity as we understand it, but God may still be active in and through them, and one should always be open to that possibility.

Second, let's assume that as a result of the image of God that every human carries and the common grace of God extended to all creation (which almost certainly has kept us from complete annihilation), people who have no Christian faith at all may be able to exercise behaviour that is so aligned with God's intention for the world that we could indeed call it *Christian*. The small acts of kindness. The willingness to serve. The motivation of love. Indeed, the generosity of the good Samaritan that Jesus talked about. Every day, in millions of different ways, things are done that are commended by God, and these activities aren't exercised by people who are necessarily committed followers of Jesus.

Therefore for both these reasons, among those we might call *non-Christians* we should expect to find plenty of human activity that takes a godly or Christian shape; these activities surely do not exclude forms of leadership. My point is: let's not continue to develop this subject with the lofty assumption that visible Christians are the only ones who can get leadership right, or even the ones who get it most right. Even if eventually we have to say some unique things about a Christian person's identity and how Christian people access the resources to lead *Christianly*, let's not miss the myriad ways people behave in ways aligned with the character and intentions of God. Let's celebrate that, draw attention to it, and continue to explain where we should look to find these things most perfectly.

Why leadership really is for all

As we come towards the end of the middle section of this book, so we should now be able to see why leadership really is for all. If the heart of true leadership, stripped back from all the connotations of *archon*ship, excessive authority, self-aggrandizement and the rest, is fundamentally about participating in the God–human project of renewing the world, then of course we all have a role to play. Whatever role we play in the human communities we are part of, whether volunteering in a care home or as CEO of a multinational enterprise, we all have the ability to exercise influence on those around us. When that influence becomes *hopeful*, when it is aligned with the advance of God's Kingdom, when it helps others see, participate and experience life in increasing measure – as it is meant to be under the lordship of Jesus – then we see the essence of what leadership is really about. More than that, whatever activities we find ourselves doing as *leaders*, it is vital to remember that the true leadership bit is found in our Hopeful Influence and not necessarily in the other functions that we often associate with those roles. This clarity about leadership is vital at a time when there is significant confusion over the true nature of leadership and also because our capacity for human pain through poor leadership is greater than at any other moment in human history. So vital is it, that I would argue that as Christians, we need to stop talking about leadership unless we are able to frame our conversation theologically in the kind of paradigm offered by Hopeful Influence. Given this, and that true leadership really is for all, then there are at least three things that followers of Jesus need to hear afresh.

First, Christians should opt in to leadership. I know that for many that will feel heavy and burdensome and, in isolation, perhaps it is. But in writing this book, I have wanted to reshape the notion we have of leadership and, to some degree also, the notion we have of ourselves as people who can exercise leadership. Reworking the leadership picture from what we have created will take a lot more than a book of course, and perhaps we are entering a season of life where the Church will be more on the front foot in presenting radically different language about what true leadership looks like. If someone reading this book has been so burned or overwhelmed by the broken concepts or experiences of leadership that we've created, then perhaps opting straight back into leadership isn't quite the right approach. However, I want to say that being a Christian, participating in God's renewal of the world, unavoidably takes us to the leadership question, and that there is a way of thinking about the essence of leadership that is life-giving, freeing and inspiring and, despite the fact that leadership is also unavoidably hard, is also extremely good for us. Ultimately, we need to opt in, and Hopeful Influence gives us the theologically robust and safe ground to do that.

Second, as well as opting in, some Christians exercising leadership really need to slow down. As we said in Chapter 2, there is a group of leaders who know by conviction that leadership is essential, and who are frustrated by those who eschew the term or who seem perpetually bent on undermining the necessity of leadership. For these leaders, there is a strong temptation to just stop listening to the critiques and to crack on regardless. I believe that for many of these leaders, there is a real need to slow down. By this, I'm not advocating exercising leadership with less energy and conviction, rather that we need to get absolute clarity on how the Hopeful Influence at the heart of our leadership activity gets expressed. We won't do this unless we create space to reflect together with others. A case in point is the contemporary implementation of various forms of managerialism within the Anglican Church's leadership structures. The best forms of managerialism enable efficiency and clear communication as well as creating space for appropriate oversight and the training required to achieve it. Clearly, at its best, there is significant overlap with Hopeful Influence in all that. However, the dissenting voices know that there are forms of managerialism in the world that don't overlap quite so well with God's purposes for leadership, and that we need to use theological paradigms like Hopeful Influence to continually critique and inform our actual practice of leadership, of which some forms of managerialism can certainly be a part. It may have been adequate, without a theological framework for leadership, to just get on with things. However, into the future, the terrain God is inviting us to navigate will require continual theological reflection as to how both our leadership is exercised and also what is happening internally in a leader's own soul and personality on their journey back to God. We won't achieve that by speeding up. Those of us who self-identify as natural leaders probably need to slow down.

Third, while we are called to debate, I believe on the issue of leadership God is calling the Church to stop fighting and to rally together on some agreed common ground. On one side of the fence we have the group who simply get on with leadership, deeply frustrated by those who eschew the term. On the other side of the fence, we have those who see the power plays, the forceful authority and worldly underbelly, and who feel compelled to challenge and sometimes usurp leaders and their structures in the pursuit of something they believe is more godly. In between these camps, and with deep overlap into both, I believe we find the essence of true leadership that is the Hopeful Influence we have explored. It is no longer sufficient to stand on one side of the fence and hurl accusations at the other camp. It is time for both camps to move into the centre ground, to stand together on the firm foundations of God's renewal of the world and our participation in that. To agree together that there is a form of influence, which is about leadership in one way or another, to which we need to make space for all to engage with well. This is the unifying potential of this book, and it is a potential for which we need more focus and further contribution.

And finally, while leadership is for all, if I've given the impression that as Christian people we can easily discern God's will and submit to it, that stepping into Hopeful Influence is simply a grasping of the intellect, then I am straying into inaccurate territory. Our experience of the Christian life is very dependent on the other Christians we journey with and the influences to which we have been and are still exposed. Having listened to baby boomers talk of their experience of Christianity, many of whom have now opted out of Christian community and even Christian identity, it seems to me that the church expressions available to that generation often fell so far short of true Christian community – in their theological understanding, activity of worship, quality of spiritual friendships and missional engagement – that it's a wonder Europe and America moved into the twenty-first century with any inherited Church at all. The majority of those who survived seemed stiff, frumpy or legalized, a passive laity ruled by a small group of highly religious control freaks. I can understand why so many de-churched Christians don't want to come back, and it may be another generation or so until they do, when hopefully enough of our churches will have caught up with the underground reformation that the Western Church has begun to experience. The tragic reality is that even now, many Christians in Europe and North America are experiencing something that is called Christian in name, but is a poor shadow of how our faith is meant to be lived out in our current world. In these places we often find death where we should find life. But that doesn't undermine the reality that God still has a plan for how we can join in with the renewal of the world or, that despite our failures, every Christian person is called to embrace forms of Hopeful Influence for themselves. Leadership really is for all, for that is part of what it means to be human.

Developing a manifesto of Hopeful Influence

As we've seen then in our journey through the second part of this book, Hopeful Influence is an eschatological form of social activity, the potential for which we find at the heart of human interactions everywhere. Hopeful Influence is the moment we enable someone's imagination to be stirred so they can better see the shape of the world as it should be. Hopeful Influence is the moment we help other people to purposefully join in with the actual advance of the Kingdom, enabling Jesus' lordship to become more manifest. Hopeful Influence is the moment we help people get a taste of how life should be, when the vision and activity come together to enable an actual change in how we live well together. Hopeful Influence happens person to person, but in that sense it can also happen between human institutions and across the complex array of people groups that form society and the wider world. In simple terms, Hopeful Influence is the activity that enables the Kingdom to advance in the lives of others.

As we've seen in this chapter, Hopeful Influence has a remarkable ability to unify some of the divergent strands in the leadership discourse. It also helps to sharply critique leadership forms and teachings that are inadequate or insufficiently Christian. Hopeful Influence brings clarity and coherence to the Christian leadership subject, and appears sufficiently broad to find resonance across some of the more well-developed strands of thinking. As we reflect back on how far we've come in the first two sections of this book, and draw our assessment of current forms of leadership and the theological exploration of Hopeful Influence in the general sense to a close, what we can now say is that things are significantly worse, and significantly better, than we might have realized.

Worse because we've consistently misunderstood the purpose of human leadership and we've exercised our influence in inappropriate, misguided and downright selfish ways. We find ourselves at a moment in history when our potential to cause human suffering and the destruction of the planet has increased beyond anything previous generations might have imagined. Terrible things are happening all around us and our shared understanding and consensus for change, and very particularly how to lead into change, often resembles a muddled mess.

Better because God has promised to sort it all out, and God's invitation to first the Church and then to all of humanity to co-participate in the renewal that we need is as strong as it has ever been. In fact, just as our social and technological developments have created huge potential for suffering and destruction, so within those developments lies the greatest potential for well-being and human flourishing. What we need to do now is explore specific ways Hopeful Influence can take shape in some of the different spheres of our shared life together.

My intention is that with increased theological understanding and practical reflection, we can begin to operate more effectively as people who lead; for all Christians everywhere to reflect on and sharpen their exercise of Hopeful Influence. We started out by making the theological case that there is a human vocation to pursue the well-being of humanity and creation and that Hopeful Influence is the activity of leadership that helps us move together into a God-shaped future. In the last part of this book we will consider the role different spheres of life play in this movement into the future. In summary terms at least, what is God doing in each of these spheres? As we understand that, so another question emerges. What shape does our Hopeful Influence take within that sphere? As we explore these questions, we should begin to see the kinds of Hopeful Influence God is wanting to release. Our understanding of each sphere should inform our realization of these distinctive forms of Hopeful Influence and, as we get to grips with that, in essence we are starting to move towards a manifesto for Hopeful Influence. We can do little more than skim the surface of these deep and far-reaching questions, but perhaps we can say enough to make the way ahead a little clearer.

Comment
Andy Flanagan, Executive Director, Christians on the Left

How much do you know about Obadiah? If you're anything like me, not very much. He was a behind-the-scenes guy – the sound guy to Elijah's worship leader. King Ahab has been leading Israel astray and Elijah has been told to challenge him to stop dabbling with other gods. But Elijah doesn't just rant about it from the desert, screaming into the ether on social media or shouting through mass emails, drumming up signatures for his 'Down with Baal' petition. He connects with a person.

Obadiah managed all of Ahab's palace and affairs. As a believer, one suspects it will not have been easy for Obadiah to be present at the heart of a regime that was doing such damage to God's honour. But he stayed. He was faithful. And at the right moment he bumps into Elijah and is perfectly placed to broker the unlikely meeting between Elijah and Ahab. The distant is brought very close.

So the rap battle to end all rap battles takes place on Mount Carmel. The prophets of Baal suffer total humiliation and an impossible bonfire that Bear Grylls would be proud of leaves a lasting impact on the consciousness of the people of Israel. It is now dramatically clear whose god is God. But it wouldn't have happened without the event management skills of Obadiah. It's as important to be holding the clipboard as it is to be holding the microphone.

Elijah continually confronted King Ahab from outside the court. We need people like him. But fewer of us are working on the inside like Obadiah. Let's face it – it's much more exciting to see soaked altars burst into flames than to be forwarding emails around a government department. Elijah gets the Sunday school stories told about him. Obadiah – not so much. We can refine our message until it's perfect, then pump it out with every piece of technology we can find, but if we don't have people of influence in the right places with the right relationships, it may be fairly pointless.

The difference between noise and influence is relationship.

If the very nature of God is a set of relationships, could it be true that the kingdom never moves faster than the speed of relationships? Yes, you can enact change faster than that, but it may not be kingdom change. We live in a noisy world. So much information, and not much wisdom. Fake news and fake people. How do you know which words to believe? Who do you believe? You believe what's said by people who you know and trust. So as Christians, why do we think people who don't yet know and trust us will believe what we say, just because we say it really well?

Noise makes you move away from some-thing. Relationship draws you closer to a some-one. Noise helps us get things off our chest, which is good for us but maybe not so great for the rest of the world.

Do we long to just feel like we've done our duty or do we genuinely want to have real influence? If so, we need to do the hard yards of relationship-building. It may not be fast and it may not be pretty, but we will learn and be changed in the process, and it may just lead to moments when impossible and beautiful things cause everyone to stop and stare and say, 'There is a God.'

My major sphere of influence is politics. Politics is just people serving people and, for a Christian, nothing should be more natural. I write this from within the Houses of Parliament in full knowledge of expenses scandals, Westminster elitism and liberalism running riot, so my glasses are not rose-tinted; this is not naive dreaming, but genuine vision. God has promised to redeem and restore all of creation, and politics is merely the way we organize ourselves in the midst of it. God's perfection *is* the future. It will happen. The only question is how soon. You can be certain that we're the ones who will be the limiting factor, not God. Yet we have the privilege of being partners with him in his project of 'making all things new'.[10]

In the next decade I see churches everywhere becoming more missional in their DNA. People continually serving their communities. Understanding that this is a vital part of the discipleship deal, rather than a fun summer extra. Engaging with friends and community, even to the point where it breaks our hearts and forces us to our knees. Highlighting where broken lives are a product of a broken society, so action is required not simply to mend individual lives, but to mend the context in which they attempt to grow.

Young people at the leading edge of an eschatological shift that has spread to the whole Church. Seeing themselves as partners in God's restoration and redemption of all things and agents of the Kingdom in the here and now. At gatherings people are commissioned to bring heaven on earth, rather than being cajoled into buying an escape ticket for heaven. They're ruthless in their desire for justice and righteousness to burst forth in schools, parks, youth clubs and the Internet. They refuse the old *either/or* of denominational or ecclesiological boundaries in favour of *both/and*. They are just as comfortable lobbying a supermarket to pay fair wages as they are praying for miraculous healings in the aisles of that supermarket. And just as comfortable speaking in the town hall as a local councillor as they are speaking in tongues in a brightly coloured prayer room.

For politics, that shift will come when people see *politics as mission*. When we put politics in the missional part of our brains and hearts. When we encourage, pray for, emulate, visit and support those in politics as we would a 'missionary'. We'll say that things changed when politics is presented as something exciting, countercultural and subversive rather than the maintenance of the 'establishment'. May there soon be a day when it is as normal for a Christian young person to be pursuing a life in politics, as it is for them to aspire to being a worship leader.

So become an influencer for the kingdom in whatever sphere you find yourself. Be part of helping others step closer to God's perfected future.

Notes

1 Henry Kissinger, www.brainyquote.com.

2 John Pritchard, *The Life and Work of a Priest* (London: SPCK, 2007).

3 Simon Sinek, *Leaders Eat Last: Why Some Teams Pull Together and Others Don't* (New York: Penguin, 2014).

4 2 Peter 3.13.

5 1 Corinthians 3.10–15.

6 John C. Maxwell, *The 21 Irrefutable Laws of Leadership* (Nashville, TN: Thomas Nelson, 2007), pp. 55–6.

7 James Lawrence, *Growing Leaders: Reflections on Leadership, Life and Jesus* (Abingdon: CPAS and The Bible Reading Fellowship, 2004), p. 90.

8 Lawrence, *Growing Leaders*, pp. 103–10.

9 1 Timothy 3.1–13.

10 Revelation 21.5.

Reflection

Joining the Dots

1 Corinthians 13.8–13

Love never fails. But where there are prophecies, they will cease; where there are tongues, they will be stilled; where there is knowledge, it will pass away. For we know in part and we prophesy in part, but when completeness comes, what is in part disappears. When I was a child, I talked like a child, I thought like a child, I reasoned like a child. When I became a man, I put the ways of childhood behind me. For now we see only a reflection as in a mirror; then we shall see face to face. Now I know in part; then I shall know fully, even as I am fully known.

And now these three remain: faith, hope and love. But the greatest of these is love.

Questions

1 In what ways has this chapter helped clarify your understanding of leadership?
2 Does theological depth bring convergence to seemingly opposed opinions about leadership? Has your own reaction towards, and definition of, leadership changed?
3 Can we see the ways the Kingdom is becoming more manifest within and around us and our freedom to operate within that?
4 Are there leadership concepts or models to which you could apply Hopeful Influence? Does Hopeful Influence sharpen your understanding of these?
5 Is there a link between the reductionist gospel seen in the recent European and American context and unbridled capitalism? If so, what needs to change?
6 Is leadership for all? Why?
7 Do you need to opt in, slow down or find more common ground on leadership?

Prayer

Father God, thank you that you are helping us to grow up in you. Thank you that you reveal yourself to us and the plans and purposes which you invite us into. Thank you that the closer we move towards you, the clearer we are able to see and the more the confusion of the world is overcome. Thank you for the invitation to join in with the advance of your kingdom; help us to be people who respond well to that invitation and help others join in too. Give us wisdom to know how to be better leaders and courage to follow your lead in the lives of others. In Jesus' name, amen.

PART THREE

How Might a Manifesto of Hopeful Influence Develop?

7

Church

If you have raced with men on foot and they have worn you out,
how can you compete with horses?
If you stumble in a safe country, how will you manage in the
thickets by the Jordan?
Jeremiah 12.5

At the church I'm part of, St James, we meet in a derelict Anglican building in the centre of Liverpool. At the time of writing, we're just in the
process of spending quite a lot of money fitting up the building with a
kitchen, toilets, entrance porch, interior refurbishments, external signage
and lighting. After six years of carrying every drop of water into church
before each service and removing every drop of whatever needs removing
from our composting toilet afterwards, it's an important step forward.
However, funds are limited, we can only do so much, and part of my role
is to keep us focused on the specific eschatological reasons for developing
the building and to help us navigate the conflicting priorities that flow
out of this.

The primary reason we are developing the building is to enable our
mission and ministry as a church family. Specifically for us, this means
we are trying to make the building more useable, and we want to let
people know what's happening by making ourselves more visible. There
are lots of things we want to do to the building that we can't do at this
moment in time. We need to repair the church tower. We'd like a floor
that won't break. Decent heating would be nice. The dilapidated galleries
need completely reworking. We'd like to restore the tower clock. To say
nothing of better facilities for our children's work. My job as a leader is
to help marshal our imagination around what is most important now,
and to help us navigate together the financially realistic set of next steps.

Of course I share this job with other leaders around me, and one of the
things we are currently debating as a team is whether we should include
one, or even two, disabled-access ramps. Of course we need the ramps,
every building should have disabled access, but where do they fit in the
wider set of priorities? We don't legally have to fit them. We do have
very limited disabled access already, which we currently use to enable
wheelchairs to get in, although it's awkward. Some organizations won't

use our building because the access isn't better, but the limited disabled access doesn't really affect our ability to grow as a church. The building is 250 years old and spent 40 years closed before we reopened it; we certainly can't do everything in this early phase of redevelopment. One day we will build the ramps – the question is: should we build them now?

I should also say that people have given very sacrificially to this project, and we have limited financial funds. We need to be very wise, certainly at this early stage in our church's life, in making sure our limited funds go primarily on things that will eventually lead to church growth, otherwise we may end up having to financially cut back on the main event of mission and ministry. In a slightly odd way the Church can function a bit like a business in that sense. The decision on whether to build access ramps is therefore a complex judgement call. We will certainly get a good price for the ramps if we do them now as part of the rest of the works, but we might be able to get a grant for the ramps in the future if we defer the works, which would mean we wouldn't have to spend our congregation's sacrificial giving on the work at all. What should we do? And equally, how does the decision-making, the application of power, work among us as a team to ensure all voices are heard but that we make the best decision for our shared future?

I find myself taken back to a moment among our church leaders when we prayed into the possibility of these works almost 18 months ago and dreamed together. At that time, those two important words emerged: usability and visibility. Anything outside of this may be really important, but isn't for now; no matter how politically correct or morally defendable the work might be. Together, and collective discernment is vital as we've seen, we need to decide whether the inclusion of the ramps is of a sufficient priority now within this framework of usability and visibility. If it isn't, then, as difficult a decision as it is, we can't do them. My leadership role up to the decision point has been to try and help our wider leadership team understand this context for making a decision. As I do this, I'm trying also to keep the discussion harmonious, conscious that disabled access is an issue that people can hold strong opinions on. In the final sway, we recognized as a group that the ramps would also double up as better access for pushchairs. We have one or two on Sundays, but we are also about to launch a ministry for families with pre-school children, and so the ramps would therefore serve as an important welcome to both people within and without the church family. In the end our decision was unanimous, but was it the right one? Only time will tell, but the increasing peace, unity and mutual positivity we had together as a leadership team has increased our confidence.

Hopeful Influence of the Church and the ordained leader

At the end of the second part of the book, we said that to understand the shape of Hopeful Influence within any sphere of life, we had to understand first the role that that particular sphere has to play within God's wider renewal of the world. In a sense, we need at least a summary grasp of the Hopeful Influence that each sphere of life offers within the wider spectrum of our shared life together. How does each sphere offer a lead to the other spheres of life as we journey back to God? The easiest place to start with this question is to look at the Church, because we did the bulk of this work in Chapter 4, principally by looking at the contribution of Lesslie Newbigin and the image of the Church as a worshipping community tasked with acting as a sign, instrument and foretaste of the Kingdom of God to the wider world. Within God's movement of renewal and re-creation, the Church is a pilgrim people who are tasked with stepping back into their God-given role to steward creation under the lordship of Jesus (part of becoming disciples) as well as drawing others into that movement of renewal (part of making disciples). This means that the Church has two particular functions of Hopeful Influence. First, towards itself, as fellow Christians help each other see, participate and experience the Kingdom as the redeemed people of God under the power of the spirit. Second, towards the world, as we call out to the rest of humanity and try and help them, in a variety of different ways, see, participate and experience life in a relationship with Jesus and as active agents within the Kingdom of God themselves. We remind people everywhere about the vision God calls us to; we help others join in and we celebrate with them as people experience it for themselves.

We've looked already at the contribution of Graham Tomlin's *The Widening Circle* as a means to unify some divergent thinking on the theology of ordained church leadership. It's worth revisiting this now as it will help us see the connection between the Hopeful Influence of the Church and Hopeful Influence for ordained leaders, and because we can also make some adjustments to this model with a better understanding of Christian leadership more generally. As we saw, in *The Widening Circle* Tomlin argued that humanity is a subset, or circle, within wider creation; the Church is a subset of humanity, and ordained church leadership can be understood to be a subset within the Church. Humanity, Church and ordained leadership all exercise outwards a different shape of priestly ministry, which Tomlin helpfully presents as different ministries of blessing. For Tomlin, there are widening circles of blessing whereby God's people extend blessing to the rest of humanity and then humanity as a whole extends blessing to the created order.[1] At the centre of this is a smaller circle of ordained leaders, which Tomlin argues is a priestly ministry within God's people, set apart to fulfil a ministry of blessing to the rest of God's people. The movement of blessing therefore essentially moves from church minister, to wider Church, to humanity and to the world; or through these widening concentric circles of blessing as Tomlin would picture it. As we've seen, this theological picture has appealed to Catholic and Protestant understanding alike, because it emphasizes the priesthood of all believers but it also locates ordained church leadership as having a unique priestly shape and function beautifully located within a much wider movement of God's blessing to the world. In introducing this picture, it is probably important to say that the ministry of blessing is about servanthood, so the fact that ordained leaders are at the centre describes their function to serve rather than implying an inflated sense of value – although the usual inappropriate temptations to elevate church leadership apply.

However, if we bring Tomlin's material into conversation with our picture of Hopeful Influence, then I think there are some specific things we need to say that give the picture an even clearer shape. Tomlin speaks of blessing: the blessings of God made manifest within the world. While he locates those blessings within Jesus, and even to an extent within humanity's movement back to God, he doesn't unpack the underlying meaning of blessing and very specifically he doesn't define it, as we have done, as a form of eschatological assistance in the journey of renewal towards and into the Kingdom. Even though Tomlin doesn't frame this in terms of Hopeful Influence, actually that is precisely what he is talking about. What the widening circles tell us is that the function of the ordained leader's ministry is to enable the wider Church to realize its own function of Hopeful Influence on humanity, such that we and the rest of humanity can exercise our Hopeful Influence on the world. Tomlin is right that the movement flows through the wider circles of blessing, but we have now located this blessing in the eschatological advance of the Kingdom: the blessing is the very activity of Hopeful Influence. This is illustrated in Figure 8.

This is an important picture showing how Christians and Christian ministers are to locate themselves in the world, and it's worth high-lighting some important implications. First, as well as being a Christian minister, I am also a Christian. Therefore, while the lion's share of my time might be given over to a priestly ministry of blessing to the Church, I am still called to exercise eschatological influence on the world through my status as a Christian person. That's another way of saying that being a Christian minister doesn't mean I abdicate personal responsibility for evangelism or service to others beyond the Church. Equally, as well as being a Christian minister and a Christian, I am also a human being. As such, I cannot abdicate my responsibility to exercise Hopeful Influence on

Figure 8: Tomlin's widening circles of blessing reframed within the movement of Hopeful Influence

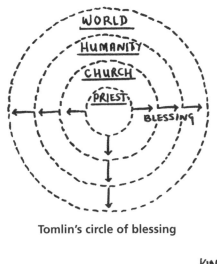

Tomlin's circle of blessing

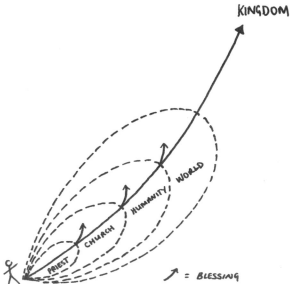

The circles of blessing, within the movement of Hopeful Influence

the wider creation, as well as my responsibility to exercise it on humanity and the Church.

Applying Hopeful Influence to Tomlin's widening-circle imagery has now helped us answer our earlier questions. We can say that the Church is meant to exercise a form of Hopeful Influence on the rest of humanity, such that humanity can move further towards the Kingdom of God. In addition, we can say that the Church, by virtue of its own humanity, is meant to exercise a form of Hopeful Influence on the rest of creation, but that it is meant to do this with, through and in partnership with the rest of humanity also. Third, the Church is meant to exercise a form of Hopeful Influence upon itself, as it journeys in community, a pilgrim people, into life under the lordship of Christ. Equally, locating the ministry of ordained leaders within this wider picture has made it clear that the Hopeful Influence of ordained leadership, and in a sense of all leadership within the Church, requires at least two strands to it. The first is to help other Christians travel faithfully towards the eschaton or, in language more in keeping with what we've said before, to inhabit the Kingdom of God with greater wholeness. The second is to equip the Church to help humanity and the rest of creation come more fully under the lordship of Jesus itself, which is what we've said above. This is the kind of Hopeful Influence that God wants the Church to exercise, and it's the context therefore through which all Christians within the Church make sense of their own forms of influence. The next thing to explore is how the activities of helping others see, participate and experience the Kingdom can take shape within this sphere.

See: imagining the future of the Church

One of the things that divides opinion in leadership, particularly church leadership, is when numbers are used to define vision. The first objection to the use of numbers is that we, very rightly, don't want to reduce the humanly rich, cosmic vision of God to numbers on a balance sheet. There is a huge danger to our culture as a Church if we start to reduce our ministry among human beings to the pursuit of numerical growth, yet some of us are perhaps a little quick to play the numbers game. The pastorally minded types are helpfully quick to call it out, but then they are accused of not thinking strategically. The question remains: should, and how, do we talk about ministry in terms of numbers, particularly aspirational numbers?

If numbers are used as a form of target (e.g. 'How many people might our church grow by this year?'), then another question emerges: where do the numbers come from? Did you pray as a group and God gave you the numbers? Is that how it works? It seems to me that there is a fairly significant division over the use of numbers within our church; people on both sides of the fence have important things to say, and applying our lens of Hopeful Influence can help us navigate through this division.

Let's take an example from within the Liverpool Diocese of which I'm part. As a diocese we are asking God for a bigger Church to make a bigger difference. At the time of writing, this breaks down into stated aims of seeing 1 person brought to church by every existing member; 10 acts of service per person; 100 new congregations; 1,000 new leaders and 10,000 new disciples. Numbers, numbers, numbers. Clearly this kind of approach appeals to some and not to others. While I didn't contribute to this vision statement, I can tell you pretty much where it came from. It didn't come from a hotline direct from God. But it did emerge from spiritual imagination, which, I believe, is precisely the kind that God invites church leaders into.

The backdrop is that our diocese has, for a while now, been very open about communicating the need for the Church to grow. Jesus called us to make disciples. Healthy things grow. The Church should, by definition, be growing. And so one very appropriate place for this to start is to encourage every person to invite one other person to church. It's almost the smallest starting point, but an important place to begin. So that's what we've done. Equally, a church that grows but that doesn't make a difference in the world is hardly a true expression of Church. In fact, the call to make a difference is in many ways a much more immediate and accessible call than plucking up the courage to invite someone; so a number of acts of service per person feels like an appropriate emphasis towards the *bigger difference* rather than the *bigger Church* part of our wider vision. We currently have a diocesan resourcing model geared around planting new congregations, which is part of the means by which we aim to grow the whole Church in our region, and coupled to this are some plans around larger church renewal and church planting. The sky is the limit on how many congregations and churches we might plant, but there is a sense of a specific number of opportunities in the immediate future and 100 happens to represent an achievable target over the next few years. In addition to resourcing these new plants and the widening opportunities for growth within existing churches, we will require more leaders. Each congregation will need one or more leaders, and the wider Church, if it is growing as planned, will need more leaders too. As a diocese we have good pathways for equipping lay and ordained missional church leaders and, while the answer won't be exactly 1,000 as one imagines the future, this number feels well aligned with the rest of the vision. As a final aim, which is the resultant growth in the Church, if the other numbers come close to being realized then the ambitious target of 10,000 new disciples suddenly doesn't seem that far off.

Now, no one in their right mind is saying that we can identify precisely the number of new disciples, leaders, congregations, acts of service or guests at our services even for next month, let alone over the next five to ten years. What happens though is that our core group of leaders, for each of these aspirations, engages in an appropriate sense of godly imagination. Not necessarily looking for a *thus saith the Lord* moment, but instead trying to discern together a sense of where we are now, what the future might hold, and what might be the appropriate *next steps* towards this over a five- or ten-year view. When the core team within the diocese allowed their shared imaginations to run, they arrived at numbers that felt exciting, informed and appropriate and they began to see a fairly memorable and easy way of communicating the vision numerically. One option is to relegate it all to human fancy, as if to imply that unless God gave those numbers in some rapturous moment of encounter then they can't be trusted. Another option is to see behind the figures to the work-ings of the Spirit among church leaders operating in a particular context, and to see the exciting possibilities that emerge out of our current reality and that God has entrusted our leaders to call us into. The second option seems much more akin to the Hopeful Influence that I'm advocating.

There are some caveats though. There are expressions of Church – networks and movements within the Church – that have caught on to the power of our imaginations, but are too quick to apply it without using the anchor points that I laid out in Chapter 5. Our imagination needs to be marshalled by a biblically informed vision of the world. Our imagination needs to be carefully handled so we avoid unhelpful over- or under-realized eschatological imaginings. Our imagination also needs to be communally discerned. I've certainly sat in Christian conferences where I've simply been invited to dream without much attention to any of these anchor points, and I think to that end we need to be very careful. We run the risk of descending into fairyland or entertaining subjective projections of what we alone think is right. Equally, there will always be those who feel disconnected from a leader's vision. There are people in our diocese who feel, from their own experience, that the diocesan vision has little or no resonance in their own context, and they might not be wrong. There will always be local contexts of life and ministry where the challenges are very different from the bigger picture within which we are located, and I'm not suggesting we all necessarily try and squeeze our contexts to fit with the larger whole. But despite these and other caveats, let's keep imagining, keep casting vision and let's not be afraid to be specific – even when it includes numbers.

Participate: accountable power as an expression of Hopeful Influence

Another aspect of leadership within the Church that is worth reflecting on is how well we build accountability around the specific eschatological goals and personal integrity of positional leadership. This goes for every positional leadership role, but it's particularly important for the role of pastor, lead minister, vicar and so on. There may be accountability structures within the local church community, but these aren't always as effective as they could be, often because of Christian communities' propensity to be *nice* to each other, but also because of the myriad destructive ways that power is held and used, as we saw earlier. We don't tend to seek out the more challenging conversations, the power dynamics at work in any given context often dictate how things happen, and even when supportive structures exist, we don't always use them to implement accountability.

Take the Church of England as an example. Behind the historical obscurity of our naming conventions there is some good logic to the geographical construction of dioceses, archdeaconries, deaneries and parishes; similarly, the forms of governance alongside these like synods and chapters, and the roles such as bishop, archdeacon and area dean. Despite the antiquated terms, if these areas, structures and roles didn't exist we would probably invent them in very similar forms to how they currently exist. The question, though, is: how are these structures used to facilitate the good application of Hopeful Influence and, very specifically here, how do they enable accountability among the power holders in office to ensure that good application of Hopeful Influence is happening?

As an example, I have hardly ever seen performance reviews for vicars or other church leaders or leadership teams geared into these structures. We don't require a creatively discerned vision from our leaders; we don't require rigorous reflection on our response to that vision; we don't identify training or development opportunities when the vision seems to get away from us and we don't require changes in office when evidence suggests a leader isn't a good fit for the role they are in. And we certainly don't use a leadership paradigm like Hopeful Influence as a frame for how church leaders are meant to be operating, nor one within which we can locate appropriate forms of accountability. Having come from a commercial environment where this kind of accountability was normal, I have been surprised to see such an unwillingness to use it within the Church. It's also a great shame because, unlike the corporate world, the Church doesn't have to adopt simply growth, often the lowest common denominator, as its paradigm for successful leadership. We've got a lot more to say about successful leadership than that but, rather than creatively mapping an accountability process, we tend to duck it altogether. I do recognize the complexities though, particularly as I've got more used to the environment of full-time church ministry.

The first complexity is that church life is so broad that any objectives in ministry need to be set within a very informed view of the local context. The worst of managerialism is that we set top-down objectives through a chain of managers who don't fully understand the complexity of the roles that they oversee. Within commercial environments, that normally results in either a hire-and-fire culture or a high degree of tension between those in coal-face leadership roles and those above them in a managerial chain of command. You could imagine the frustration of a local minister, tasked with a growth objective for their church completely out of sync with the particular pastoral needs of the community. Any objectives need to be brokered sensibly within the Church as well as beyond it.

Another complexity is the extent to which a minister's life is tied into their parish in a way that is fundamentally different from most commercial roles. Most ministers will have moved into their parish. Perhaps their children now go to a local school. Their partner may have changed jobs and found employment locally when they took up the role. This isn't the kind of family upheaval that normally goes alongside a change of employment. Most people live in a geographical region and will be open to job changes within that region that won't necessitate moving home. Structures of ministerial accountability need to factor this in. People need to be given time to work out realistic objectives, and then time to gauge whether they are the right person to fulfil them. Moving people out of roles needs to be done carefully, with much greater awareness and respect for the family situation than in a normal commercial situation. These are all good reasons to protect ministers in their roles, for an appropriate period of time at least, but they aren't reasons to avoid accountability and the benefits to all of moving someone on into a post more suited to them.

The third complexity relates to the existing culture within the Church of England and certain assumptions about the implicit authority of the local minister. We have been used to ministers exercising a huge amount of autonomy, which appeals to the human condition in potentially dangerous ways, as we've already explored. Quite frankly, we just aren't very open to harder forms of accountability and so we resist them. We don't prepare ministers for accountability in their training; we don't utilize our existing structures to facilitate it and we don't help ministers to critically reflect on their own abilities enough. We also get confused between a person's calling to ministry more generally and their effectiveness in a specific context; we should be able to differentiate between these. Generally speaking, our autonomy as leaders has made us too defended to engage with a more challenging accountability framework.

As we look to the future of ordained leadership and the facilitation of Hopeful Influence within that role, we need forms of accountability that will ensure ministers are fulfilling the role that they have been given and that is right for them. However, as we do that we need to be mindful of the peculiarities of the minister's role and the ways in which managerialism can undermine both the complexities of the role and the committed, incarnational nature of it. Equally though, we need to find ways of resetting a culture of excessive autonomy and protectionism. This is part of what it means to marshal the power required to help local churches participate in the renewal of the world to which they are called.

Experience: playing in Church

My wife Hannah was recently appointed as the Anglican chaplain to two of Liverpool's universities. As part of her role she oversees two part-time chaplaincy assistants who, in an interesting ministerial experiment, also happen to be students at the two different universities. When Hannah was appointed, we talked about how to start the role and the kinds of things that needed to be communicated within the team. We talked at length about vision, what the team was trying to achieve and how it might do that. We talked about the challenges of working with two staff members who were undergraduates and the structures that might help to ensure they were productive and fruitful. Hannah was excited about the future and I was glad to be working with her and encouraged that my experience of leading a church with a large and growing student community was helpful in the formation of how she understood her role. I was a bit surprised, then, when the first thing she did with her team, instead of outlining vision, strategy and terms of reference, was to take them bowling. What had she understood about leadership that I can easily miss? Her basic assumption that travelling well together means prioritizing fun and making space for investment in relationships isn't always at the forefront of our leadership thinking.

In some ways, this relates quite closely to my whole experience of doing church. As I've shared, I had a very powerful experience of God in my early twenties which has gone on to shape my whole life and direction. I know that Jesus is good news to everyone and I know that Jesus' followers are meant to gather and do life together in a committed way. However, if I'm honest, it's taken me many years to actually enjoy the experience of Church, particularly the experience of gathered Church on Sundays or during the week. Part of this, I'm sure, is to do with forms of Church that don't resonate well with my personality. I've often felt too passive in church. Some expressions of Church can feel like a damp attempt to offer meaning and fulfilment. I'd rather be climbing a mountain, kicking a football around or down the pub. But there's something else as well. In my desire to follow Jesus faithfully, I can dangerously turn godly obedience into doing what I think others think I should be doing. In specific practical terms, I can turn *going to church* from having fun with God and my friends into a form of slightly cold, religious duty. I now, in a slightly ironic sense, find myself as a church leader called to help others reimagine Church for the next generation. Enjoying Church, really enjoying the experience of gathered Church, is something I am on a journey with, and that I think is central to the challenge of leadership within the Church in my wider cultural context. How do we play well together? In our church experiences, this seems to be a vital question to answer in responding to that challenge.

For the first six years or so of ordained ministry, I had the privilege of working under a remarkable church leader-evangelist. Someone who was passionate about sharing their faith with others, and who consistently, year on year, led people to Jesus. I also have a calling to evangelism, and I was encouraged and challenged by their fruitfulness. We would talk about the best strategies for evangelism. The merits of different Explorer courses. How to equip the other evangelists in our church. How to equip the whole Church for an invitational culture and to share our testimonies with friends and family. It was an inspiring partnership from which I learned much. One question sticks out in my mind though from all that zeal and talk between two fellow evangelists: what's the most essential thing for a church to grow? I knew my own thoughts – what would my colleague have to offer? 'Well, that's easy,' he said, 'we just have more fun than anybody else.' What a remarkable observation from someone with decades of ministry experience behind them and a natural inclination to emphasize overt forms of evangelism. Does our theology stretch that far? Do we know the kind of life God wants us to inhabit? Are our expressions of Church enablers to that? Outposts of that? Constantly evolving playgrounds informed by a deep theology of what it means to experience the Kingdom of God today? These are some of the questions that Hopeful Influencers within the Church are grappling with today.

Towards a manifesto for Hopeful Influence in the Church

So we have said that the Church has a unique role in offering Hopeful Influence both to itself and also towards the rest of humanity. Leadership within the Church needs to reflect this and this seems to resonate with the kind of language the New Testament uses in its different leadership functions. Apostle, prophet, evangelist, pastor and teacher[2] could all be thought of as different applications of this kind of leadership, as the Church imagines and discerns the future world towards which we head, equips itself for our involvement in that and as we help others locate themselves under the lordship of Jesus and experience life in a renewed sense.

The Church, then, should function as a hotbed for Hopeful Influence. Creative imagination about the future and ours and others' roles in it should be normal. This can take the form of vibrant, ambitious and clearly defined goals within church life, of course including the use of numbers. It also needs to find forms where the Church speaks out to people everywhere about the possibilities for our shared future, and where imagination and creativity are sparked in others to grasp where God is calling us.

Throughout our church communities there needs to be an acknowledged sense that we are here to participate in the renewal of the world, and we need to take a lead in equipping ourselves and those beyond the Church for this purpose. Within the Church this manifests, in part, through clearer accountability around suitability and performance for those in leadership positions. To this end, Hopeful Influence offers an alternative to the simplistic metrics often used to evaluate that. Much broader than that though, having cast a vision of the future, the Church is called to create space for others to find their active place in God's work of renewal. This requires leadership that will step aside, that won't coerce and that can remain optimistic and upbeat despite the limitations of the present.

Finally, church communities are places where we must find life. Despite the temptation to reduce our existence to activity, and despite the temptation to translate obedience into passive conformity, we need to be a people who have the experience of full-life front and centre. More than that, we need to be a people who allow the shape of life that we enjoy to be informed by the pages of the New Testament, the conviction that the spirit brings, and challenged and affirmed by those in community around us. As we hold all these things together, and help others embrace them more fully, we will be a people who exercise the Hopeful Influence to which we are called.

Comment
Rt Revd Ric Thorpe, Bishop of Islington

When we were invited to lead a church plant into the East End of London, we went with so much more than a vision to see a church come back to life. We went with a vision to see the wider Church flourish. In 2005, the Bishop of London invited me and my family to lead a team from Holy Trinity Brompton to revitalize the about-to-close St Paul's Shadwell, Tower Hamlets. We went with a group of 100 people, most already living in the area, but some moving house and relocating from West London. It was a generous and sacrificial gesture from Holy Trinity Brompton, giving away leaders, people and funding. But they also embedded within us a bigger vision of how God saw the Church as a united, beautiful, generous and loving Church that was called to serve the local area with the good news of Jesus Christ.

We worked hard to partner with other churches in the Anglican deanery, across differences of tradition and practice, as well as churches in other denominations. We did this because on our own we could do very little, but together we could do so much more. And our diversity did not need to be a problem, but rather a blessing so that even more people could be reached in diverse ways.

Within a few years, we had the chance to send leaders, teams and funding of our own to revitalize other churches in the borough. We knew we wanted to stay in touch with each other and we knew we did not want to lose the friendships, fellowship and enormous skills that each of those leaders had to offer. So we set up a monthly learning community so that we could encourage each other, learn from each other and pray for each other. Each of the church leaders brought their own leadership teams and we created a very flat environment where we could both teach and learn from each other. Our values of audacity, generosity, humility and unity worked themselves out in this new network of churches and we were so much the stronger as a result. We saw meeting together not just as a way of adding up best practice, but of multiplying ministries and opportunities. Together was so much more fun than doing it alone!

Leading in this way – by giving away power to enable others to flourish – led to new gifts being discovered, more leaders emerging and our churches being far more effective than they would have been alone. That network continues to meet years after we moved into a new role. There is strength by doing it together.

In my new role, as Bishop of Islington, my remit now stretches across the London Diocese and across England, where I am responsible for encouraging church planting – the starting or revitalizing of churches – in the Church of England. I have brought those same values of audacity, generosity, humility and unity in a more strategic way. We are seeing an extraordinary movement emerging of courageous, pioneering, creative leaders who love the ancient Church of England but who want to 'do church' in new ways, reaching new people in new places. And as they plant, we are encouraging them into new learning communities to share their learning and strengthen their churches as a result.

These learning communities bridge across existing networks, forming an even stronger lattice of relationships and learning experiences like a national web. This in turn is showing us that networks have a huge part to play in supporting and developing churches and planting new ones, and we need many more networks across the whole Church. I find myself encouraging new networks to start where there are none, and existing networks being introduced to others so that learning across differences becomes rich and generous. Fear of difference isolates and divides; confidence of identity with a generous spirit unites, strengthens and diversifies.

This kind of thinking needs to be led top-down so that it is seen and invested in in order that the whole organism can thrive. This is the great opportunity we have to bring when we are appointed and invited to lead. We can encourage those around us to find a common mission and to face that mission in an outward way, so we stand shoulder to shoulder, rather than facing each other acutely aware of our differences. Side by side, we realize difference is an asset and learning from others a strength.

So we need leaders with these visionary values working deeply through us in order that the whole Church can thrive. I continue to reflect on how these values work in my own life so that I can encourage them to be worked out across the whole Church. Imagine a Church that has audacious Kingdom-minded and God-sized goals; a Church that is generous inside and out, giving away the gospel and planting new communities by giving away their best; a Church that is humble, honouring difference and preferring others; and a Church that is united across that diversity, enjoying being together in teams and learning communities; and all for the glory of God! How could the Church not impact the world?

Notes

1 Graham Tomlin, *The Widening Circle: Priesthood as God's Way of Blessing the World* (London: SPCK, 2015), p. 143.
2 Ephesians 4.11.

Reflection

Fruitfulness

John 15.1–8

'I am the true vine, and my Father is the gardener. He cuts off every branch in me that bears no fruit, while every branch that does bear fruit he prunes so that it will be even more fruitful. You are already clean because of the word I have spoken to you. Remain in me, as I also remain in you. No branch can bear fruit by itself; it must remain in the vine. Neither can you bear fruit unless you remain in me.

'I am the vine; you are the branches. If you remain in me and I in you, you will bear much fruit; apart from me you can do nothing. If you do not remain in me, you are like a branch that is thrown away and withers; such branches are picked up, thrown into the fire and burned. If you remain in me and my words remain in you, ask whatever you wish, and it will be done for you. This is to my Father's glory, that you bear much fruit, showing yourselves to be my disciples.'

Questions

1 In what ways does this chapter resonate with your own experience and observations of leadership in the Church?
2 Does Hopeful Influence help sharpen some of the activities of blessing that we saw in Tomlin's *The Widening Circle*? Does the diagram adjustment help?
3 What are some of the distinctive forms of influence that the Church needs to exercise on the world and itself?
4 How might your church, or the ministries of which you're part, signpost the Kingdom of God more effectively? How do we dream together?
5 How might your church, or ministries of which you're part, help others participate more in the Kingdom of God? How can we share power better?
6 How might your church, or ministries of which you're part, help others to experience the Kingdom of God more fully? How do we have more fun together?

7 How might your church be a place where the Hopeful Influence of everyone is nurtured and developed?

Prayer

Father God, thank you that you are the perfect gardener. Thank you that, in Christ, we are part of the true vine of life and love. Teach your Church afresh how to exercise true leadership, both in the world and within itself. Help us to be a people who dream well, include and empower others and step together into your Kingdom life today. Help us to remain in you and to bear much fruit for you. By the power of the Spirit and in the name of Jesus, we ask it. Amen.

8

Politics

Power, in a nutshell, is the ability to get things done,
and politics is the ability to decide which things need to be done.
Zygmunt Bauman (1925–2017)[1]

At the time of writing, the British government is locked in uncertainty around Brexit. It's a huge political moment and one that goes far beyond the analysis that this book can offer. However, I think there are at least three areas of leadership failure that have categorized the Brexit political process and one area of tremendous leadership opportunity that hasn't been particularly well recognized.

First, there has been a poverty of vision. In the build-up to the referendum, neither the Remain nor the Leave camps mapped out, in a positive sense, what life could be like if they were successful. There was a real failure of positive imagination in the presentation of the cases for both sides, and neither side evoked the kind of inspirational, hopeful vision of the future that was required to win the day convincingly. Admittedly the sensationalist, profit-driven media channels are always more interested in presenting bad news, so perhaps it wasn't entirely the politicians' fault, but it was insufficiently positive all the same. Perhaps because of this, and certainly related to it, a second failure has been both sides' preferred use of the politics of fear to develop support for their cause. For the Leave campaign, this tended to involve imagery around the threat of unmanaged immigration, the financial cost to the British taxpayer of being in the EU as well as an undermining of national identity through political rule and oversight from Brussels. For the Remain campaign, this was typically portrayed as our inability to function in a more isolated and autonomous state away from our nearest neighbours and the impending economic crisis that would result if we decided to go that way. Almost certainly, neither of the bleak pictures presented by either campaign are true. The third failure has been the inability to work out, both before the referendum and certainly after it, the appropriate shape that Brexit should take. The referendum was unclear on this and the political infighting after the result has been intense and damaging. Up to this moment, there is still no consensus on what Brexit will involve.

These areas of failure are in some sense failures of the different roles that the political arena is meant to fulfil. As we've touched on already and will continue to explore, the political arena is meant to be a breeding ground of positive, creative ideas about our future where vision is birthed and shaped. It is also meant to be a space for helpful and informative discussion which appeals to the best human aspirations and values. Finally it is also the place where that vision, after robust discussion, can be fleshed out and ultimately agreed and applied. At all these levels, on the Brexit debate at least, the British political system has fallen far short of its duty to the electorate.

However, there is also a tremendous leadership opportunity. If we can get our heads up for long enough to see the current crisis amid its historical and contemporary backdrop, what we find, I think, are long-held tensions around local versus global identity and a degree of confusion about the best political structures to navigate these tensions. If the challenges of Brexit – with all the underlying issues of national identity, immigration, international governance and trade – were being worked out in a more volatile and polarized country than the UK, then the likely outcome would probably be an unhealthy mix of violence, increased prejudice and economic collapse. However, with all our heritage, and I unashamedly also say all of our Christian heritage, the very fact that these deep questions that hang over much of the world, and which in many ways will determine our global future together, are being worked out in a significant way in the UK gives me cause to hope. Because of our Christian heritage I want to say that, in all sorts of interesting ways, being British has always included having the potential to lead. It's the same in this case too. And before this sounds triumphalist, this fundamentally means of course that we have the potential to serve the wider world in sacrificial ways through that leadership. Before this particular Brexit story is complete, amid the confusion and the easy critique, perhaps we will have offered other nations some Hopeful Influence on how to navigate these important tensions.

Hopeful Influence in politics

As with the other spheres of life, understanding the role politics has to play within wider society as we journey into God's renewal of the world is the vital starting place; we therefore need to understand the kind of Hopeful Influence that the political sphere has to offer. As we said in Chapter 2, politics is about marshalling social partnerships that lead to the greatest common good: creating space for discourse to decide the shapes our shared life will take and then marshalling power to achieve them. The goal of Hopeful Influence in politics is therefore about the establishment of policies and structures that enable a shared, societal, movement towards a better future. It's a sphere that has been given a particular mandate to broker imagination for our collective future, enable steps to realize it and to ensure that members of society have sufficient opportunity to pause for breath and enjoy the world we are creating. The important point, at least in the UK, is that we have a political structure that has been geared around social and economic renewal and that attempts to be representative of the wider society with clear limits around any individual's use of power.

In a liberal democracy like that of the UK, which of course emerged out of a predominantly Christianized society, Christians have a voice at the table to contribute to these goals like every other person. In truth, because of our history, we also have recognized privilege, primarily through the established Anglican Church, because we have a long history of winning the argument that followers of Jesus are good for society and that our perspective often brings great value within the political debate. However, conversely, we are also on the back foot in contemporary times, because we're perceived as being overly traditional on some social issues, we haven't morally kept our own house in order, and because we are a community consistently declining in number. The Church as a political force doesn't have the relevance or credibility of previous generations. But any Christian can be at the table and, when we leverage our privilege appropriately, we can speak with a loud voice. These facts are important for Christians wanting to serve in political leadership. Whether you're an MP serving your constituency or holding a particular brief; whether in the House of Lords or in the civil service; whether in local government or working for a government agency, you somehow fit within this larger brief for wider societal movement into a renewed quality of life.

Political people, and certainly Christians working in politics, are invested with power to make changes, and their service is meant to be towards all citizens and institutions of the land. This is the big end in mind: the purpose they serve. Christians in politics therefore need to continually bring their work activity into conversation with a truly Kingdom-of-God-shaped vision of renewal. Let's consider some examples of this and how we help others to see, participate and experience the Kingdom as agents of a political structure tasked with facilitating societal movement.

See: the imagination of Hopeful Influence in British politics

Let's begin by thinking about the application of imagination. We've made the theological case for imagination and discernment to be the starting place for a leader's influence, but how does it play it out in practice?

Well, every local councillor, city mayor and MP that I've spoken to has suggested that a disproportionately small amount of their time is actually spent on imagining the future. Instead of brokering long-term transformational plans with communities, businesses and local stakeholders, most local political leaders are unnecessarily bogged down in small-scale problem-resolution, essentially firefighting issues of malaise in their communities, often raised by people with the loudest voice. Of course, good MPs and councillors will have a sense of diligence and personal justice to help steer them towards the issues of greatest need, but there is a strong sense in which the institutions of political leadership haven't been geared adequately to enable strategic vision and planning. In practice, key decisions on employment, education and local infrastructure seem to happen as a result of wider socio-economic factors, sometimes purely market driven or taken by centralized government away from the coal face, and often haven't been sufficiently tested with residents and the wider set of local stakeholders.

In addition to this, the lack of spiritual or moral consensus, and the slightly vacuous nature of our current expression of secular multiculturalism, make identifying the strategic steps towards human flourishing more difficult. We need to work much harder to broker relationships of trust and mutual understanding before we can journey together. This is worthy of a bit more comment, because it plays to the contemporary challenges of doing politics in a diverse society. There are probably some Christians who bemoan the lack of moral consensus and would prefer a form of theocracy, where Christians decide the wider moral framework and everything ripples down nicely from there. However, I am not arguing for that, and I don't believe that idea for the world gives sufficient weight to the autonomy and individuality that God has put in human hearts. Neither does it recognize the essential space that we need to create for free choice, supremely the free choice of loving God and our neighbour that God wants to foster in all people. Society can't be forced to live well; we need to choose it through forums of debate that allow everyone to play their part, which is both extremely risky yet also a remarkable opportunity for the wider Church.

Therefore, I am not arguing that Christians should have de facto privilege in having our voice heard, but each generation can earn forms of political privilege through our service and good citizenship within wider society. Nor am I arguing that contributors from other faiths and none shouldn't be able to bring their philosophical or religiously informed visions of the future to the table either. We need their voices, and sometimes they see things that an occasionally muddled Church does not. Fortunately, because of its Christian heritage, secularism understands the vitality and beauty of diversity amid our common identity of citizenship. Confident and wise forms of secularism also understand that people will disagree about the future but that the process of disagreement can be healthy and, marshalled well, will ultimately lead to a better future. This in many ways creates fresh opportunity for the sensible Christian to contribute.

For Christians in politics to play their visionary part in transforming society, we need to win the confidence afresh of the secular power holders. This is probably easier than it sounds, in part because we just need to get a bit better at telling positive stories of the Church's contribution, which is huge, in a language the world understands. We also need to be exemplar models of the boundaries of power and sexual propriety among people who often aren't. Equally, we need to be able to say sorry and move on when our historical misreading of Scripture paved the way to injustice. The rights of women and the treatment of people with same-sex attraction are two areas where our theological understanding and pastoral care got stuck in under-developed theology and practice. As a final appeal, the established Church, of which I am part, has had a shockingly poor connection with the rhythm and pulse of contemporary culture: outdated forms of music, language, style and tone going hand in hand with quasi-religious forms of human moralism. While the ability to address these issues may lie more with church leaders than with political leaders, Christians in politics need to help the Church understand how its wider witness plays into the political landscape.

Amid all this complex landscape of challenge and opportunity, Christians in politics need to be people who consistently dream of a better future and who encourage others to do the same. In the city where I live, there is enough energy in the local tidal estuary to power the surrounding urban area many times over. In the homes of this city there are migrant people who haven't been allowed to work in this country for years. On the roads in our city, there are damaging levels of pollution that could have been countered ten years ago, let alone today. On the streets of our city are homeless drug addicts to whom we give unfettered freedom and choice without the intervention that could save and change lives for ever. In some schools, a small number of children aren't given the specialist education and wider social care they need to enable them and the rest of the class to flourish to its true potential, thereby reducing future GDP by millions to say nothing of the infinitely more important human value. The solutions to these challenges aren't easy, but may Christians in politics be a confident people who believe that spirit-inspired dreams are the birthplace of tomorrow's reality.

Participate: hard and soft power in local government

If imagination is the beginning of Kingdom change, then of course Hopeful Influencers need to affect change by enabling others to participate. Once a vision begins to emerge, there is the brokering of conversation, the corporate exploration of how to move forwards, and the implementation of that movement. For a more light-hearted way into this, consider our relationship to the seagull. Now I love family holidays, and family holidays close to the sea are, for me, the best. Over the past few years we've spent quite a bit of our summer time on the north Cornish coast, in Pembrokeshire and southern Ireland. I don't need to get on a plane: I love it here. But one of the things that troubles me is when it's clear that those blessed seagulls rule the roost. You're walking on the prom, enjoying eating ice cream with your infant son or daughter when all of a sudden, if you're not careful, those aerial monsters circle and take that scoop of creamy delight right out of your hand.

So what should the leaders in local government do? Cull them? Well, let's first imagine the future world. Will those rogue seagulls make it into the world to come, or will they perish in the lake of fire? Well, I wouldn't want to comment on the personal salvation of any specific seagull (although I can think of at least one that is perilously close to missing out), but I do want to say that as part of God's creation there is no reason why the new heavens and the new earth will not have plenty of space for redeemed seagulls, as well as redeemed cats, dogs, hamsters and every other living thing for that matter. That will hopefully have been clear from the theology laid out earlier in the book. But I strongly suspect that in a redeemed creation the seagulls' natural habitat will be out over the sea, not pilfering from humans or being reduced to scavengers in an urban environment. That second bit, frankly, is more of our doing. Going for an early morning run in a seaside town, which I've done many a time, reveals the extent of rubbish that we leave out. No wonder so many seagulls loiter with intent – we've unhelpfully developed an unnatural feeding ground for these opportunists. Fair play, one might say, to that rogue seagull who spurns the rubbish, and has the courage to follow their natural instincts to catch an ice-cold treasure from the hand of an unsuspecting tourist.

So the seagulls are in the wrong place, eating the wrong food, and would be much better off moved out into their more natural environment. As stewards of the world, and specifically as stewards of that picturesque little village by the sea, we are surely entitled to take measures to discourage the birds from their greed and lethargy and get them to take flight to more appropriate parts. However, if we cull the birds, we might get some short-term gains, but have we really moved the situation forwards eschatologically? Next summer a different crop of birds will be back, unless we also take action on the street pollution that draws them in such numbers. A cull is only legitimate if we combine it with better steward-ship of our mess. Measures to improve street bins and commercial and residential garbage storage and collection. Fines for people violating the measures. Signs discouraging the feeding of seagulls. Even perhaps a food disposal area out of town to draw the birds away if a temporary diversion is required. Think of that as a benefits system for those birds unable to fish as successfully. Only once we've reordered the structural deficiencies that led to the problem in the first place can we legitimately authorize the culling – although perhaps by that point we'll find we don't have to?

The real point here is about navigating pathways into the future that recognize the holistic connection between different aspects of our shared society. It's about understanding cause and effect and making an unbiased assessment on our own contribution to the current poverty of the world. It's about drawing people together to take concerted action against something that is wrong. And it may also be about making tough choices to forcefully take us into a better future. These are some of the shapes Hopeful Influence needs to take as we help others participate in the political renewal that we seek.

Experience: truly helping people live better

And as well as helping people participate in the coming Kingdom, we help people experience it. That, I suppose, is the goal of all good politics. We want to shape our society so that people everywhere experience the best quality of life. That is why we serve, and that is why forms of politics that seem to be more about the aggrandizement and to the benefit of the political class make so many of the public angry and disenchanted with government. All attempts to signpost and enable others to participate in change will ultimately be judged on how that change becomes manifest in people's lives. That's why politicians need a rigorous understanding of what is indeed good for people and what human flourishing genuinely looks like.

It would seem appropriate at this point to make some reference to the benefits system, and how government provides for people who aren't able to participate in normal working life. While I realize I am venturing into highly politicized territory, I must say that I am tremendously proud of our welfare system in this country. Of course, it's rightly open to constant critique, and as political priorities shift there are sometimes mistakes and appalling injustices, but the notion that society will provide financial support for you if you are too sick to work, need to take time off to have a family, are made redundant, or simply don't have the qualifications or experience to get a job is a wonderful thing. It speaks of the worth and importance of every human being despite our current contribution. Society needs you and, if work isn't an option, society should extend an arm to help.

However, we do seem to have brokered a slightly odd framework for assessing people's eligibility for state support and the levels of provision therein. One particular critique is that we haven't gone far enough in encouraging people who aren't able to participate in regular employment to find other ways to participate in society as a whole. When speaking into a community that had a problem with idleness and sloth, the apostle Paul wrote that 'The one who is unwilling to work shall not eat.'[2] Now, as with all Bible interpretation, context is key and Paul is applying a well-known phrase of the time to a particular problem that was arising within a Christian community. Clearly this isn't a phrase to apply en masse to all people unable to work for a variety of good and valid reasons. Nor, perhaps, is it fully conclusive that an implication is that lazy people shouldn't receive any state benefits at all. Set alongside this verse is the wonderful truth that sun and rain are made available to all within God's economy,[3] and perhaps it is part of God's generosity that even those who refuse to contribute positively to society should still reap some harvest from it.

However, I think we can still learn something very important from this phrase about how society looks after those unable to contribute within the particular state-market economy of the day. Working in the most general sense – not being idle and having some contribution to make within the wider whole – is a really important part of what it means to be human. How unimaginative to create a benefits system where people can just rock up for a hand out. What a complete misunderstanding of the human condition. What a strange, peculiarly liberal, idea that this could ever be an expression of true love or generosity, or even indeed be helpful to those who know they are made for something more. What if, instead, the state created a smart framework, with businesses and the third sector, to enable people to volunteer in a wide varieties of ways that contributed to the common good? What if people could gain experience, learn new skills, develop social awareness, show employability and get a great reference through coordinated volunteering? How much economic benefit might this bring in the long term? How much easier might it make the discussion over taxation levels if the higher earners knew that the vast majority of benefits support went on adding value to society as a whole? What unifying potential might initiatives like this bring to a strangely fractured electorate? It can't be done, say the sceptics. With theological and social clarity, the permission to dream and the growing power of technology, what cannot be done? Hopeful Influencers in politics will be burdened by the desire for greater human experience, and will be able to think creatively and act collaboratively to achieve these goals.

Towards a manifesto for Hopeful Influence in politics

So we've outlined the sphere of politics as a place that facilitates social partnerships, creates space for public discourse and marshals power to achieve change. Into this theologically informed picture, we've said that Christians in politics are called particularly to help our shared societal journey keep on track with God's renewal of the world, and that to achieve this we need to do a whole load of politically smart things to help others see, participate and experience the Kingdom.

Within the contemporary British political system that task is perhaps harder than it should be, but Christians within politics do have remarkable resources, not least historical, to draw on. While current structures don't necessarily help, restricting the space to imagine and discern the future, we do need to have confidence in presenting a Christian understanding of human society as something life enhancing. We need to be much more creative and theologically informed in the solutions we propose, and we need to be braver in speaking truth to power when the needs demand it. We need to have a theology of personhood and particularly human flourishing, and we need to translate this into a language the world understands. Alongside all this, we should be structurally agile and seek to renew the forms of political power to marshal the complex environment in which we live.

Finally, we need to retain our optimism, even amid the darkest human challenges. Perhaps it is in this sphere more than any other that we need to remember and stand firm on the promises of God. There are times when the tempestuous waters of human society rise up in the most fearful ways, but it will not always be like this, and even in the most explosive moments, God has put limits around those negative forces. The more Hopeful Influencers speak justice, fairness, compassion, opportunity, generosity and peace on the different platforms they occupy, and the more they translate these values into practical, sustainable, embodied experiences, then the more human souls across our lands will experience something of the light. These are the great goals of human development before us. It is a battle that will be won. And we need theologically informed Christians at the centre of our political structures working to make this a reality.

Comment
Stephen Timms, Labour MP, East Ham

Tom Wright has observed that 'people who believe in the resurrection, in God making a whole new world in which everything will be set right at last, are unstoppably motivated to work for that new world in the present.'[4] We need that kind of motivation to be influencing politics, as people who believe in Christ reflect it in their work. I want to reflect separately on three spheres of work that I undertake as MP: first, dealing with constituents who approach me for assistance; second, in making representations to the authorities on behalf of my community; and, third, in developing proposals for how our society should be governed.

Accepting the argument that Christian leadership happens when, through our influence, we help people see, participate and experience the coming Kingdom, it often strikes me how much scope there is for the exercise of Christian leadership in the first of these three spheres. I represent a community in the East End of London, and am approached continuously by constituents whose experience of officialdom is grim. Officials they encounter – perhaps through overwork – seem to have very little interest in what my constituents tell them, or in the problems that trouble them, and even less interest in trying to help. If the politician approached in those circumstances – often as a last resort – can at least be interested and attentive, and be seen to try to do something to help, even if ultimately the problem is not solved, it is remarkable how appreciative constituents will frequently be. I think that is an example of people whose everyday experience is of the absence of the Kingdom having instead an experience of it, and of being immensely appreciative, albeit that they will not usually attribute their positive experience to God's Kingdom.

In the second sphere, in making representations to the authorities on behalf of their community, Christian leadership can provide a quality of hope. The conviction that, ultimately, things that are clearly wrong today are going to be put right is a very hopeful conviction. It is one that Christians who believe in the coming Kingdom can hold, when others often can't. It means that representations which we make can be suffused by hopefulness – and, when they are, they exhibit Christian leadership.

In the late 1980s, I was chair of the planning committee in the area where I am now MP. I picked up a suggestion floated by what we then called British Rail, and started a campaign to bring to Stratford in East London a station on the planned high-speed rail link from London to the Channel Tunnel. It seemed a bit far-fetched – at the time, the rail line was planned to run south of the Thames rather than north. But the local community saw that, if we could achieve it, the station could bring new economic vitality to an area that had had the stuffing knocked out of it by de-industrialization in the early 1980s. It took over ten years for the campaign to succeed, but then it opened up the possibility for the UK's successful bid to host the 2012 Olympics, with the Olympic Stadium at Stratford, providing a powerful catalyst for the eastwards shift of London's centre of economic gravity which is under way at present.

In the third sphere, in developing proposals for how our society should be governed, the potential for the exercise of Christian leadership – to make changes that enable people to get a taste of the coming Kingdom – is readily apparent. The reality of delivering, however, is much harder. But we need Christians to be making the attempt. Among the institutions established by British governments, it is perhaps the National Health Service and its unconditional care and support that most strikingly provides a foretaste of the coming Kingdom. And that observation should encourage us that demonstrating Christian leadership in politics is not an impossible task.

Notes

1 Zygmunt Bauman, 'Politics, the Good Society and "Westphalian Sovereignty"', *Social Europe*, 25 May 2012.

2 2 Thessalonians 3.10.

3 Matthew 5.45–46.

4 Tom Wright, *Surprised by Hope* (London: SPCK, 2007), p. 226.

Reflection

Discussion, Power and Partnership

Mark 10.35–45

Then James and John, the sons of Zebedee, came to him. 'Teacher,' they said, 'we want you to do for us whatever we ask.'

'What do you want me to do for you?' he asked.

They replied, 'Let one of us sit at your right and the other at your left in your glory.'

'You don't know what you are asking,' Jesus said. 'Can you drink the cup I drink or be baptised with the baptism I am baptised with?'

'We can,' they answered.

Jesus said to them, 'You will drink the cup I drink and be baptised with the baptism I am baptised with, but to sit at my right or left is not for me to grant. These places belong to those for whom they have been prepared.'

When the ten heard about this, they became indignant with James and John. Jesus called them together and said, 'You know that those who are regarded as rulers of the Gentiles lord it over them, and their high officials exercise authority over them. Not so with you. Instead, whoever wants to become great among you must be your servant, and whoever wants to be first must be slave of all. For even the Son of Man did not come to be served, but to serve, and to give his life as a ransom for many.'

Questions

1 In what ways does this chapter resonate with your own experience and observations of leadership in politics?
2 Can you think of ways Hopeful Influence has been exercised to establish policies or structures that enable the Kingdom's advancement?
3 How would you describe the role of Christians in politics? Are there ways every Christian can contribute in this sphere?
4 How could you facilitate discussion on the conditions for greatest flourishing and wholeness in local or national politics? What biblically informed vision can you share?

5 How could you bring together stakeholders to make the best decisions about our shared future? What compromises might we need to make?

6 What partnerships need to be forged to get things done? How do we celebrate our collaborations and successes?

7 How can we encourage more Christians to be politically active?

Prayer

Father God, grant us a vision of your world as your love would have it: a world where the weak are protected, and none go hungry or poor; a world where the riches of creation are shared, and everyone can enjoy them; a world where different races and cultures live in harmony and mutual respect; a world where peace is built with justice, and justice is guided by love. Give us the inspiration and courage to build it, through Jesus Christ our Lord.

(Anon.)

9

Business

*Our society has come to see that a strategy to build shareholder
value, without a clear mission based on robust ethical values,
is a complete nonsense. In fact, it has proved one of the
fastest ways of destroying an entire global business.*
Patrick Dixon, Building a Better Business[1]

I lived in East London for most of my thirties and, alongside working as
a business consultant in the city, served part-time on the staff team of the
local church which I was part of. That season of my life was marked by
huge contrasts. In the borough of Tower Hamlets where I lived, a very
poor community was bordered by the city on one side, had the towers of
Canary Wharf to the other and was essentially surrounded by businesses
and people living in extreme affluence; mostly gated, out-of-reach and
well protected against the impoverished urban community on their doorstep. Within this community where I lived, among these great symbols
of wealth, were very high rates of child poverty and large-scale problems
around social integration and reduced opportunities for employment or
higher education. I can remember campaigning for affordable housing in
our local borough, hearing stories of families with five or more children
sharing a one- or two-bedroom flat, and then going into the office to
hear executives on six-figure salaries complaining about the amount of
tax they had to pay, and, from their isolated worlds, how unjust they
perceived the taxation system to be. I occupied the strange position of
inhabiting two very different worlds: close in proximity but forcefully
separated by human constructs of finance, education and power.

A few years into my time there, the global financial crisis of 2008 hit
and suddenly these seemingly invulnerable banks began to look shaky.
There were all sorts of contributing factors behind the strength of the
financial crisis, but for many, it seemed like a moment had come when
the financial industry that had become so consumed by its own increase
in wealth was finally having to experience the consequences of its institutional selfishness. There they went, cap in hand to the government, forced
to seek help from the only power holder in the land who could force them
to rewrite the practices that had caused such disaster. Surely this was
the moment when fairer and sustainable foundations could be laid, that

wouldn't just protect against another financial crisis, but would pave the way for a much more equitable society, perhaps leading to the erosion of the kind of gulf in wealth that was so brazenly on display in Tower Hamlets? That was the hope at least.

In some ways it was a crisis of capitalism. The imbalanced and unrestrained focus on financial growth, so prevalent in business communities up and down the land, had permeated into the very financial service structures that supported the fabric of business life. The desperate need to grow quicker and faster, drowning out the voices of good practice and deeper business and financial purpose. Working in a business connected to the financial industry I felt close to all of this. I also knew there were other Christians scattered across the industry in a variety of influential positions. It was an opportunity for Christian influence, but it was also a hopeful moment that gave way to disappointment. Disappointment in the government for failing to redefine the banking industry as a genuinely accountable service within the wider community of which it was part. Disappointment in big business, for not recognizing more publicly and substantially the underlying greed and failure of purpose of which it too had been just as guilty. And disappointment also in the wider Church of which I was part.

In our busy lives, within the limited shape most churches carve out for Christian community, we actually offered so little to equip people in banks and businesses for their specific role in the world. We, the wider Church, could have done so much more to enable theologically informative discourse on the questions the banking industry and the wider capitalist structure were facing. In a microcosm of it all, that moment when the 'Occupy' movement decided to camp out at St Paul's Cathedral epitomized a missed opportunity for the Church to host a national debate about the ethics of the financial structures that had grown out of an unfettered, dog-eats-dog marketplace. While I want to point the finger at others, as a church leader I have to say we simply weren't on our toes sufficiently for the huge discipleship opportunities in our midst; we didn't know how to help people find the best God-shaped solutions in their workplaces.

Hopeful Influence of business

Before we can look at the details of how Hopeful Influence is best expressed within the sphere of business, we need to locate business activity as a whole in God's wider movement of renewal in the world. In a sense we are asking: what is the role of Hopeful Influence that the business community is meant to fulfil in relation to other parts of society?

As we've seen already, part of following Jesus means being restored to our proper role as stewards of the world. As the Kingdom advances, so we get to play a working part in the renewal of the world, helping other people live and operate in life-enhancing ways that give glory back to God. And, of course, utilizing the planet's resources well and co-existing alongside the natural world as we do that. In the realization of this we need to build, market and distribute goods that improve life. We need to provide services that make a positive impact on people's lives. We need to create opportunities for entrepreneurs to start things, employ people and produce and provide things that offer real value to people everywhere. And we need to create employment, satisfying expressions of work that utilize the best of our God-given potential. These are the roles of the business community at its best, and the more Christians are able to exercise influence within the sphere of business, as well as the other spheres that are influential and mutually dependent on business, then the more businesses are able to properly reflect their true role in a society moving into the Kingdom. For a fuller theology of work, see Ken Costa's *God at Work*[2] and other material like it, but this in essence is the theological purpose of business.

It is true, of course, that most people don't see business in these terms, and many Christians don't either. We haven't resourced a practical theology of work in contemporary life particularly well, and the loudest voices within the business community often seem to be those that want to build up their own small tribe of senior employees or shareholders at whatever wider cost. We assume that a business operating in a free-market economy has a moral validity of its own, and we often allow it to trample over humanitarian and environmental concerns in its pursuit of profitability. We need to find more effective ways of articulating the theological purpose of a business, which should, within its own sphere of operations, be to consistently and increasingly operate in a way that makes the world a better place, both on the inside of the business and the outside.

Businesses therefore, properly understood, are vehicles for the Kingdom and should operate eschatologically, moving into a renewed future that anticipates our greater future to come. As with the other spheres of life, sometimes this is about compromise; sometimes it's about pruning and renewal; sometimes it involves decisions that seem to move the business backwards on the eschatological journey, but that are necessary for the business to renew and reposition itself so that forwards movement is then possible. The important point here though, is that there is a purpose beyond shareholder value that defines what the business is for, and this is vital for the self-understanding of any organization, in contrast to the ideas of Thomas Murphy and others which we have visited already. As Ken Costa summarizes, 'the world of work belongs not in the slipstream of twenty-first-century Christian spirituality, but in its mainstream. That's how God meant it to be.'[3]

See: defining and communicating the vision of a business

Within the Hopeful Influence of business that we've briefly explored, the financial viability and therefore sustainability and growth of a business hinges on the demand for goods and services that are at least perceived to offer value to people with particular desires for the future. A truly Christian business should therefore revolve around delivering goods and services that offer value within a God-shaped vision of the future. Every Christian working in a business should understand this eschatological potential that the whole business has, and understand the ways in which their Hopeful Influence within the business can be aligned with that potential. The overriding meaning of a company's endeavour that leaders need to articulate, and which will capture the imagination of customers and employees alike, is this eschatological potential. Every business begins with a dream, and the best businesses pursue God-shaped dreams.

What might a toothbrush look like that is more aligned with the ultimate purposes of God? What materials would it be made from? How would it be constructed? To whom would it be available and how might that be made possible?

What kind of cars are we meant to be driving in a world where humankind exercises proper stewardship over creation? What fuel would they use? How long would they last? How would individuality be expressed in their form?

What kinds of material do we use to build and package our products? How are these materials sourced and how are they disposed of? How far should we be transporting physical goods across the globe? Where do we draw appropriate boundaries on the energy footprint required to bring them to our doorstep?

What kind of services, many entirely electronic, are helpful as we build a faster, more connected society? Which services detract from and undermine our humanity and how can this be changed? How is advertising marshalled in the new virtual world in which we inhabit? How are abuses of these new technologies weeded out amid the plethora of generally positive activity?

And finally: what kinds of jobs are we as humans meant to be working on, that enable our greatest flourishing? Societies at different stages of development may tolerate certain repetitive and potentially de-humanizing forms of employment, but what forms of employment should we be aspiring to and how do we get there together?

These are just a flicker of the beautiful questions that hover over the businesses of the present. In the business world, perhaps more than any other, we are in desperate need of leadership as Hopeful Influence properly understood. And, when the answers to questions about a better future are brought together into a compelling package that customers can understand, market share and long-term profitability will increase. We should be on the front foot and confident about that. And, to avoid misunderstanding, this isn't to understate the importance of shareholder value to any business either. Shareholder value may still be the best single measure of a business's health and the concept of shared ownership is of course what attracts investment. Neither is this an argument not to go for profits that can remunerate hard-working employees and be invested back in the business. But it is an argument to relativize shareholder value and profit to their proper function: they are important dimensions of a business but they do not define its purpose.

So the challenge, at least at this point in our discussion, is to understand how an employee, a shareholder or an owner of a company can help others see the eschatological potential of the business. This might seem like a complex challenge, but I would suggest that most businesses are already aligned in ways that make this more possible. To this point, we've argued previously that the world is slowly gaining a growing revelation of the eschatological reality within which it sits, and that people have generally figured out through a combination of trial and error, common grace, latent Judeo-Christian influence and their own *imago dei* potential a whole host of stuff about how to do life, and certainly lead businesses, in ways that facilitate effective movement forwards. In that sense it should not surprise us to find business leadership structured in ways that enable movement. Indeed, we should expect to find a level of excellence, even in a theological sense, in the methodology of leadership in business, particularly where that methodology aids the realization of the business's purpose. Unfortunately, because of the brokenness of the world, we should also expect to find a level of deprivation in the methodology, particularly where people can still maintain the business's purpose but exploit their own roles within the business for excessive personal gain – and of course we find plenty of that, as we looked at in Chapter 1. But it is very interesting to see the excellence in leadership that much of the business world has managed to develop.

Take for example the way businesses, certainly larger ones, generally organize themselves. There is a senior leadership function, which is essentially tasked with the question, 'Where are we going as an organization?' The business has a current state of operation, but in which direction will it move and how will this lead to a positive form of renewal? This overlaps directly with leadership that helps people see the future, or at least a particular vision of the future. The senior leadership team essentially dream together how their products and services can meet the needs of a future market; hopefully doing some high-level viability on demand, financing, marketing strategy, production, employment requirements and so on. They then communicate this out to employees of the organization so there is a shared sense of where they are going together and the associated motivation to achieve. In a smart business this function will be alive and healthy. The challenge for Christians is to bring the right questions to the table within this part of the business – questions that explore the business's role within a future world that is better for all and where the case can be made for truly life-enhancing products, sustainability and good employment commitments.

All this needs to be done while ensuring that the bottom line remains healthy as investment is made and products and services change, acquisitions happen and a business diversifies or contracts to refocus. Regularly mapping the different facets of a business to understand the current and potential value therein should be a regular exercise. At every point the senior leadership needs to ask whether the business as it stands is capable of moving into a renewed future. Sometimes the answer will be yes. Sometimes it will be yes, but only if certain conditions are enabled. Sometimes it will be no, and an exit strategy from a particular market sector may be required. Sometimes, on rare occasions, the competition may be too fierce, or the stepping stones required in the market too great, so that a particular business will have to die. Even that can be a good and appropriate outcome when managed well within the wider business and employment landscape.

One final scenario is also worth comment because I suspect it happens a lot. Sometimes movement forwards in vital areas of the business is only possible if conditions are met that result in backward eschatological steps in others. An example might be where competition on production costs force a company to move production to a country where employment conditions are significantly worse, where quality will decrease or there will also be a significant environmental impact. To keep the business alive, to preserve its competitiveness, the company needs to reduce costs, but to achieve this it needs to move backwards in other areas. In these situations, the company cannot function in isolation but needs to dialogue with other organizations and with government bodies to prevent this backwards movement. Perhaps it might be appropriate to create a framework where imports are only allowed if foreign workers' rights are protected and steadily improved. Perhaps it might be appropriate to create industry bodies to monitor quality and inform customers of any significant decrease in reliability or longevity. Perhaps it might be appropriate to require businesses to pay significant taxes to offset increased environmental impact. Imagine the betterment of our shared life if government and businesses had done the hard work on these questions over the past twenty years.

Once the business is clear about its vision and difficult decisions have been made about where it needs to move forwards, it then needs to communicate out the particular merits of its products and services to its customer base through marketing. It needs to exercise Steven Croft's 'outward-facing leadership' that we looked at in Chapter 1, and essentially convince the potential market that what it offers is part of an appealing vision of the future. Effective marketing that is also true and honest is another subject beyond the scope of this book, but it is interesting that many of the most successful advertising campaigns don't start with the basic questions of 'what?' and 'how?', rather they try and connect with the deeper 'why?' question; this is the question that resonates best with the kind of life that the products or services are facilitating and are attempting to be aligned with. It's also why marketing that is an adjunct to a company's production and service departments is so often a step behind marketing that is directly geared into a company's senior leadership and vision. Again, it's about communicating the journey into a better future. How businesses paint this picture without lapsing into self-centred world views that pamper to a customer's ego is all part of the challenge to identify truly Hopeful Influence with all the Christian resources that we have. Again, dialogue with government and consumer groups to ensure true and accurate messaging will certainly be required.

Participate: empowering decision-making throughout the business

In many ways it is the vision of an organization that sets its resonance with and contribution towards God's renewal of the world. However, alongside the senior leadership function, and the marketing role that flows out of it, positional leadership is farmed out across the business to ensure the timely production of goods and services and the appropriate quality of the different tangible outputs of the business. Essentially asking the question, 'What do we have to do to get to where we want to go?' This is the functional leadership if you like, and it overlaps with Hopeful Influence when business leaders help their employees participate in the God-shaped future towards which they are aiming. Employees of the business are paid to help make the intended future a reality, and positional leaders throughout the business are tasked with ensuring that the business moves forwards as planned. Leadership within analysis, design, testing, production and delivery all fall into this category, as does leadership in managing accounts, process improvement and quality control. Christians exercising influence in these areas need to be constantly asking the question, 'How do we get to where we want to go in faster, more effective and less costly ways?' But they need to answer this by making sure that all facets of that better future are upheld. If there are ways of doing things that are more aligned with a future where Jesus is Lord, then Hopeful Influence at this point is about influencing others to join in with that.

When I was working in the financial services sector I was continually struck by how little Hopeful Influence actually permeated into the functional leadership within the business. The story I shared at the beginning of Chapter 5 is a case in point. I remember having to fight tooth and nail internally to free up resources to prove the value of an integrated fraud solution to a particular client, despite the fact that it was such an obvious business opportunity. Most businesses seem to want to keep employees focused on delivering against a set of predefined business outputs, without contributing to the wider discussion around direction of travel. Rarely is there space to bring construction, delivery and other business activities into conversation with what constitutes a better future. It's as if senior leaders generally don't trust those closer to the coal face with the ability to see future opportunities as they arise, adjust elements of strategy accordingly or kick back when they are asked to do things that are morally compromised. I want to argue that making space for every employee within an organization to grapple with the strategic questions of how to move forwards better releases them into a proper *participation* in that wider movement into renewal. It therefore unlocks the potential for true Hopeful Influence. Otherwise, middle-tier managers and shop-floor workers become the passive upholders of a broken status quo and perpetuators of the malaise so often found in the workplace.

One only has to read the story of INEOS[4] to see the fruit of a company intentionally trusting and releasing its middle-tier leadership into the possibility of Hopeful Influence. I wonder whether the senior leaders of that company understand the profoundly theological leadership culture they are setting when they give responsibility away to the leaders of business units and, in so doing, model something to be passed on to other employees? Most law firms operate in a similar way. The focus is about appointing people who understand the DNA of the organization and who can propagate this kind of decentralized ownership and responsibility deeper into the organization. In other words, it's about appointing and developing middle-tier leaders instead of middle-tier managers and ultimately inviting a whole company to engage in leadership activity.

Some businesses empower decision-making well, some don't. What very few seem to do is to help employees connect the activity they are participating in with that wider journey towards the world as it should be. When I worked for an information company, within a business unit that specialized in fraud prevention, I was often struck by how little we talked about the value we were delivering to the wider economy or the increase of justice and fairness that was being achieved through our technologies. When we met as a business unit, the talk so often was of profit and loss, bottom-line value, new technology solutions that might help us increase market share, and so on. There was so much potential to motivate and excite staff, to tap into our collective desire to contribute to a better future, and yet we failed to tell our own story properly. It was interesting to see management struggling with the challenge to increase staff positivity and achieve wider productivity and yet they were often failing to help people connect with possibly the greatest core motivator. We were making a real difference in the world, preventing fraud, combating lies and helping apprehend criminality. Yet we didn't use this reality as an advertisement for future employees and we failed to draw attention to and celebrate the work that we were doing in its proper eschatological sense.

Experience: the real purpose and breadth of HR

In my first graduate job, I was working within a team of software developers working on a flight and data-link simulator for the Royal Air Force Tornado. It was a really enjoyable first job. The software was pioneering. The people were talented. The remuneration certainly adequate. And yet, somehow, the team as a whole were unhappy. We were part of a larger business unit, but we'd been located away from the wider group and we'd developed a sort of edgy, slightly separate identity. We looked down a bit on the technologies other groups were using. We didn't like their antiquated development methodologies. We resisted oversight and the interference of senior managers. We grumbled about others but we didn't have much fun together ourselves; most people were out of the door by 5.30 p.m. The real killer was that leadership within the group wasn't entirely clear and there was no one to draw us together around the positive narratives of which we were part. During my first eighteen months within the team almost every single member left and was replaced. Out the door they went, convinced that life would be better elsewhere. Eventually, more as a result of us now being massively behind schedule, we were physically relocated alongside the rest of the business unit and given a management team who would bring us together around shared goals and with some social energy. It made all the difference. A highly skilled but degenerate team became well motivated and positively integrated together. In a sense nothing had changed, but in another sense, everything was different. There was a human resourcing dimension, a stepping-into-life movement, that needed to happen for us to function well.

Alongside senior and functional leadership roles within a business, the other, distinct leadership function is in the area Human Resources, or HR, essentially the function that ensures that staff members have a sufficient quality of experience in their roles. This HR responsibility is shared by positional leaders across the business and in larger businesses is complemented by a specific business unit. The essential question being asked is, 'How do we work well together on our journey into the future?' I want to suggest that this overlaps with the requirement for business leaders to help people experience the future for which they are aiming, a future that looks inward on their shared quality of life as well as looking outward to the business purpose. This is where the third strand of Hopeful Influence – helping people within the business experience an improved future – can become realized. As with the senior leadership and functional leadership areas, there is often a lot of HR that is about preserving an agreed status quo and performing activities that essentially keep the show on the road – things that aren't particularly *hopeful*. However, the Hopeful Influence opportunity is when HR leaders see the possibility of moving their employees' experience forwards in ways that renew and improve their quality of life.

Appropriate remuneration is unavoidably a key part of this. Employees who take their work seriously will want a pay that properly reflects that. A salary change that provides an increasing financial reward helps people to experience a better future for themselves; it's not wrong for that to be part of our motivation to work. HR leaders exercising Hopeful Influence will want to facilitate appropriate remuneration, despite business pressures to reduce costs to maintain competitiveness, because they understand the importance of an employee's whole working experience. Equally, I don't think bonuses are intrinsically bad, and I experienced the pleasure of a hard-working, successful year finishing with an increased financial reward. The level of bonus reward is of course contentious, and bonuses that are grotesquely large and that are solely driven around one metric of a business's success are rightly problematic. Alongside remuneration, taking steps towards a better quality of working environment, improved team relations and increased flexible hours to fit with different lifestyle demands are all examples of Hopeful Influence which helps others experience a better kind of future.

The most successful companies seem to start with the premise that improving employee experience is a vital component of a business's overall success; indeed, the offices of Microsoft or Google were always places of fun and play and high reward, even before the huge profitability those companies went on to enjoy. In contrast, for some companies their employees' experience is simply something that needs managing to prevent staff attrition: how little can a company get away with and remain competitive? Two completely different approaches. Leaders exercising Hopeful Influence gravitate to the former, and they know that it is when they help others experience a better future that truly eschatological movement within a business happens.

Towards a manifesto for Hopeful Influence in business

In summary, then, we need to resource business leaders everywhere with a theology that identifies the role their business plays as an active agent in God's renewal of the world. In fact, more than that, we need every Christian working in the business sector to understand this role and to be resourced to help others in their workplace see, participate and experience the Kingdom in ways that relate to their business. It's about understanding the eschatological potential that the business has, and the ways in which their influence can be aligned with that potential. This is something for every Christian in business, but it's particularly important for Christians in positional leadership within the business community.

Interestingly, the generally secular business community has been around for enough time to have worked out how it needs to structure itself to enable effective movement into the future. The areas of senior leadership, functional leadership and HR fit together quite neatly to enable people to see, participate and experience the future respectively. Where businesses need an abundance of help is to work out how these leadership functions become expressions of truly Hopeful Influence – not just because that is what is right and good, but because the only sustainable and mutually beneficial future is a future where Jesus is Lord, and all pretensions against that will ultimately be dashed on the rocks of our eternal reality. As the world's financial system almost discovered. The best opportunity, then, for Hopeful Influencers in businesses is to locate ourselves within these functions and structures and help the business understand how these structures work best in an eschatological sense. It's about joining the fight to maintain a growing business that has holistic alignment with a better future for all.

As a final reflection, there is a point about limitation that is often heard among contemporary social commentators.[5] Given the propensity of this current world to curve in on itself and to produce leadership that is very much not *hopeful*, we will need, as we move into increasingly new ground within the business community, a greater number of rules. Some may hear this as increased red tape to restrict the agility and creativity of pioneering new businesses. However, that is not what I'm talking about. What we need are sensible social partnerships, that do require rules, for businesses to resist the propensity to act greedily and without accountability under the pressures of a competitive marketplace. And very specifically, we need sensible dialogue with government bodies to ensure that our commercial movement into the future is indeed a movement into a better future for all. This won't be easy, and globalization and the pace of technological development mean that sometimes we're playing catch-up on how to do this well. However, at the centre of this dialogue, just as at the centre of business life, we need people of Hopeful Influence, informed by a rich, holistic, biblically informed vision of the future, and who can make the case for those rules of engagement that take businesses through the narrow door to life.

Comment
Eve Poole, Church Commissioner
and former lecturer at Ashridge Business School,
Berkhamsted

In business, Christian leaders should be at a considerable advantage, because of the hope that is in them. Daniel Goleman, the behavioural scientist, says that optimism is a core emotional competency, because people follow leaders who give them hope. While the rhetoric is often more about vision and strategy, hope is what this really means, because any vision or strategy that does not contain hope will not be compelling enough to attract affiliation, and will not inspire excellence from others. Hopeful leadership is therefore about how well leaders offer hope to others, and about how leaders themselves remain hopeful and optimistic. In service of the latter, a Christian leader without a prayer life and whose faith is weakened is holed below the waterline in terms of personal resourcefulness.

Ashridge's John Neal has a well-known visioning exercise, in which he asks people to close their eyes and imagine teeing-off on a golf course. The context is about future success, and about the use of visualization in sports coaching. But when he asks the room to indicate whether any of them imagined a hole in one, no one puts their hand up. Many people imagine sub-optimally if they are not helped by their leaders to dream big. Dreaming big is about taking off the blinkers. The human brain is used to the habitual editing out of crazy ideas, but these seemingly 'wrong' answers might actually be the seeds of something that is right. Most creativity tools are simple overrides for this editing process, so that potential solutions are not discounted until the very final stage in the thinking process. Hopeful leadership is about taking the filters off, and trusting God. If you had all the time in the world ...? If you had all the resources you would ever need ...? If you did not care what people thought ...? Answering these questions with hope might just produce the germ of an idea for a way forward. Hopeful leaders need to dream big for their organizations and to help suspend the filters of their colleagues until the very last minute.

Hope is vital in the nurturing of followers, because being able to guard the image of Christ in them guides the leader into wise decisions about development, deployment and discipline. A steady hope that God has a plan for each and every one, helps the leader to discern paths to the future and never to write anyone off. Hope keeps the leader focused when times are tough, and hope cheers the team whenever there are setbacks. As it says in 1 Peter 3.15, 'Always be prepared to give an answer to everyone who asks you to give the reason for the hope that you have. But do this with gentleness and respect.' Christian business leaders have an advantage if they draw on the hope that is in them, because it makes them reliably optimistic. Yet the gentleness and reverence are also vital, lest the hope become hubris. Wise leaders always take feedback, in the sure hope that a better future is always possible, both for themselves and for all those around them.

Notes

1 Patrick Dixon, *Building a Better Business: The Key to Future Marketing, Management and Motivation* (London: Profile Books, 2005), p. 237; emphasis in original.

2 Ken Costa, *God at Work* (London: Bloomsbury, 2007), p. 2.

3 Costa, *God at Work*, p. 17.

4 Jim Ratcliffe and Ursula Heath, *The Alchemists: The INEOS Story – An Industrial Giant Comes of Age* (London: Biteback, 2018).

5 Jordan B. Peterson, *12 Rules for Life: An Antidote to Chaos* (London: Penguin, 2018).

Reflection

Trusting and Growing Well

John 21.1–14

Afterwards Jesus appeared again to his disciples, by the Sea of Galilee. It happened this way: Simon Peter, Thomas (also known as Didymus), Nathanael from Cana in Galilee, the sons of Zebedee, and two other disciples were together. 'I'm going out to fish,' Simon Peter told them, and they said, 'We'll go with you.' So they went out and got into the boat, but that night they caught nothing.

Early in the morning, Jesus stood on the shore, but the disciples did not realise that it was Jesus.

He called out to them, 'Friends, haven't you any fish?'

'No,' they answered.

He said, 'Throw your net on the right side of the boat and you will find some.' When they did, they were unable to haul the net in because of the large number of fish.

Then the disciple whom Jesus loved said to Peter, 'It is the Lord!' As soon as Simon Peter heard him say, 'It is the Lord,' he wrapped his outer garment around him (for he had taken it off) and jumped into the water. The other disciples followed in the boat, towing the net full of fish, for they were not far from shore, about a hundred metres. When they landed, they saw a fire of burning coals there with fish on it, and some bread.

Jesus said to them, 'Bring some of the fish you have just caught.' So Simon Peter climbed back into the boat and dragged the net ashore. It was full of large fish, 153, but even with so many the net was not torn. Jesus said to them, 'Come and have breakfast.' None of the disciples dared ask him, 'Who are you?' They knew it was the Lord. Jesus came, took the bread and gave it to them, and did the same with the fish. This was now the third time Jesus appeared to his disciples after he was raised from the dead.

Questions

1 In what ways does this chapter resonate with your own experience and observations of leadership in business?
2 In what ways are businesses you know or are involved in geared towards the fulfilment of human purpose and well-being?
3 How would you describe the role of Christians in business? Are there ways every Christian can contribute in this sphere?
4 How is the business you are part of a participation in God's renewal of the world? Are there important boundaries to the business's activity? Where should it innovate?
5 How might your business foster greater participation in its strategic direction and in its general self-improvement? How might you contribute more to this?
6 How is quality of life promoted and celebrated in your business? How do you travel well together?
7 If you were starting a business, what goods and services of a better tomorrow would you like to develop?

Prayer

Father God, thank you for the part businesses play in making your world a better place. Inspire our imaginations so that businesses we know and are involved in might operate in ways that are more aligned with how life is meant to be. Help leaders across our business communities to know and trust you more. Help us to avoid fear and the life-destroying capacity it has to prevent us from innovating and moving forwards. Help us to foster generosity in the business communities that we are part of, and may we always promote quality of life for employees everywhere. In Jesus' name, amen.

10

Third Sector

I do not think in the last forty years
I have lived one conscious hour
that was not influenced by the thought of our Lord's return.
Anthony Ashley Cooper, 7th Earl of Shaftesbury (1801–85)[1]

During my time on staff at a church in East London we developed some
great relationships with local charities and social enterprises and at times
the church was a bit of a hothouse for third sector workers and volunteers. There was tremendous energy for justice and change, and seeing a
group of adults, predominantly young, mobilized by the organizations
they served in was hugely inspiring. At one point, we began a conversation with one of the larger charities about a more formal partnership.
The charity was an obvious fit. It had a long-standing presence in the
local community. It was geared around young people and increased
opportunity, which was an important goal that our church shared for
an often under-resourced demographic. It was also, importantly for us,
founded on a Christian ethos and run by a management team predominantly made up of committed Christians. Could we, as a church, partner
with this organization more: share ownership of projects, encourage
more volunteering or start new initiatives perhaps? As we got into the
discussions, there were different flavours of partnership we felt we could
explore: from light-touch support through to long-term embedded prayer
and action partners. In the end, disappointingly I felt, we settled on a
much more light-touch approach.

I think it's fair to say that our decision essentially boiled down to one
conversation about discipleship. Within the church staff team, amid
competing priorities and limited resources, we were used to reminding
each other that the Church's primary role was about making disciples.
We could already celebrate the goodness inherent in having members of
the church working for businesses and third sector organizations across
the city, and how these people were fruitful without having particularly
formal links between their organizations and our church. For our church
as an organization to strongly partner with a third sector organization,
so the argument went, there needed to be very clear alignment around a

shared goal of *growing disciples*. It's not an unreasonable argument by any means. Unfortunately, when this argument was presented to one of the leaders of the charity, their response kind of sealed the death of a fuller kind of partnership when they said, in effect, 'As an organization, our charity isn't primarily geared towards growing disciples; it has a much wider set of aims than that.' And so ended the discussion.

When I reflect on that, I am not without sympathy for the argument that won the day, and the conclusion may well have been right for both parties at that moment in time. However, I do want to ask the question whether the equation was run adequately, and whether the language of *growing disciples* was sufficiently understood by both sets of parties. More broadly, and I can think of other churches and church networks that have run similar equations with similar results around their links to specific charities and social enterprises: do we need to dig deeper into the *discipleship* touch-point between organizational Church and third sector organizations? Is there a case, particularly from our exploration of Hopeful Influence, to say that many charities are more in the business of *growing disciples* than they might realize? And, therefore, more in the business of being Church than we might recognize?

Hopeful Influence of the third sector

As with the other sectors we've looked at, we need to locate the role of the third sector within the life of the Kingdom. Within this big picture in many, perhaps surprising, ways the third sector operates in a similar way to the sphere of business in broader society. As with business, the third sector often employs people – it certainly mobilizes them around shared goals – it evaluates areas of need, creates products and structures of service delivery and can facilitate meaningful relationships to achieve change. The third sector, as a contributor to the renewal of the world, is trying to enable life in richer and fuller forms and is about caring for people and the wider creation, particularly when other structures fail to do so.

The big difference, of course, between the business sphere and the third sector is that businesses operate with the intention of creating wealth for their owners. As we've explored, some businesses are exclusively and unhealthily tied to the generation of profit, but others relativize profit within a wider paradigm of the properly human purposes which they serve, many of which would be shared by organizations operating in the third sector. Either way, the major difference between business and the third sector, be it charities, social enterprises, voluntary organizations or the delivery of forms of social services, is that third sector organizations do not generate profits. Any funds raised are reinvested back into those same services. In this sense, the third sector is perhaps free to function more like the political sphere. It can identify and respond to aspects of brokenness and missed opportunity within the wider societal whole and provide services without the required financial carrot of potential profit. As long, of course, as it has sustainable resources to do so.

It is often assumed that the third sector is, by definition, about providing free or cheap stuff to those who need it, but actually that is an occasional dimension of a much wider whole. More widely, and this is part of its potential function within the emerging Kingdom, the third sector has a unique role in dovetailing with the political and business spheres to provide care for those who benefit least from the civic and commercial status quo. It is like both sectors, but it is also different from both sectors. It participates in the renewal of the world, but it does this through the overspill of justice and compassion to those who need it most. In many ways people of Hopeful Influence in the third sector sphere are therefore asking the same type of questions as those in the business sphere and in the political sphere; it's just that they are asking them with a particular concern around what state and market are already doing or not doing. In that sense, the Hopeful Influence of the third sector is best understood as the manifestation of God's reactive concern against societal movement that only benefits more privileged sub-groups. Wider society understands something of this, and the funding opportunities, tax incentives, peppercorn rents and other benefits in kind that the third sector can enjoy is testimony of that.

Having said all that, it is important to be clear that the third sector also has a vital role in speaking prophetically back to politics and business and showing the damaging gaps, perhaps I could say the damaging eschatological gaps, as state and market help formulate society. If it fails to do this then the third sector risks colluding with the power holders in permeating broken societal structures. Equally, there is a huge challenge for the third sector to work out what helping people truly looks like on a shared journey into life under the lordship of Jesus. Having a clear theology of human personhood, understanding the difference between doing things *with* and *for* someone and having the wisdom to know how to achieve sustainable positive change are all deeply important for Hopeful Influence to be properly manifest. As we saw in Chapter 1, Robert Lupton is one of the best recent commentators on how charitable structures can get this wrong. Lupton shares his own journey of self-revelation as he begins to spend more time with some of the recipients of his own charitable projects. Suddenly he sees how the easy gifts, the distribution of excessive wealth, all given at arm's length, are actually demeaning and disempowering to many of the recipients. Through the story of a father who becomes conspicuously absent on Christmas Day, Lupton offers a particularly poignant picture of how misunderstood and inappropriately channelled forms of generosity can be so destructive; a wealthy family knock on the door to give the father's children the gifts that he could never have afforded.[2]

As a vehicle for Hopeful Influence, many Christians don't realize that the third sector is there to act as both a safety belt and a parking brake on inappropriate developments within wider society. Or that the third sector can, at its worst, collude with broken power structures and operate in ways that heighten the injustice and poverty that people experience. Or, for that matter, that in playing a part in the renewal of the world itself, the third sector is free to lean on private sector methodology, political activism and even the pursuit of financial gain for oft-needed reinvestment. The third sector caricature is much more akin to the paternalistic charity, providing free services to the institutionally poor, eschewing all forms of business acumen, ranting at injustice but not engaging with the existing structures to drive meaningful and lasting change. Many charities and the like are much smarter than this, but that has been the backdrop to much of third sector life in recent times, against which the opportunity for more meaningful forms of Hopeful Influence sits.

See: plugging the gaps

Because we've said that the third sector is primarily about activity that responds to the eschatological shortcomings of wider society, resultant from the brokering of market and state, the first activity of Hopeful Influence that a third sector organization needs to engage in is an analysis of the deficiencies of the status quo and imaginative enquiry as to how these gaps can be filled. Whereas a business often begins by dreaming the future, and then working out the pathways to it, a third sector organization often begins by seeing the poverty of life experienced by a few and asking the question, 'How might they be able to experience life a bit more like everyone else?' Beyond human needs even, how might we take better care of animals and the environment when state and market fail them? As the Kingdom advances in the world, the third sector dreams of a better life for all and is then tasked with overturning the results of structural injustice.

So just as with a business, the primary resource for every Christian working in a third sector organization is theological reflection on the eschatological potential that the organization has and how their activity of Hopeful Influence can be aligned with that potential. Just as with a business, every third sector organization begins with a dream, a dream fuelled by a desire for justice and that imagines a world where those who suffer under the current system can be set free to enjoy a much richer kind of life. How might basic living resources be deployed to those outside employment? Particularly, how might resources be deployed to those unemployed for reasons society isn't sympathetic with? How might expressions of community be created for those who find themselves isolated? How might parenting resources be provided to those who didn't learn them well from their own family networks? How might children in care be provided for better than government funding seems to allow? How might education be provided to those who don't fit the current models? What forms of schooling or training could meet specialist needs which generalist, nationwide provision isn't able to? What types of employment could be created for people who find it hard to work within a normal commercial environment? How could people new to our country be better integrated so they can play a full and important part? How could people living on our streets be drawn into supportive communities that lead to life change? And in exploring the answers to these questions, how are different types of services delivered in ways that lead to greater human empowerment and self-worth and avoid the disabling feeling many have when they are treated as simply beneficiaries? Going a stage further still, how has market and state conspired together to create these pockets of poverty? How might, through provocative and prophetic activity, third sector organizations draw attention to the obvious injustices and participate in structural change that leads to eschatological movement? These are the kinds of questions that third sector organizations need to begin with and keep at the heart of their activity. Christians developing the vision of their third sector organization and who are exercising Hopeful Influence will be committing their plans to God, theologically reflecting on the emerging vision and seeking Holy Spirit-led direction, discerned through community in order to know how to move forwards.

A good example of a third sector organization whose vision resonates strongly with Hopeful Influence is International Justice Mission (IJM). IJM's existence is built on the biblical understanding that slavery is wrong, and they have a dedicated purpose of ending modern-day slavery. In that sense, they want to move people from a place of oppression into a place of genuine freedom. This *hopeful* vision has three practical dimensions to it, from which they have resisted the temptation to diversify: they help rescue slaves, they pursue jail terms for perpetrators of slavery and they work with governments across the world to erode the operational networks of slavery. They have completed the hard work on how the vision they are called to might become an achievable and sustainable reality. They have built appropriate partnerships where necessary and they are innovating in the practice of combatting slavery today and tomorrow. IJM are set up as a not-for-profit organization, but they have a recognizable business structure behind it and the usual group of senior executives tasked with steering direction and activity. They see this investment in strategic direction as fundamentally essential to the organization's long-term viability: they need to see where they are going so they invest in informed, imaginative enquiry and then review their actual activity and performance against those strategic goals. Their business operations are split between actual slavery prevention and building a movement of modern-day slavery awareness to help achieve the bigger objectives of the future. They ensure they have people with the right skills and gifts in the key positions. They are a future-led organization, with attention to the present, operating with business acumen where appropriate. They can punch well above their weight because of supporters and advocates beyond the organization. Most importantly perhaps, they are fuelled by high-quality staff with a passion for the organization's deeper purpose: if you work for IJM you know why and you are energized by it.

Participate: wisdom and hard decisions for those on the ground

So third sector organizations and workers exercising Hopeful Influence need to help others see the advancing Kingdom. Equally, they need to help others participate, join in, with the Kingdom movement that God is calling their organization into. As with businesses, alongside the senior leadership setting vision, third sector organizations have leaders tasked with working out precisely how to effectively implement activities that will see that vision realized. Unfortunately, in a manner similar to many businesses, often these leaders at an operational level within the third sector aren't empowered to ensure eschatological movement actually happens. They aren't given the opportunity to influence how resources are distributed or to reshape things when they aren't working.

As an example, I spent a year working for a mission organization in Nigeria, based in a rural village some way from the nearest city. As you drove out to the village, you'd occasionally see rusted old tractors in some of the fields, long since broken down. When I asked about them, I heard they were often the generous gift from some well-meaning church or charity, who hadn't realized that running and maintaining that same generous gift was way beyond the resources of the local farmers. The broken down rust buckets just became eyesores on the horizon, depressing reminders of the poverty of the indigenous people rather than the source of blessing they were meant to be. On another occasion, I remember driving past a huge water mill, an enormous building even by European standards. The strange thing was, I didn't notice any activity at it. Again, I enquired and found out that this too had been the gift of some foreign benefactor. A huge investment to transform a whole community. However, here the story was more sinister. Apparently the local manager of the mill had run off with all the profits and left the enterprise so greatly in debt that the mill had to be closed. In both cases, I'm sure, stronger relational investment between the charity and the beneficiary, clearer communication between on-the-ground service providers and senior leaders, as well as hard lines on sustainability and future-proofing would have gone a long way to ensuring these sad stories never happened.

As the vision of a third sector organization begins to be realized there will be hard questions about whether the particular way of delivering that vision will actually lead to genuine eschatological movement and the proper Kingdom renewal that is sought. In these examples, those helping the Kingdom movement to happen needed to be empowered to say, 'enough is enough'; and affluent benefactors, who are perhaps more interested in relieving their own debt of conscience than actually effecting change in a foreign environment, needed to be ready to change the approach. Exercising Hopeful Influence at this level requires keeping a handle on the wider eschatological movement that a third sector organization is participating in and taking action to help the efforts of the organization stay aligned with what we might call a genuine participation in that movement.

As we've seen, mutuality and empowerment are fundamental dimensions of Hopeful Influence, as we help others join in with the Kingdom movement of which we are part. There is some responsibility though, when we invite others to come alongside us, to conduct an adequate analysis of the power required to achieve something; to ensure we are inviting people to join in with activities that will result in a genuine movement towards the Kingdom. I remember a few years ago I was invited to speak at a UNISON conference, specifically on the benefits of community organizing and to explore their appetite for supporting grassroots organizing to fulfil objectives around social cohesion and well-being. It was a great gig, and I have huge admiration for what UNISON has been able to do for workers and communities the nation over – a good example of a third sector organization committed to standing up to the varied injustices that spill out through unrestrained capitalism. On that day I shared the stage with a group of ambulance workers petitioning for support over the intended privatization of some of their services, and UNISON's stance was very interesting to observe. As you might imagine, slogans like 'Save our NHS' and 'No to Privatization' abounded and the protest was made primarily on ideological grounds. Like UNISON, I struggle to believe that private contractors will deliver as good an ambulance service for less money and I'm loathe to reduce the level of service provision, particularly when our growing elderly population naturally demands more resources. However, like much of the electorate, I was sympathetic to a government trying to balance the books when the level of financial strain was so high.

However, on reflection, it seemed to me that UNISON might have had more success exercising their *influence* in a different way. Was the fight really just about idealistic notions of public vs private – somehow the private being all bad and the public being all good? Didn't that play into a confrontational power game which, given the economic climate, the union was always going to lose? At its heart, wasn't it ultimately about the quality of service that needed to be maintained alongside the efficiencies that needed to be realized, given the current government's challenges to balance the books within a financial crisis? Perhaps a campaign that focused on the nuances of this challenge would have been stronger? And weren't those nuances about ensuring that our elderly people got the necessary care and attention when they were picked up and dropped off from hospital? No one in their right mind wants an ambulance service to drop an elderly person at home without making sure the curtains are opened, the heating is back on and that they are able to sit down with a cup of tea before said ambulance team disappear. That's what was at the heart of the issues and UNISON, rightly, didn't want ambulance services disappearing after two minutes because they had a commercial target of drop-offs to fulfil. As an alternative headline, perhaps 'Helping Grandma Get a Cuppa' might have struck the necessary chord: campaigning to ensure that commercial agreements to privatize some of the ambulance service came with cast-iron guarantees that when the elderly were dropped off they had someone to help them get settled in their home. For me, UNISON didn't build their mutuality and empowerment around activities that had the best chance of enabling true movement forwards, and therefore didn't exercise the Hopeful Influence that might have been possible.

Experience: true service and meaningful change

The next strand of Hopeful Influence in a third sector organization revolves around the experience of its own employees and volunteers, as well as the experience of those the organization tries to help. Internally, much like the HR strand we explored in the sphere of business, third sector organizations need to do a good job of helping their workers enter into the joy of the renewal they are facilitating and ensure they have a really good experience in the workplace. I am always encouraged when I hear about friends and church members in the third sector taking time out to celebrate what they are doing together. Because the needs are so great, and the resources often too small, third sector organizations can become relentlessly driven places. Maintaining a theology of play for our organizations, ensuring that we celebrate and enjoy our time in this environment seems vital. Equally, but perhaps more subtly, there is something in the human condition that wants to earn God's, and others', approval – often at great personal cost. Charities and philanthropic organizations can get sucked into this subconscious posture of earning our value and self-worth. Unless organizations are rooted in a theology of personhood and well-being, which includes those within the organization as well as without, we are left deeply unsatisfied and run the risk of burn-out. For Christians, reminding one another that following Jesus means entering into something wonderful, which includes our own experience, would seem an important expression of Hopeful Influence in many third sector organizations.

This relates, in part, to the vitality of finding peace amid the things that seem unchangeable. We get angry and frustrated when we don't see the change that we long for. Within this anger and frustration, often, is the positive energy we need to fight for change and to keep going in that struggle. However, this anger and frustration, if not well managed, can spill over into the environment in which we work. Third sector organizations, at their worst, can be angry and frustrating places to work; they need tempering with the grace and wisdom to know that even our smallest efforts demand celebration and that without our involvement the world would be a much poorer place. I don't want to undermine the very deep challenges that those working in areas like health care or education might face, but I am often surprised to hear people so bogged down in the struggles of the day that they miss the extraordinary good that they are participating in. Yes, let's work for improvement and call out inadequate structures and resources when we see them. No, let's not become so demoralized by the challenges we face that we fail to see and celebrate the remarkable good that we are participating in.

It is important also to say something theologically about the nature of service unto others. When we serve others out of a genuine other-person-centred desire for life and well-being, then we find ourselves feeling good – such is the paradoxical nature of love. In fact, the more we enter into the life of the Godhead – generous, compassionate and kenotic as we explored earlier – the greater our own sense of identity, significance and fulfilment in the world. In that sense, you could say that the more we step into the Kingdom, the more we experience it. However, within the third sector, even this experience of the Kingdom needs some care. Serving at food banks, a remarkable initiative hugely resourced by local churches, is a great thing to do. But if we stop there, if we don't seek to overthrow the unjust structures that trap people in such poverty that they require food banks, then at best we limit the extent of our Hopeful Influence, and at worst we collude with the power holders so that change is no longer required. One slightly worrying aspect of this is that employees often move on from third sector organizations when they realize these eschatological limits, only to be replaced by the next bright young talent, full of enthusiasm, ready to champion the same kinds of initiatives without looking to effect the deeper change that is required. Rather than giving up on organizations because of their perceived limits, we need to constantly evaluate the eschatological movement that our initiatives are facilitating and be ready to diversify, change tack, build power-alliances or simply start things anew if we see our efforts becoming ineffective or compromised.

And of course, helping others experience the Kingdom is what a third sector organization is really all about. In the church I'm part of, one of the partners we work with is a very small charitable organization helping women who have experienced trauma: often asylum seekers new to the city and sometimes women who have escaped domestic abuse. They run a variety of different projects, but at their heart is the theological idea that we become more fully alive when we do things with others who share our passions and interests. You could call it friendship, perhaps. But for people who have been isolated and who have experienced appalling abuses, a simple structure to enable them to come alongside and get to know others while expressing themselves in a way that is inspiring and freeing has been found to be completely life-changing. The organization struggles for resources, the change they are effecting is just a fraction of what could be possible with stronger financial backing, and yet their workers are full of fun, optimism and joy as they faithfully commit to the relatively small work they are doing. Their activities are geared, without compromise, on facilitating the development of friendships through shared interests, and they consistently make the space to celebrate life together. Because they are so focused on relationships, and have done the hard work on how they can add eschatological value, they are more effective than some organizations much larger than they are.

Towards a manifesto for Hopeful Influence in the third sector

To enable leaders to exercise Hopeful Influence in the third sector, we need to further develop the theology of God's activity within it, and the unique role it has to play in wider society. Specifically this, as with the business sphere, is about understanding the eschatological potential that a third sector organization has, and the ways in which people's *influence* in this sphere can be aligned with that potential. This principally means plugging the gaps left by market and state and speaking prophetically back to both to ensure that there are appropriate partnerships in place to ensure a better future for all.

In so doing, one obvious area where the third sector hasn't been as effective as it could be, is that in playing a reactionary role against market and state it can sometimes condemn much of the practice found in those spheres without thinking through some of the theological underpinnings that make those spheres effective before God. Third sector organizations need to function well, and there is much to be learned from other organizations, particularly businesses, that doesn't compromise a third sector organization's overall purpose. Third sector organizations need senior leadership that understand the eschatological role the organization can play and that are shrewd enough to see beyond the societal constructs or partisan politics that can sometimes inhibit their effectiveness.

To really enable the third sector to plug the eschatological gaps as market and state move society forwards, and to campaign for market and state to make the structural changes to eradicate these gaps into the longer term, we need to foster deep and searching imaginative enquiry. Understanding how market and state make provision for human flourishing and a sharp eye and a listening ear for who and how people get left behind is vital. This is sometimes a lengthy process that requires participation with multiple stakeholders and often needs a level of genius, or Holy Spirit-led imagination, to enquire of fresh and creative ways to plug the gaps that are there. Again, the sharp edge of Hopeful Influence isn't just about delivering ongoing services that make a difference, as vital as that is, but about facilitating movement in others that leads to sustainable Kingdom renewal. Leadership is always about stepping into a new future, and participating in campaigns that lead to structural renewal has to be part of this sharp edge. Regular assessment of a third sector organization's impact on ongoing eschatological movement within wider society is a necessary part of this as the status quo moves and develops.

At a service and delivery level, third sector organizations need Hopeful Influencers to drive this regular assessment. These workers need to develop their voice and, as with the business sphere, find ways of raising concern and sharpening the detailed vision that the organization has been set. The best third sector organizations will understand this and make space for this more organic activity as the organization responds to the challenges around it. Equally, third sector organizations often need to build power to effect change, and the opportunities to create mutuality and empowerment among others needs to be appropriately tempered with a power analysis of what can be achieved together. Sometimes there is a temptation to drive forwards on ideological principles, when compromise and pragmatic assessment of what is achievable would better serve the immediate next steps.

Finally, third sector organizations often need to travel better together, with a theology of play that impacts their own quality of life as well as those that they serve. Resisting the psychological pull to works-righteousness is vital for the experiential health of an organization, as is fostering a maturity that is peaceful about what cannot yet be changed amid the plethora of broken societal elements. And, when all of this is put together in effective forms, there is still the danger of falling into a hubris over the positive changes we are making and missing the wider call to participate in the overthrow of the structures that led to the human poverty in the first place. To journey into the Kingdom means keeping the joy that we have been called to make a difference – and that very calling, and the assurance of ultimate victory, is something for constant celebration.

Comment
Hannah Bowring, Church Partnerships Manager, Tearfund

At Tearfund, we feel we have a role as a prophetic voice to the UK Church. In the UK, we don't see enough signs of the Kingdom coming in ways that change whole communities. In Western churches there is often a lack of confidence in the ability of the local church to bring holistic transformation to this world. Our connection with churches overseas gives people the opportunity to see the *dunamos*/dynamite of the Holy Spirit at work in and through the local church. When people see churches tackling injustice, reconciling across divides and communities beginning to thrive, it inspires hope and raises confidence. It points clearly to the need for leadership that understands the holistic nature of the gospel and salvation. It challenges people to think more broadly about the scope of the Kingdom of God to beyond personal salvation – to the restoration of *all* things.

Church leaders, quite rightly, place emphasis on their local community, but the third sector has a role to keep the wider and even global poor on the agenda. We need to pray for God's Kingdom and renewal to come and to give financially in emergency situations and towards long-term development. But we also need to bring challenge around issues of justice. What is the part we have to play, both as individuals and church communities, to see God's justice come in our world? How can we challenge unjust structures and speak up for the rights of the poor and the oppressed?

A key example of this is climate change. As people of God we are called to be good stewards of his world and therefore should be leading the way in how we treat it. We know that climate change has the greatest impact on the poorest people and we know that our God encourages us regularly in Scripture to pay specific attention to this group of people. What is our response as the people of God? How can the Church, led by the spirit, imagine a better way to live – where everyone has enough to thrive and creation is well cared for? How can we begin to model this better way, through the way we live and eat and travel, through the way we operate in business, government? And how do we speak with courage and confidence for the changes we know we're called to participate in bringing about?

I hope for a world where the Church is a leading voice in the area of climate change. Where our congregations are full of people making changes in their daily lives, thinking about their impact on our global community and all of that underpinned with a great theology of creation care. Imagine a world where the Church is known again for its care for the poor, both locally and globally, showing God's love in tangible ways.

Alongside other third sector organizations, our role at Tearfund is to inspire the Church, but also government and businesses, with this Spirit-led imagination. Believing a better world truly is possible, we call that out from the way we live as Christians, and from how governments and businesses act and the decisions they make. We can inspire a better way, a way more like the Kingdom, when we're led by the spirit and speak boldly into these spaces.

There was a programme in Tanzania using solar panels to help rural people get electricity. By proving the concept, the World Bank were successfully petitioned that this is an effective and affordable way to get electricity to the poorest communities. A project in Pakistan models good waste management, which enabled dialogue with governments to invest more into this work globally.

When businesses are brought to the table, the push and shove of our commercial culture can be brought into greater alignment with the Kingdom. Because some businesses were inspired to imagine better stewardship of food, leading supermarkets in the UK have been influenced to do things differently. Through campaigning, enough people said they'd switch supermarkets based on their stewardship concerns and desire for action on food waste. As a result, supermarkets began to shift and make commitments. Again, a powerful witness to turn the tide and realize a better future for all.

Notes

1 Anthony Ashley Cooper, 7th Earl of Shaftesbury, in John Stott, *The Incomparable Christ* (Downers Grove, IL: Inter-Varsity Press, 2014), p. 169.
2 Robert B. Lupton, *Toxic Charity: How Churches and Charities Hurt Those They Help (And How to Reverse It)* (New York: HarperOne, 2012), pp. 31–3.

Reflection

Plugging Gaps and Changing Structures

John 9.1–12

As he went along, he saw a man blind from birth. His disciples asked him, 'Rabbi, who sinned, this man or his parents, that he was born blind?'

'Neither this man nor his parents sinned,' said Jesus, 'but this happened so that the works of God might be displayed in him. As long as it is day, we must do the works of him who sent me. Night is coming, when no one can work. While I am in the world, I am the light of the world.'

After saying this, he spat on the ground, made some mud with the saliva, and put it on the man's eyes. 'Go,' he told him, 'wash in the Pool of Siloam' (this word means 'Sent'). So the man went and washed, and came home seeing.

His neighbours and those who had formerly seen him begging asked, 'Isn't this the same man who used to sit and beg?' Some claimed that he was.

Others said, 'No, he only looks like him.'

But he himself insisted, 'I am the man.'

'How then were your eyes opened?' they asked.

He replied, 'The man they call Jesus made some mud and put it on my eyes. He told me to go to Siloam and wash. So I went and washed, and then I could see.'

'Where is this man?' they asked him.

'I don't know,' he said.

Questions

1 In what ways does this chapter resonate with your own experience and observations of leadership in the third sector?

2 In what ways are third sector organizations you know, or are involved in, plugging the gaps in our societal movement forwards? How are these activities aligned with a biblical picture of God's renewal?

3 How do these third sector organizations speak back to the spheres of politics and business to overcome structural injustice?

4 Within these third sector organizations, how is vision shared and communicated? What particular areas of 'quality of life for all' are they focusing on?

5 Does the activity of these third sector organizations ever hold people back from their own development? How do we avoid being overly paternalistic?

6 Are these third sector organizations healthy places to work? How do we develop the right motivation for our activities? How do we avoid burn-out and travel well together?

7 If you were starting a third sector organization, what eschatological potential would you like to focus on? What would being Jesus' hands and feet look like in that area of life?

Prayer

Father God, thank you for the abundance of third sector organizations around us and thank you for the amazing pioneers who lead and work for them. For people in these organizations, help them to constantly evaluate the role the organization is playing. Give them a vision for how they can plug the gaps, but also ensure society truly moves towards you. Protect us from disempowering people and keep us aligned with your vision for a new and better world. In Jesus' name, amen.

II

Next Generation

A hundred times every day I remind myself that my inner and outer life
depend on the labours of other [people], living and dead.
Albert Einstein (1879–1955)

I'd got up fairly early, and by 6.30 I was working in my study on something I was keen to get finished that morning. It was a struggle. I'd gone
to bed later than planned, was a bit more tired than I thought I'd be, and I
just couldn't think as clearly as I wanted to. Mentally I felt distracted, not
really present with the job in hand; a variety of other thoughts were competing for my attention and it was not the start to the day that I'd wanted.
I persevered for a bit, joined my wife and children for breakfast and had
another go. Most of the time working at my desk is pretty easy. I sit and
get on with it. Then sometimes, for no particular reason, it's a slog.

At about 8.30, Hannah and the children were ready to walk to school
so I spent a few minutes with them talking about the day to come. We
went outside and it was a beautiful day. Our house is in the grounds of
the Anglican Cathedral, and as we stepped outside it soared majestically
up above us. I decided to walk with them down our little close for the first
100 yards or so of the walk to school. At the other end of the driveway,
in the opposite direction past our house and some distance from where
we were walking, there is a moveable cone. This cone indicates to people
in the adjacent cathedral car park that parking in a way that blocks the
drive isn't a helpful thing to do. Almost immediately, my seven-year-old
son spotted that the cone was out of its usual position. Straight away he's
running off to remedy the situation.

'Hold on a moment please, Jake,' I called, but there was no stopping
him. On one level I tried to remind myself that he was trying to do a good
thing. On another, I knew that part of what was happening was that Jake
was wanting to assert himself against the adult priorities of the morning,
namely getting to school on time, and that annoyed me. I was also a little
concerned that there were cars manoeuvring themselves the other side of
the cone right at that moment. Back he came, having moved the cone.
'Don't get angry,' I told myself, 'just talk to him.'

Having previously started the walk to school, by this point we were
now back by our front door. We stepped back into the house and I knelt

down to his level. 'Jake,' I said, 'I know you were trying to help, but you didn't listen to me when I called you back.' Jake looked kind of sheepish. 'We need to go to school now, but I'd like to talk about this when you get back,' I said. I walked out of the front door and looked round for Jake to follow. It was at this point that I realized Jake hadn't got the message. He was half in the hallway, half outside, scowling a bit, swinging the door, and saying something about how he hadn't heard me and that my abilities as a father were somewhere close to the bottom of the list of all fathers in the world and down through human history. Maybe he had a point, but by now I'd also stopped listening. 'Come on now, Jake,' I said. Well he didn't. And it was at that point that I flipped. I marched back into the house, half carrying, half pushing Jake ahead of me. Slamming the door behind me I gave him a full-on telling off. My voice was loud, authoritative, my words were challenging, harsh. This time he'd got the message, and suddenly I felt a lot better.

Half an hour later, as I reflected on what had really happened, I wasn't feeling quite as good. The truth of the morning's tale was that I'd had a frustrating time at the desk, I was angry at myself for my own lack of mental discipline and I was ready to blow. Jake had deliberately not listened to me, but his intentions had been good. He'd wanted to move the cone, and I'd ignored the kindness at the heart of his actions. In addition, I hadn't been particularly direct or urgent in asking him not to run up the driveway, and when I confronted him over it I could have had a great deal more understanding and humour. Not only that, but my loud, authoritative voice and forceful, controlling posture was a show of strength, linked I suspect, to my own lack of mental control displayed in the morning's slow start. Jake was now in school having had a roasting from me without sufficient time to resolve and make up. Well done, Dad.

Hopeful Influence for the next generation

As with the other chapters in this final part of the book, the first question to ask when thinking about a particular sphere of life is to ask what role does Hopeful Influence in the sphere of the next generation play in the wider world? As we considered in Chapter 1, we are defining the next generation very specifically as those people who will, at some point in the future, inhabit forms of influence similar to our own. Our Hopeful Influence towards the next generation isn't, then, just how to help others advance the Kingdom of God in their general activity, but more specifically how we relationally influence others to inhabit roles like ours for that same purpose. With that perspective, as an ordained minister I have a unique opportunity to facilitate someone else's journey into ordained ministry. A doctor will have a unique opportunity to help others following them into the medical community. Someone running their own company will have the opportunity to pass the baton on to other entrepreneurs. As a parent I have the unique privilege of helping my children grow in their own humanity. When these kinds of influence are directed towards the Kingdom we can say that Hopeful influence for the next generation is being expressed. Therefore, regardless of the sphere of life I am operating in, there is a dimension of Hopeful Influence that is focused on passing on what we have learned and, more deeply, passing on what we have become to those who follow us. In a sense, in every role we occupy we have the opportunity to pass this baton on to the next generation. Our roles at work, at home, in our community, our role as Christian people, our role as men or women, our role simply as people; in each role we can exercise a very particular form of Hopeful Influence to those who will take up those same roles.

At its most basic, perhaps, Hopeful Influence to the next generation requires a certain amount of self-awareness regarding the journey we have travelled and the ability to influence out of that. What sat beneath our own sense of vision and calling to this particular role? Why do we do things the way we do them? How have we found joy and sustainable rhythms within these roles? In general terms, what have we learned and how can we communicate that? Part of the Kingdom's economy seems to be that each generation doesn't have to start from scratch. We can lean on each other. There is a responsibility even, on those who have travelled a certain distance, to help others make that same journey: to influence those among the next generation.

And yet things aren't quite that straightforward either. As I alluded to earlier, the dynamic of Hopeful Influence between generations brings into sharper focus the way that leadership, unavoidably on our shared journey towards the eschaton, has to have a two-way dimension to it. Leadership that is always from a particular leader to particular followers does fundamental disservice to what is actually happening in the realms of leadership. We are journeying together, and God has gifted us in community to one another to aid that journey. This means we all have the potential to move closer, to evolve into, to become more fully the kind of people doing the kind of things God wants us to, and Hopeful Influence is the shared dynamic that enables this.

Therefore, as we briefly explore what it means to help the generation coming after us to see, participate in and experience the Kingdom of God more fully, we have to be particularly alive to the possibility that they have something very important to offer and say to us. Most parents will know this. We start out in our parenting with a generosity of spirit; a desire for the betterment of others and a certain aspiration for altruism.

Those who last the distance, at least with a degree of attention to our own personal transformation and a willingness to embrace that, are often surprised by the increasing depths of that same altruism and related qualities. Parenting has a tremendous potential to help us become better people. As does marriage for that matter, and any other role in life where we get to exercise significant influence on those around us. We encounter pushback. We realize others are further ahead of us in myriad areas. We have to change approach. We realize that the things we learned and embraced in our formation aren't necessarily the right things for those who come after us. The spotlight shines on the negative influences we embraced. And even when we got things right, sometimes life, culture and society changes and demands different qualities from those in the generations behind us. So with a short reflection from my own experiences of handing on the baton, let's now explore the three movements of see, participate and experience through the particular lens of influencing the next generation.

See: dreaming together

Early in my own vocational journey, I explored a variety of different forms of work and service. I was working for a creative technology company, exercising, over time, an increasing level of leadership responsibility, which enabled me to use certain gifts and abilities. Within my church community, I volunteered to help with children and young people, led a midweek group and joined in with different roles within the Sunday services. I loved sport and helped run football teams. I was energized by evangelism, and so worked with a couple of different mission organizations to explore this further. As I journeyed into my late twenties, while I thoroughly enjoyed all of these things, I was still unclear about what I really wanted to do into the future. When I first began to take these questions of vocation to the Church of England, as I shared earlier, my initial framing of a possible vocation as 'leadership within the Church' wasn't received particularly well. What I needed help on was being really clear about what I meant by leadership, and doing the necessary theological and experiential reflection to know that I was really talking about forms of service that enabled the wider Church to inhabit its own identity more fully. As a good friend with a few years of ordained ministry behind him helpfully put it, 'Jude, you are passionate about the Church!'

I now have the privilege of helping others through this same discernment process and leading a church of predominantly young adults brings me into relationship with quite a few people who are actively thinking through their own sense of vocation. Right through church history, God seems to set people aside to exercise a particular ministry towards the wider body of the Church. There is some sense in which that ministry is unavoidably public and sacrificial, with a whole host of significant implications. And yet with each person, elements of that calling are different, and with each generation certain aspects or distinctives within that calling are often emphasized. Part of my role is to help people imagine the best shapes of their own ministries. Very specifically, part of my role can also be about helping people imagine the best shape of their whole life calling and how they might fulfil that within the role of an ordained minister. If, then, I've presented Hopeful Influence as a leader's permission to dream and then create reality around their own imaginings of the future, I've limited the fullness of its true theological shape. Yes, part of our life as a leader is to imagine a better future. When it comes to how this is passed on – and particularly how we release others into leadership, which is unavoidable and necessary if we want any real traction on our hopes for the future – we have to move beyond just our own dreams and towards a posture of facilitating others' dreams and of bringing them into conversation with our own.

As a city-centre church, we have been asked by our diocese to be missionally intentional among a younger demographic, and to achieve this we have fairly well-formed strategies for evangelism and discipleship through which we have been consistently growing. One thing we've observed is that we have been particularly fruitful, as you might expect, among those who live in the centre of the city and close to the location of our church. There are other large residential areas where people in our key demographic live, and it is definitely harder to make the journey to our church building from those areas. In response to that, I've been dreaming about church planting and the planting of missional congregations into those areas. Now, there's a whole body of work around how new initiatives integrate well alongside what God is already doing in given areas, but that's not the essence of what I'd like to focus on here. Rather, another key leadership challenge is how to invite others into this kind of vision, and specifically to make space for others to shape and own a vision and to hear God's voice for themselves. In this particular example, there were two leaders within our church family whom I approached so we might dream together about how things could look.

As we began sketching out the shape of a new missional congregation in a particular pub a couple of miles from our church, two things really struck me. First, the hugely encouraging agreement and affirmation, from the two leaders involved, that God was speaking through the vision and that it therefore represented an exciting opportunity to grow the Church and advance God's Kingdom. Second, I found it very interesting that as these leaders began to dream together, some of the detail of what this congregation could look like began to diverge significantly from mine – or perhaps from what I thought God had been saying. I had to catch myself. In my mind, the gatherings had a particular shape and we were reworking that significantly. I was much more experienced than the two people involved. Did my experience trump theirs? How was it going to play out? Fortunately, this moment of hesitation and questioning didn't last long: my job was to let their imaginations fly, to relativize aspects of my own imagination to exactly that, and to help round the edges to make sure that they ended up with something as fruitful as it could be. From their vantage point, not least being 20 years my junior, they could see things that I could not. I needed to be mature enough to realize that, yet not give up the reins completely, so that the experience and learning I could bring was not lost.

And so we started to create something new. A distinct worshipping community, with clear avenues in and a helpful welcoming space to make it easier for people who wouldn't normally attend church to come along. As the conversations with the two leaders have developed, it's been clear that this is just one expression of a deep calling to the Church that both of them carry. At my best, I'm reflecting back to them how I think their calling resonates with the ways the Church of England historically understands the role of an ordained minister, and I'm helping them see how their passions, gifts and abilities might be realized within this particular ministry. At the same time, I'm trying to be alive to ways I might limit their sense of calling or put false boundaries on how their own ministry might develop. As we've journeyed together, they have helped me see things more clearly, and I have helped them put fresh words to the ministry they are leading on and their wider sense of vocation before God.

Participate: helping people develop

Unavoidably, part of helping the next generation participate in the future Kingdom requires a level of training and development – the deep sense of empowerment that we explored earlier. The next generation becomes more able to participate in making the Kingdom a reality when it has the right skills, character and resources to do so. As one generation looks to the next, we need to find smart ways to help those that follow us grow up so they can realize their God-given potential. Now, to an extent, some of this has been taken care of through the formation of educational systems structured around precisely those aims. Most cultures seem to have grasped the value of this and it is certainly true that the Christian Church has contributed enormously to the distribution and accessibility of education in all parts of the world. However, even within the Church, and certainly beyond it, there are a variety of conflicting views about how to train and equip people for the future and the best ways of empowering others to make a difference in the world. This is all the beginning of a very large subject of course, but a helpful element to look at within this, is the transition from school-age children into university-age adults.[1] At this transition point there is a very particular need to lead people into adulthood, or to pass on the baton of adulthood if you like. As a transition moment, there is great potential for Hopeful Influence, and I think this isn't often very well understood or resourced.

It's over 25 years since I was first an undergraduate in the UK, and a lot has changed since then. When I went to university it was sink or swim within what felt like a fairly crude survival-of-the-fittest environment. The transition in that first year into a very high level of adult autonomy was too much to bear for many. The proliferation of drugs, the peer-encouragement into a hedonistic student lifestyle, the normality and experience of sexual relationships, the didactic learning environments where turning up or not was entirely up to you and, for some, the pressures of excessive parental expectation. Most of us hadn't heard of mental health, and there were plenty who just dropped out when the going got tough. I did a physics degree, which meant quite a lot of class time, if you bothered attending. I rarely did, and ended up scraping through each year by the narrowest of margins. This, coupled with all sorts of other life mistakes, led to me experiencing something of a breakdown at the end of my university years. I don't blame the generation before me – tutors, educational leaders, parents, social influencers – for my mistakes. But on reflection, I am conscious of a lack of coaching and support through that formative time – for me and for many others like me.

Undoubtedly things have changed since then, in a variety of ways, but some things are also still very similar. I now find myself in the interesting position of leading a church with a large number of students: we pour significant efforts into welcoming students when they arrive at university, help them settle in the city and, if they want to, explore the Christian faith. As a church, we work with the university chaplaincy and well-being functions and we liaise with a number of student halls of residence to offer supportive resources to all types of different students. Within our wider church family, we also work hard to develop a supportive culture where we can help these young people make that transition into adulthood. We've been helped by the Fusion student movement, who have a very particular vision to equip the whole Church to properly look after and disciple students through university: one organization that has recognized just how important and significant this time of life is. Enabling churches to hand on the baton of adulthood, and very specifically Christian adulthood, is a vital work to ensure students survive the pitfalls of university life and are able to fulfil their different vocations to society in the wider sense.

Within this student ministry, in this development and empowerment of young adults, some of the subtleties of Hopeful Influence that we've already explored begin to surface. Young adults often think they know more than they do, at least I certainly did, and, flush with their new autonomy, they don't generally respond well to forms of moralizing or hard boundaries either. What they need are supportive relationships within the context of a consistent and meaningful community. That means a freedom to make decisions, but supported by the wise counsel of those who have been there before. What they need is not the absence of direction or encouragement, but these things offered as part of ongoing relationship and without the additional burden of other people's projected ambitions for them. For us, this means we unconditionally welcome all students who might attend our church. It means we create relational structures where people can really get to know each other and journey together. It means we formalize some of those relationships, mentors and ministry or group leaders for example, who have a particular role to play in a young adult's development. It means we entrust our students with roles and responsibilities themselves, and give them room to play and find their particular identity within community. And it also means we are intentional about making room for students to say no, and to draw their own boundaries around how they want to engage with church life. That means sadness as well as joy for those who travel with our students, but it's a vital part of the kenotic space that needs to be created as we seek to pass on the baton of Christian adulthood.

It strikes me that much of this is the way we all grow up. We flourish best when surrounded by a loving community who give us opportunities, aren't afraid to speak up about what's best, and who will love us regardless. If you speak to the average secular university there is an acknowledgement that faith institutions can be helpful to those students who seek them out. However, I also find much ignorance about how much value-added benefit our church, and others like us, bring to students' experience. We protect students, we motivate them and really help them do the best they can across their whole university experience. We have a framework for human flourishing and well-being that is often lacking in other institutions, and I look forward to the day when secular universities actively invite Christian churches to promote their activities and create the broadest bridges between life in the institution and life in a Christian community for those who would wish to travel. Equally, the Church itself could do with some significant reflection on how it helps young adults transition this boundary and others like it, and how some of these foundational shapes of Hopeful Influence get expressed more widely.

Experience: the existential challenge of living well together

Passing the baton on to others and maintaining an environment of living well together brings some of the greatest leadership dynamics to a head. We've journeyed into the future and we look back and see the formative period of someone else's journey; how do we respond to failure and inadequacy? Particularly when we might have a vested interest in the achievements of those who follow us. There's a scene in *The King's Speech* where, under the threat of Nazi expansion and a possible world war, the future King George VI is battling his stammer to the huge disappointment and indignation of his father. 'Just do it, boy!' his father cries, with condescending rage. In this visualization at least, the father stands as the archetypal emotionally unintelligent male, with no awareness of how he can travel well with his son on whom so many of his own hopes and needs are projected. I find this stereotype a helpful warning for my own journey as a father, and the family is a good place to go to highlight some sharp edges of how Hopeful Influence is expressed to the next generation.

When my younger brother, George, entered his teens, he began to really struggle at school, both socially and academically. There had always been indicators of this struggle, but they didn't fully manifest themselves until his teenage years, and sadly schools weren't brilliant in those days at identifying and supporting those with mental wiring slightly outside the mainstream. He never really got the support he needed, which, for George, resulted in his leaving school early and spending his late teens and twenties struggling for work, often socially isolated and suffering all the associated mental health challenges that come with that kind of lifestyle. For George, it wasn't until his early thirties that we managed to get a diagnosis of mild autism and Asperger's syndrome, and he then began to get more appropriate forms of care and support. Even now, we are still scratching the surface of the tremendous gifts George has as a result of what society calls a 'condition', and helping him find a quality of life within which he is able to participate in a properly human way.

When I think back to George growing up, my memory is of him being a very playful child who suffered an increasing degree of volatility and internal angst when he found himself unable to engage with life on the playful terms, particularly the relationally playful terms, that he wanted. Over time, this manifested itself in all sorts of ways that were difficult and challenging for the rest of the family. When I think back to mine and my parents' influence on George, sadly, I think we often met fire with fire, arguing and fighting over appropriate forms of behaviour and wanting George to grow up and be a bit more adult. George's favourite derogatory line to me in our younger years was, 'Stop being so mature, Jude', which reveals quite a lot about us both in hindsight. I don't think

I understood that George was crying out for fun and friendship. I also lacked an understanding of why fun and play are so central to human relationships, and I certainly lacked the deeper motivations of the heart to journey with George into territory that might have been very good for me as well as for him. Given our time again, I am sure we would have all tried to work harder to ensure we travelled well together, to find peace over things that couldn't be changed and to equip ourselves for the more playful reality that George was wanting to occupy.

I share this, because it is a memory that is helpful for my own experience of parenting and because it touches on the different aspects of living well together that we've explored within Hopeful Influence already. I began this chapter with a story about a particular failing of my own as a parent, but the encouraging news is that I am normally more self-aware and sensitive in my relationship with my son. Jake is clearly a different person from my brother George, but he certainly does exhibit tendencies to want to do life on his own terms and to prioritize play over most other things. Throughout my relationship with Jake there sits this tension: how willing am I to enter into life on those terms? How willing am I to set down my adult self, the person who thinks they know how to do things, and to join Jake on his journey into newness with that same openness and fascination that he exhibits? Of course this doesn't mean that I submit to Jake's every whim, but it does mean that if he wants to do something I don't think is appropriate, then before putting up the barriers, I need to talk with him and understand why he wants to do it. It also means that, when I want to teach him things, if I reduce it to simply an exchange of information – do what I tell you Jake, and then you'll be able to do it better – then he will almost always disengage. Jake demands more of me when he's learning things. He demands more space to call the shots and more room to find his own way. In many ways he is asking for input from me that is much more akin to Hopeful Influence, and it takes a very intentional form of coaching and support from me to realize that and to help him grow.

It's also interesting for me to observe that what Jake asks of me is almost completely counter to the learning processes that I have been taught and have embraced in my own formation. Learning isn't necessarily meant to be fun. My taught assumption is that, when I am learning, my voice and innate instinct in the learning process is less important. My formation has taught me that the didactic learning style is the primary way of helping people grow, whereas Jake is teaching me other ways. My guess is that if I and Jake's other key influencers (such as teachers, the wider family, etc.) persisted with applying purely didactic forms of teaching then it would push Jake away and dangerously restrict his own development. This raises the much wider question of whether some of the children's behavioural and/or learning conditions that we now negatively categorize are exacerbated by the poverty of *influence* that we are offering them, but that is a much wider discussion beyond the scope of this book.

What this brings us back to is that leadership towards the next generation is at the very least a two-way exchange. Henri Nouwen was right: leadership does mean being willing to be led; our effectiveness as people of influence means learning to engage on terms that are informed by and are appropriate to those who we are leading. It also means that leadership truly understood has to be freed from the positional leadership structures we impose on it: when leadership becomes the gift of Hopeful Influence that God wants to be passed around between people of all roles and responsibilities, a gift meant to take us into places of fun and play. This is particularly vital when we consider next-generation leadership, because those of the next generation will always operate in some ways that are different from ours and have particular strengths and insights of their own which reveal the shortcomings of our formation as leaders. To travel well together, to create an environment where we can all take footsteps into the future and where greater fullness of life, even life in the Kingdom, can be experienced, means embracing the existential challenges of Hopeful Influence and a willingness to go on the journey of change ourselves.

Towards a manifesto for Hopeful Influence regarding the next generation

We have defined the next generation as those coming behind us who will inhabit similar roles to our own. In a sense, we all carry a responsibility to the next generation; at the very least to help them become the best human beings they can be, which unavoidably takes us to the person of Jesus and how we become more like him in our own diversity. More specifically, in the other roles we inhabit there is a constant invitation to give others a leg up and pass the baton on well to those who will come after us. To do this, we need to know what we are doing and why, and be able to communicate that helpfully to those who follow. Equally, though, the two-way nature of leadership takes on a particular focus between generations. We are called to lead those who follow us, but we also need to be able to follow the leadership of those who come after us; to have teachable hearts willing to listen to their perspective.

Part of this means bringing our dreams into conversation with one another and, very directly, helping those who come after us discover their own sense of vision as they follow us. This sometimes requires us to hold less tightly to what we think we know, and it certainly means that we restrict the vitality of others when we force them to conform to our specific plans and purposes. There is wisdom around how we humbly communicate the lessons we have learned on the journey, but there is also an intentional giving away of the permission for others to dream and imagine.

As well as a permission to dream, we need to give and affirm the next generation's authority and power to act, supported by meaningful expressions of community. The future is a mutual future, where everyone gets to contribute, and when we hold the reins on others' development too tightly then we can restrict activity that is rightly meant to happen. So we must give responsibility away early and freely, but we also need to nurture community where truth be spoken and accountability lived out. This has particular resonance at transitional boundaries, and the transition into adulthood is a helpful case study of some of the tensions around how kenotic power is expressed and genuine altruism made manifest.

We have also said that to help the next generation experience the Kingdom requires that we are willing to embrace something that we've called the existential challenge of living well. At different points in our leadership experience we will want and desire the betterment of others, and yet be faced with the unavoidable reality that we cannot control their choices and actions, and also that there may be deep flaws in our assumed ways of leading that are hindering the influence we long to have. Rather than this being the traumatic experience that it can so often be, we need to be reminded that our influence is meant to lead to fullness of life, and that to achieve that may require a deep reworking of some of those tightly held assumptions that we carry. Beneath this existential challenge lies something joyful, because we begin to see the true purpose of Hopeful Influence as a God-ordained means by which we travel together, in a transformational way, into the eschaton. We all need challenge and sharpening, and even those in the highest positions of leadership and authority are thankfully not immune to the Hopeful Influence of those in seemingly the lowest.

Finally, there is perhaps a posture that encompasses all this: that our hopes and prayers for the next generation should truly stretch and reach to places we haven't been able to go ourselves. I can remember one of the leaders of our church once saying that they hoped that the young people in the church would one day achieve things that the leader hadn't dared to hope for themselves. As the leader spoke, I searched their face for any sense of insincerity. Did they really mean that? More pertinently, did I share that hope, really? Could I ask that of God, without some sense of actually wanting more for myself and my own future than those for whom I prayed? In truth, then, probably not. It may be that in my ministry I never empty myself quite as adequately as that particular minister, but what I do recognize is that this is part of the journey to which I am called. That seems to be at the heart of the realization of Hopeful Influence towards the next generation.

Comment
Esther Swaffield-Bray, England Director for
International Justice Mission

Since before I can remember, I have been fortunate enough to be surrounded by exceptional leaders. There are leaders who have opened doors for me and let me sit in on conversations I would never have found myself in otherwise; leaders who have prayed for me and kept praying for me, even when I didn't know it; leaders who have invited me to speak at events much bigger than I have been used to because they had more faith in me than I did; leaders who watched me agonize about the 'how' and gently encourage me to instead ask 'why'; leaders who have listened to my dreams and ideas and helped me craft them into a vision; and leaders who have invited me to stay for the weekend, just to spend time laughing and having fun together. In the varying forms it has taken and continues to take, time and time again, my experience of leadership has been characterized by generosity. The leaders who have impacted me most profoundly have been the ones who are generous with their time, wisdom, resources, humour, trust and recognition.

One occasion stands out to me. I joined the organization I currently work with a few years ago, and was still very 'junior'. A member of the senior leadership team booked two days in their calendar to visit me where I was working and 'learn from me'. What transpired was two days of rich conversation surrounding my observations of the organization – but more than that, two days of listening and finding out who I was, my own story and my ambitions for the future. I was not only blown away by the generosity of time that they'd set aside and their willingness to travel the length of the country, but also shocked at the humility of this leader, who had been a go-to voice in the sector for years, genuinely valuing my insight and reflections.

The message that I received in those two days was not only that my perspective was valuable, but that *who I was* mattered … in fact, more so than what I could do for the organization. Rather than a top-down model of leadership, this example of listening and encouraging me to dream gave me incredible confidence. I felt trusted, and this trust helped to create a relationship where I felt safe to try out new things, knowing that they wanted *me* to grow as much as the organization. It seems to me that if next-generation leadership is characterized by anything, all true leadership for that matter, it is in this mutual, generous, relational activity of helping one another travel better together.

Now, a few years later, I lead our work across England and am challenged to offer the same open-handed, people-focused, generous leadership to my team. I certainly don't have this sorted, but I do wholeheartedly aspire to be a leader who is genuinely interested in the people they are leading, much more so than any project: to be a leader who asks the question 'Who are you becoming?' more than 'What are you doing?' I aim to be a leader who is happy creating space in my diary to learn from my team, who is quick to listen and slow to speak. My dream is to emulate the leadership I have seen in order to create a safe space for my team to try new things and fail at things, sharing the joys and struggles with one another (and preferably laughing a lot along the way!).

Note

1 Lots of people transition to adulthood without going to university of course, but this helps as an example because of the often common aspects at work in this particular transition.

Reflection

Passing on the Baton

Luke 10.1–20

After this the Lord appointed seventy-two others and sent them two by two ahead of him to every town and place where he was about to go. He told them, 'The harvest is plentiful, but the workers are few. Ask the Lord of the harvest, therefore, to send out workers into his harvest field. Go! I am sending you out like lambs among wolves. Do not take a purse or bag or sandals; and do not greet anyone on the road.

'When you enter a house, first say, "Peace to this house." If someone who promotes peace is there, your peace will rest on them; if not, it will return to you. Stay there, eating and drinking whatever they give you, for the worker deserves his wages. Do not move around from house to house.

'When you enter a town and are welcomed, eat what is offered to you. Heal the sick who are there and tell them, "The kingdom of God has come near to you." But when you enter a town and are not welcomed, go into its streets and say, "Even the dust of your town we wipe from our feet as a warning to you. Yet be sure of this: the kingdom of God has come near." I tell you, it will be more bearable on that day for Sodom than for that town.

'Woe to you, Chorazin! Woe to you, Bethsaida! For if the miracles that were performed in you had been performed in Tyre and Sidon, they would have repented long ago, sitting in sack cloth and ashes. But it will be more bearable for Tyre and Sidon at the judgment than for you. And you, Capernaum, will you be lifted to the heavens? No, you will go down to Hades.

'Whoever listens to you listens to me; whoever rejects you rejects me; but whoever rejects me rejects him who sent me.'

The seventy-two returned with joy and said, 'Lord, even the demons submit to us in your name.'

He replied, 'I saw Satan fall like lightning from heaven. I have given you authority to trample on snakes and scorpions and to overcome all the power of the enemy; nothing will harm you. However, do not rejoice that the spirits submit to you, but rejoice that your names are written in heaven.'

Questions

1 In what ways does this chapter resonate with your own experience and observations of leadership to the next generation?
2 In what areas of life are you able to exercise next-generation leadership?
3 How are you trying to pass the baton on in these areas currently? How is this process strengthening and re-forming you?
4 How are you dreaming with others coming after you and helping them see a new future?
5 How do we create kenotic space around those who follow us? Where can we give away power?
6 How do we grow together? What areas of our own formation come under the spotlight when we exercise next-generation leadership?
7 How do we share Jesus with those who come after us? Could we even want more for them than for ourselves?

Prayer

Father God, thank you that you entrust us with leadership to the next generation. We are sorry for the ways that we inhibit others and miss the opportunity to be changed ourselves through this leadership. Help us to dream well with those who come after us, to make space for them to grow and flourish and to be willing to be changed as we lead them. Soften our hearts and help us to step aside and humble ourselves so that others can fulfil their potential in you. In Jesus' name, amen.

Epilogue

A few years ago we had an architect in our church, Baba, who was working on the Liverpool Welsh Streets development project, a fantastic initiative to redevelop some of the derelict homes in an area of the city. In this particular project, a large number of houses in an estate had been boarded up for nearly 20 years, and the company Baba was working with had been commissioned to complete a pilot project to refurbish a small proportion of the vacant housing stock. It was a brilliant project that has gone on to produce a number of quality houses which have been quickly filled. New residents are enjoying a quality of housing that hasn't been seen in that area for a long time.

However, towards the end of his involvement in the project, Baba began to get itchy feet. I met with him and we talked about some of his passions and interests, and it became clear that while Baba had been enthused about this project, what was really on his heart was to design and build houses differently from how they tended to be built today. As I listened to Baba talk about his fascination with wood and earth, and the ways in which natural materials could be used to develop a more effective and sustainable type of housing, there was part of me that wanted to pull him back down to that same earth and remind him what an extraordinary difference the project he was currently working on was making; surely he should stay where he was and keep working on these important redevelopment projects?

Fortunately I caught myself and tried to offer a different kind of influence. As we talked I became increasingly aware that Baba had grasped an important vision for something beyond where the mainstream housing development market was at. Over time I realized that I needed to encourage Baba to see these fresh imaginings as part of God's wider movement of equipping architects to build the houses of the future; or at least to build the houses tomorrow that would be more in line with the houses we might one day occupy in our greater tomorrow. We talked about how stewardship of the resources of creation, the properties of natural materials and a bigger vision for human homeliness and comfort all came together to create a shape of a different kind of housing from anything mainstream developers were producing. Of course, I was way out of my depth technically, but our conversation became one of theologically informed imagination coupled to scientific and engineering possibility. Because people listened and encouraged him, Baba went on to quit his job and do some postgraduate training and research at one of the few institutes in the world that could help him realize his dreams. He trusted that his ideas and convictions were from God. He dared to locate himself in the wider renewal of the world. He also exercised tremendous courage to walk away from immediate job security to pursue the higher ideals.

My sense is that these kinds of conversations should be far more the norm among Christians than they are. I long for a day when gathered communities of Christians are hotbeds for this creative, theologically informed imagination; a day where we dream, act and begin to experience the world as it should be rather than the world as it is. For this to become a reality, we need a more comprehensive theology of human activity within which to locate the Christian life and, within this, we certainly need a better understanding of our leadership contribution. To that end, I pray that my ministry will involve conversations with many more Babas.

Theology, simply put, is humankind's attempt to say something about God. In this book I've tried to say something clear about what God is doing in and through the expression of Christian leadership, and to therefore arrive at a theological motif that helps us understand and exercise leadership better. I'm not saying that there aren't other ways into the subject of leadership; that other biblical imagery or categories aren't important or that other motifs aren't necessary to elaborate the concept of leadership in all its fullness. However, to do things better and achieve a wider consensus, we do need to be clearer in our theological discourse. Hopeful Influence is an attempt to do that. In some sense this is a first word and, in that sense, it does need more examination and exploration.

As an example of this further examination and exploration, I have two particular interests in leadership at the moment. First, I want to understand, theologically speaking, why the development of healthy teams is so central to the leadership process. Second, I'd like to understand better why personality and character seem so central to a leader's effectiveness. These are questions that I want to take back to the motif of Hopeful Influence and see what answers I can find and whether those answers offer something also to the evolving shape of the motif. I suspect others will have questions like this too, and further work is essential if Hopeful Influence is to function as a unifying contribution to the important subject of leadership.

On the five spheres of life that we've looked at, my overwhelming feeling is that we need to go back to basics with the leadership question. Of course there are wonderful leaders in all these spheres leading in amazing ways. However, we need fresh understanding and language around how our activity of influence in these spheres becomes aligned with God's renewal of the world. We need to explore the movement of the Kingdom of God in these spheres and get to grips with what our Christian contribution should look like within these overarching pictures. Church leaders need to be resourced to oversee a community of people where, inwards and outwards, Hopeful Influence is the norm. Leaders in politics need to see the potential for their roles and help reshape the political structures so that the potential can be realized. Leaders in the business community need to understand the game they are in and continually bring their business's eschatological purpose into conversation with the financial and functional workings. Third sector leaders need to be clear about the role their organization plays within a wider whole and explore how Hopeful Influence helps them sharpen their contribution. Next-generation leaders, which is all of us, need to be more equipped to pass on the baton and to do this in ways that recognize the collaborative nature of our mutual growth and flourishing.

In simple terms, this is all part of the big adventure that God calls us into. To be human means many things and, as we've said already, part of this *being human* means to help take a lead on God's renewal of the world. As we follow Jesus, so therein lies the potential for others to follow us. Not in some hierarchical power play, but as an expression of loving service as we help the Church, humanity and the rest of creation step closer towards the Kingdom where the good and perfect rule of Jesus is found. May we play our part in that more fully as people who exercise Hopeful Influence, or true Christian leadership.

Index of Bible References